CW00821310

COMPTON VERNEY

&

A History of the
House and its Owners

12.10.2000

COMPTON VERNEY

A History of the House and its Owners

EDITED *by*

ROBERT BEARMAN

SHAKESPEARE BIRTHPLACE TRUST

First published
in the United Kingdom in 2000 by

The Shakespeare Birthplace Trust
Henley Street, Stratford-upon-Avon
CV37 6QW

ISBN: 0 904201 03 1

Design: Alan Ward @ Axis, Manchester
www.axisgraphicdesign.co.uk

Typeface: Vendetta by Emigre Type Foundry
Print: Craftprint International Ltd, Singapore

COVER IMAGE
Compton Verney, c.1655: detail from a drawing by Wenceslas Hollar,
published in William Dugdale's *Antiquities of Warwickshire*.
(The complete drawing is given as Plate 36).

CONTENTS

PREFACE

This volume presents, in edited (and in some cases, expanded) form, the papers which were given at a two-day conference held, in the summer of 1998, at Compton Verney, the former ancestral home of the Willoughby de Broke family. The family papers, housed for many years at the Shakespeare Birthplace Trust Records Office, have provided many historians with a rich resource, be it for the study of the medieval settlement at Compton, the evolution of the present house and landscape, or the careers of individual members of the family. In the mid 1990s, it became clear that Compton Verney, after years of uncertainty, was to be completely refurbished as an art gallery and opened to the public for the first time. This made it an obvious venue for a conference to celebrate both the rescue of the building and the unique importance of the family papers. Lord Willoughby de Broke was most supportive and the Compton Verney House Trust extremely generous in making the house available to us over a weekend in the summer of 1998 when the building, still only partly restored, was opened to the public for a trial period.

The Shakespeare Birthplace Trust, as the organiser of the conference and the custodian of the archive which provided the contributors with much of their material, has undertaken publication of the conference proceedings in order to bring them to the attention of a wider audience. This would not have been possible, however, without the willingness of the contributors to re-work their papers, the patience and good humour of Alan Ward of Axis Design, the helpful support of Richard Gray, Director of the Compton Verney House Trust, and the pair of very experienced eyes of my colleague, Robert Smallwood, which proved invaluable at proof stage.

Robert Bearman
Shakespeare Birthplace Trust

FOREWORD

by

LORD WILLOUGHBY DE BROKE

I am delighted that the Shakespeare Birthplace Trust is preserving in book form the papers which were presented to a weekend conference at Compton Verney in 1998. As an amateur family historian I was deeply interested in what our distinguished contributors had to say about my family and its long association with Compton Verney and eager to learn more about the house, its architecture and landscape.

My own perspective of Compton Verney has inevitably been coloured by my grandfather's book, *The Passing Years*, in which he painted an elegaic picture of life on the estate in the last flicker of its days as our family seat. The beef roasting on the kitchen spit, the ton of coal burned in the house each day and the private brewery: all are described fondly but without sentimentality, as is his relationship with estate workers and tenant farmers, whom he saw as friends and neighbours and who I think returned his affection and respect.

I suppose that successive generations have always felt that it was their forefathers who had the best of things, as indeed my grandfather wrote in the opening lines of *The Passing Years*: 'As soon as I could hear anything I was told that I was born with a silver spoon in my mouth... I am not quite sure what has happened to that silver spoon now.' He was writing in 1923, two years after the sale of Compton Verney. The reasons for that sale have been well documented, not least by David Cannadine in his scholarly book *The Decline and Fall of the British Aristocracy*, in which our family name appears with all too depressing frequency.

During my boyhood in Kineton, Compton Verney was all round me – pictures, photographs in the family album, books in the library kept back from the sale, and the house itself, past which I used to ride or drive nearly every weekday in school holidays. It was always the same, silent, shuttered, unkempt but with a remote and timeless tranquillity.

My own memories of Compton Verney go back well beyond my school days. During the war our house in Kineton was commandeered by the War Office for use by the Czech Army – I was brought up in a cottage at the end of the garden, Fox Cottage. My mother had volunteered to drive what was called a mobile canteen round the local army units, including Compton Verney, which the Army had been lent to play with for use as the School of Smoke Camouflage. Only the War Office could have dreamed up using Adam and Gibbs buildings for smoke training, a decision which even Evelyn Waugh might have found beyond parody. I enlisted or was pressed, I really cannot remember, to be Mother's Little Helper: we used to go to the YMCA hut in Kineton, and stock up with tea, cakes, sweets and cigarettes to dispense to the troops. My role was reduced to dropping the cigarettes in the tea, eating the sweets and being taken for rides in bren-gun carriers.

So I can fairly say that Compton Verney has been with me for as long as I can remember – and in my adolescent dreams it was all too easy to imagine what might have been. The dreams quickly evaporated under the reality of what was actually happening to Compton Verney. The sale of the house in 1958 was when the rot, which started under government occupation, became entrenched and widespread. Chopped up into lots, the property was dismembered – the Lower Water and land went one way, the park to a timber merchant, the house and its curtilage to Harry Ellard. Twenty-five years of neglect ensued. I remember the occasional visits and deeply depressing they were; rusting barbed-wire fences, hungry alsatians barking in the James Gibbs stables, and evidence of neglect everywhere; crumbling masonry, gaping holes in roofs, even a sapling growing from one of the dormer windows – and nobody needs reminding of the fate of the Adam ceiling over the Great Hall.

When Ellard died in 1984 he left the house, increasingly dilapidated and dangerous, to the Masons – this was a gift horse whose mouth they examined and found to be rotten – who put the house up for sale once again, when it was bought at auction. The stable block was restored and converted into flats, and emergency repairs were carried out to the main house. A deal was cut giving planning permission for the old walled garden above the chapel to be developed with the attached condition that the resultant profit, or a good part of it, should be spent on repairs to the house. It turned out that the sum needed for such repairs far exceeded any profit from the development sale and a further period of uncertainty ensued.

When in 1995 the ownership of the house passed to the Moores Foundation I was cautiously pleased. Brian Hayton, the then Director, was kind enough to show me round the house three or four years or so ago: it was virtually a shell – most of the roof was being replaced, while floors and ceilings were gone, eaten by rot, also to be replaced. Good though most of the stone is, sixty years' lack of maintenance had taken its toll. When Peter Moores and his team took over, the house was in a critical state – another winter or two and it would have been beyond salvation.

I think it is worth pausing to consider exactly what Peter Moores has done at Compton Verney. He is carrying on a great British tradition – the tradition of the Grand Tour – but with a difference; he has been on his own Grand Tour and is bringing the evidence back not for his or his family's private enjoyment, but for everyone who can now visit Compton Verney. It is a quite extraordinarily enlightened use of resources and I am delighted that Compton Verney is the chosen site. Not only has the house been restored by the expenditure of a very considerable sum of money, but a further sum has been set aside for maintenance and running costs; and let us not forget the capital cost of the collection itself and of future acquisitions. This is patronage on a Medici scale and an achievement which I believe to be unique in post-war Britain.

A vote of thanks is in order to Peter Moores and everyone who has contributed to the regeneration of Compton Verney. This is I believe as happy and elegant a solution as could have been reached. Robert Bearman too deserves congratulations for his commitment to putting these papers together in a single volume, and their several authors for being tempted down the tributaries of our family history. Their interest does honour not only to the family but to those who have so diligently maintained the archive throughout Compton Verney's long history.

LIST OF ILLUSTRATIONS

PLATES

Chapter 1

Chapter 2

Chapter 3

FIGURES

TABLES

LIST OF CONTRIBUTORS

Robert Bearman is Senior Archivist at the Shakespeare Birthplace Trust and is author of *Shakespeare in the Stratford Records* (1994) and editor of *Charters of the Redvers Family and the Earldom of Devon, 1090-1217* (1994) and *The History of an English Borough: Stratford-upon-Avon 1196-1996*, 1997.

Steven Brindle is an Inspector of Ancient Monuments and Historic Buildings at English Heritage and is co-author of the *Blue Guide to the Country Houses of England.*

Christopher Dyer is Professor of Medieval Social History at the University of Birmingham. His most important articles, many with a Midlands bias, have recently been re-published under the title *Everyday Life in Medieval England* and among his other works is *Lords and Peasants in a Changing Society: The Estates of the Bishopric of Worcester, 680-1540* (1980).

Martyn James joined Compton Verney for its 1998 Preview Season. He now works at Sudeley Castle in Gloucestershire.

Roland Quinault, Senior Lecturer in History at the University of North London, has written extensively on British political and social history of the late nineteenth and early twentieth centuries, building on his D.Phil. thesis which examined in depth Warwickshire politics in the Victorian period.

Geoffrey Tyack is Director of Stanford University in Oxford and the author of the definitive *Warwickshire Country Houses* (1994). He has written many other articles on related subjects and his other books include *Sir James Pennethorne and the Making of Victorian London* (1992).

Philip Wise, recently appointed Curator of Archaeology at Colchester Museums, was formerly Keeper of Archaeology at Warwickshire Museum, contributing many articles on archaeological and historical subjects to the *Transactions of the Birmingham and Warwickshire Archaeological Society*, *West Midlands Archaeology*, and *Warwickshire History.*

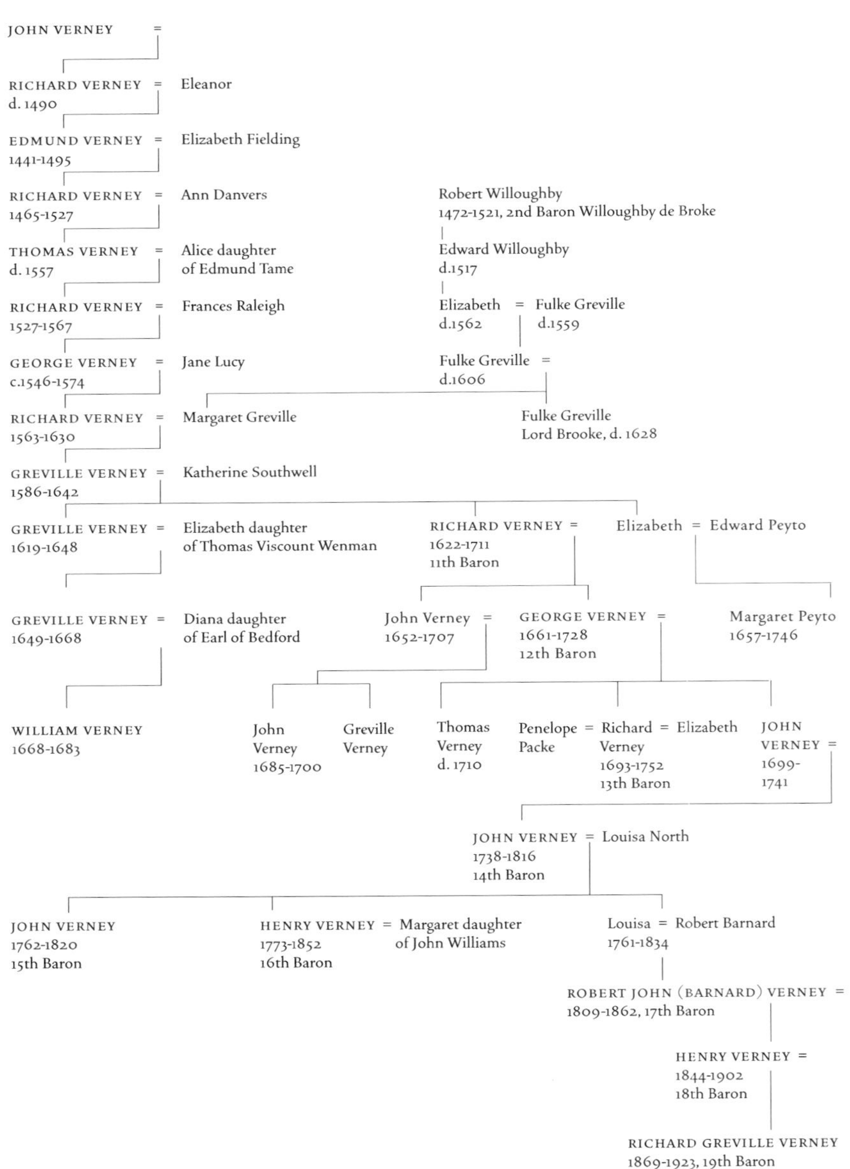

FIGURE 1

The Verney Family

Barons Willoughby de Broke from 1696

Entries in capitals indicate holders of Compton Verney

CHAPTER ONE

MPs, JPs and The Occasional Rogue:

THE VERNEY FAMILY OVER SIXTEEN GENERATIONS

ROBERT BEARMAN

For nearly 600 years, from the 1430s until 1921, the manor house at Compton Verney, albeit extended and rebuilt over the years, was in the ownership of a single family, the Verneys, sixteen generations represented by twenty members. For just under half that time, from 1696, they also enjoyed the title of Barons Willoughby de Broke. With the exception of the last, the nineteenth baron, none have attracted the attentions of a biographer. For the most part, they lived out their lives in unspectacular fashion, playing the parts expected of them, firstly as landed gentry and then as members of the peerage, with the orderly descent of the property interrupted from time to time by typical family quarrels, minorities and commissions of lunacy. Some achieved more than others, and several have found their way into general works which deal with particular periods in Warwickshire's history. Others have received more than a passing mention in books and articles concerned with the fabric of the house and the layout of the estates, albeit as background to architectural and landscape themes. However, no satisfactory history of the family has yet been written, an essential prerequisite for a proper understanding of the house and estates, whose fortunes are but a reflection of the fortunes of the people who owned them. It is the purpose of this chapter to outline, for the first time, the fluctuating circumstances of the Verneys over six centuries, and in so doing to provide a context for the detailed studies of particular episodes which follow.

Until the last fifty years of our six centuries, the general impression of the Verney family is of an upwardly mobile one, and it might be as well to remind ourselves of the relative position the family achieved before its dramatic downfall. A survey of 1883 ranks the Verneys second only to the Leighs of Stoneleigh Abbey in the extent of their rolling acres within Warwickshire, some 12,600, yielding an annual income of around £16,510.[1] In addition, and in common with many leading Warwickshire landowners, the Verneys held estates outside the county, boosting their income to a grand total of nearly £24,000. Taking these out-county estates into account, there were, amongst Warwickshire's landed families, more than just the Leighs who outstripped them but they all lived in the north of the county. In the south, the Verneys were pre-eminent, for no other family with their main seat there enjoyed such an income. Their nearest rivals were the Throckmortons of Coughton with an income, in 1874, of some £3,000 more; but their main estates lay outside the county and their obstinate adherence to the Catholic faith had damaged their social prospects. The Shirleys of Ettington were also rich by Warwickshire standards, but their estates within the county totalled a mere 1,800 acres, and it was only their Irish lands, with a yield of £23,000, which brought them into the same bracket as the Verneys. Nor had the Shirleys made it into the peerage. The only other major landowner in the area was the marquess of Northampton but his main seat was over the county border.

On the other hand, it is worth recording that no Warwickshire family, not even the wealthiest, was amongst the country's super-rich, the thirty or so families with incomes of over £76,000.[2] The Verneys may have been an influential family in south Warwickshire, but were not that highly placed in the country-wide league table. And this, of course, is reflected in the house today: certainly one of the more ambitious in south Warwickshire, but of modest scale when set against such establishments as Woburn Abbey, Chatsworth and Blenheim Palace. What follows is an attempt to explain how the family came to occupy this position, wealthy and therefore influential in a local but not a national context.

An ambitious family could improve its prospects in a number of ways. Service in the royal or a noble household could produce dramatic results, though nobles, of course, could fall out of favour, bringing down their dependants too. Marriage to an heiress was another well recognized means of augmenting family income. Then, the wealth of many landed gentry had its origins in business, the profits from trade having been invested in land which came onto the market on the Dissolution of the Monasteries. Sir Thomas Leigh, who bought Stoneleigh Abbey in the 1570s, came from just such a background. Judicious management of one's estates did not necessarily, by itself, produce dramatic results, although, in the fifteenth and sixteenth centuries particularly, conversion of arable to sheep pasture often proved highly profitable. This was the basis for the rapid rise of the Spencer family of Wormleighton. And there could also be, of course, strokes of sheer luck. Over the centuries, the Verneys built up their resources through one or other of these means, and, unlike some landed families, never had their position seriously undermined by the excesses of any one head of the family.

1. These figures, and those which follow, are derived from *Return of Owners of Land*, Parliamentary Papers, 1874, lxxii (2), and J. Bateman, *Great Landowners*, 1883; but, for Warwickshire, are conveniently summarized in Geoffrey Tyack, *The Country Houses of Warwickshire 1800-1939*, Warwickshire Local History Society, Occasional Paper no. 7, 1989, 59-61.

2. For these, see David Cannadine, *The Decline and Fall of the British Aristocracy*, revised edn, London and Basingstoke 1996, 710-11.

The origins of the Verney family are obscure, and indeed cannot be traced back with any certainty beyond John Verney, who makes his debut in the records in 1422 as an officer in the household of Richard Beauchamp, earl of Warwick, at that time one of the most powerful figures in the country.[3] He appears to have been related to a minor landholding family of Great Wolford, but how he had come to Beauchamp's notice is at present unknown. The advantages of such a patron soon became apparent. John, his younger son, went into the church and Beauchamp used his influence to secure him a number of ecclesiastical appointments as well as, in 1432, making him supervisor of his own lands and receiver-general of accounts. By the time of his death in 1457, he was dean of Lichfield and archdeacon of Worcester, a combination sufficient to earn him a reprimand from the Pope which he had, however, ignored.[4] His elder brother, Richard, was also employed by the earl, from at least 1428, and it was he who acquired Compton Verney and set the family on its career as landed gentry. Here again, it was Beauchamp who provided the necessary help. Verney's first purchase, in fact, was Kingston, in Chesterton, by 1432. Compton Verney (or Compton Murdak as it was then called after the family who had held it in the twelfth century) followed in 1435.[5] Beauchamp was overlord of both these manors and, by one means or another, had persuaded the previous owner, Robert Skerne, to part with them. Indeed, it was later quite openly stated that Beauchamp had helped Verney buy both properties. The deal was, apparently, that on Beauchamp's death, Verney would grant Kingston to the church of St Mary, Warwick, to help fund a chantry in Beauchamp's memory. In fact, Verney reneged on this, preferring, after a long dispute with Beauchamp's executors, to pay £550 or so for the manor rather than lose it.[6] Be this as it may, there is no doubt on the main issue, that the Verneys had become landed gentry through the patronage of the earl of Warwick. John the elder's efficient discharge of his duties in the earl's household had led, in his son John's case, to preferment in the church and in his son Richard's to acquisition of the nucleus of a landed estate. To this Richard added some lands in Lighthorne around 1436 (again a manor where the earl of Warwick was overlord) and one or two other freeholds in Compton Murdak soon afterwards, including the sub-manor known as Durvassals, in 1437.[7]

3. Christine Carpenter, *Locality and Polity: a Study of Warwickshire Landed Society, 1401-1499*, Cambridge 1992, 130n, 690.

4. *Ministers' Accounts of the Collegiate Church of St. Mary, Warwick, 1432-85*, ed. Dorothy Styles, Dugdale Society xxvi, 1969, 1n.

5. Shakespeare Birthplace Trust Records Office (SBTRO), DR 98/97-9,460, 462, 471. Due to the complexities of medieval conveyancing, whereby the names of real owners were concealed behind those of feoffees (or trustees), it is not easy to pinpoint the dates when he became outright owner.

6. Carpenter, *Locality and Polity*, 126.

7. SBTRO, DR 98/680-5,100-2.

Richard Verney, by all accounts, was a ruthless and ambitious man, bent on securing maximum return from his estates, and forever quarrelling with his neighbours. The most striking example of this was his long-running dispute with Richard Dalby, a neighbouring landholder in Brookhampton, Combrook and Kineton, who was as anxious as Verney to make capital out of his estates by conversion to sheep pasture. But as the national situation deteriorated, with rival factions struggling first over who should control the increasingly incapable Henry VI, and then over who should succeed him, the gentry found it necessary, if not advantageous, to align themselves behind powerful political figures, giving what had been local disputes a new dimension. Verney, of course, was a member of the Beauchamp clan but the Dalbys acknowledged as overlords the earls of Buckingham, rivals to the Beauchamp interest within the county. Verney's dealings with Dalby therefore reflect to some extent this struggle at a higher level. Richard Beauchamp's death in 1439, for instance, presented the Verneys with problems, for the earl's successor, Henry, was only fourteen years old. Clearly, this would not have been a good time to have picked a quarrel with Dalby, if to succeed he needed the support of a lord in favour at court. But in 1444, the young Henry was made premier earl and the following year, in April, a duke. So it was probably no coincidence that a month later, Verney's quarrel with Dalby first comes out into the open, with an accusation, manufactured if not invented by the Verneys, that Dalby had abducted the daughter of a local Northamptonshire yeoman.[8] But the Verneys' hopes that their affinity with a young and powerful duke of Warwick would stand them in good stead received a serious setback on the duke's premature death in June 1446, leaving an infant daughter to succeed. On her death three years later, the title passed to her aunt, Anne, and through her to her husband, Richard Neville, known to posterity as the Kingmaker. Young and inexperienced and a stranger to the county, his advent coincided with a conflict at the highest level over control of the king. The gentry for a time appeared wary of aligning themselves too obviously with one side or the other. But with the triumph of the earl of Warwick, as head of the Yorkist cause early in 1461, and the proclamation of Edward IV as king, Verney decided to press the Dalbys harder. With his son Edmund, just turned twenty, he was accused of assaulting Dalby and his wife on their way back from church in Kineton, of attacking Mrs Dalby in a similar incident and stabbing one of her servants in the churchyard, and of plundering Dalby's estates in Kineton and Brookhampton.[9] The earl of Warwick, although distracted by the crisis in national affairs, could not ignore this, and other anarchic disturbances in his county, and Verney spent a short period in gaol. But his harassment of Dalby continued into 1464, leaving the latter to complain that 'Sir Richard is a common oppressor of ye kynges lieges and of so grete myght and power in yat countree that yor sede besecher [i.e., Dalby] is not of power to justifie w[t] hym by ye kynges lawes'. In the meantime, he had also formed an alliance with Simon Mountford, the greatest non-noble landowner in the county. In 1462 we find him implicated in an ambush on Richard Clapham, with whom Mountford was quarrelling over land in the north of the county, and in 1465, he was involved in another fracas between Mountford's men and Clapham which ended in the murder of one of Clapham's servants.[10] The earl of Warwick was again forced to intervene and Verney spent a further four months, from October 1465 until the following January, in

8. Carpenter, *Locality and Polity*, 416-17.

9. Carpenter, *Locality and Polity*, 495-7.

10. Carpenter, *Locality and Polity*, 499-501, 503-4.

PLATE 1
Brass marking the tomb of Richard Verney (died 1527)
and his wife, Ann Danvers, in the newly-extended church at Compton Verney;
from a drawing in Dugdale's *Antiquities of Warwickshire*.

PLATE 2

Glass from a window in Compton Verney church, in commemoration of Richard Verney and his wife, Ann Danvers.

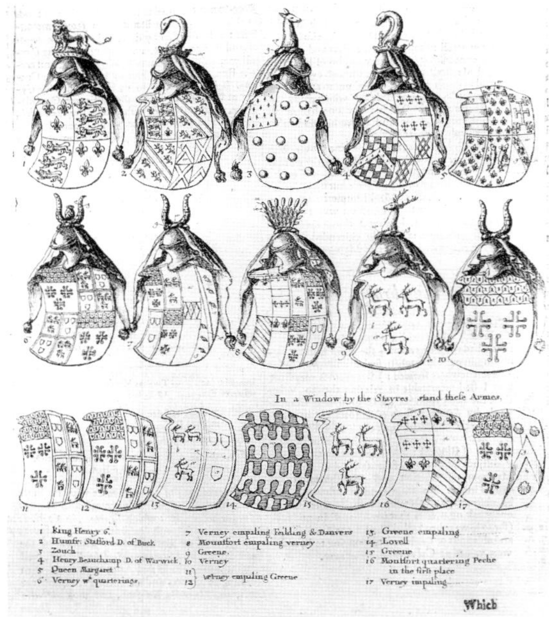

PLATE 3

The sequence of heraldic glass once in the window of the hall at Compton Verney; from a drawing in Dugdale's *Antiquities of Warwickshire*.

the Marshalsea prison. But his cause suffered no lasting damage. After two years of wrangling, he was acquitted of any wrongdoing and in 1468 regained his position as Justice of the Peace. He was now in his sixties, and seems to have lost his taste for violent confrontation, although with his son, Edmund, he was once more threatened with imprisonment, this time in 1474, during a dispute between him and another Warwickshire neighbour, John Peyto of Chesterton. This was over pasture and enclosure, and the quarrel rumbled on into 1477 with accusations of illegal entry on each other's lands and the setting of dogs on sheep.[11]

Verney lived on for another thirteen years, dying in 1490. He was buried at the church of St Andrew, Northampton, where two years earlier, he had made arrangements for masses to be said for the safety of his soul.[12] Under Beauchamp's patronage, it was he who had set up his family as a landed one, and the exploitation of his newly-won estates shows a man determined further to advance his position. This had brought him into conflict with other landowners, at a time when the collapse of central authority had encouraged a similar breakdown in law and order locally: as a result, his career reads today almost as gangster-like. It could also be argued, however, that these were troubled times and that, had Richard not taken the law into his own hands, he might have lost ground. When the greatest in the land were wrangling over the crown, we should not really be surprised to find their social inferiors conducting, or reviving, their own feuds, sometimes even to the death. In any event, Richard handed on to his son, Edmund, a position on which to build. It comprised, according to a survey taken on his death, some 340 acres in Compton Murdak, worth £20, 340 acres in Kingston also worth £20, and some smaller parcels in Burton Dassett, Lighthorne and Whitnash.[13]

Richard's wife, it is said, was Eleanor, daughter of John Loutham of Northampton[14] which, if true, might have a bearing on the family's origins and explain Richard's choice of burial place. His heir, his son Edmund, was forty-nine when, in 1490, he eventually succeeded his father. Though implicated, as we have seen, in his father's escapades, he had, by the more peaceful 1480s, turned to less violent means of securing his position. He was involved in the administration of the late duke of Clarence's estates during the minority of his son, Edward,[15] and was in royal service as escheator for the counties of Warwick and Leicester from 1481. However, there is no evidence that he had added anything to the family estates before his death in 1495, only five years after his father.[16] In his will, he gave instructions to be buried in the church of the Dominican Friars in Warwick 'betwixt the Altar of our Lady, and the Altar of S. Dominick, on the north part; appointing that by the care of his Executors, a Lamp should be continually maintained burning in the Chancell of the Church, before the host'.[17]

Edmund had married Elizabeth, a daughter of William Feilding of Newnham

11. Carpenter, *Locality and Polity*, 533.

12. SBTRO, DR 98/125.

13. *Calendar of Inquisitions Post Mortem, Henry VII*, ii, 656.

14. *Collins's Peerage of England ... greatly enlarged ... by Sir Egerton Bridges*, 9 vols, London 1812, vi, 694.

15. *Cal. Pat. Rolls, 1476-85*, 91, 540.

16. The inquisition held on his death valued his estates in Compton Verney and Kingston as worth less than they had been in his father's time (*Cal. Inq. P.M., Henry VII*, i, 1052).

17. William Dugdale, *Antiquities of Warwickshire*, 1730 edn., i, 565.

Paddox, in 1457, and his heir by her was a son, Richard, aged about thirty on his father's death.[18] His years as head of the family (1495-1526) were to witness a quiet consolidation of the family's position. We find him buying up pieces of property in Kineton, including the windmill, a large estate in Chesterton and further land in Lighthorne.[19] The capital to make these purchases came, apparently, from the profits of a continuing policy of conversion to pasture for sheep farming.

18. *CIPM, Henry VII*, I, 1052. He was, however, stated to be only 36 when his mother died twelve years later: *CIPM Henry VIII*,iii,238, no. 376.

19. SBTRO, DR 98/131,660-1,697.

His will is also of interest, for in it he provides for his burial in the new chapel which he had built on the north side of Compton church. The brass in his memory and that of his wife, Ann (Plate 1), a daughter of William Danvers, still survives and the marriage was also commemorated in two panels of stained glass (Plate 2). His father and grandfather, as we have seen, had chosen to be buried at Northampton and Warwick respectively. But the enlargement of the church to serve as a family mausoleum is evidence of a growing pride in an estate which the family had now held for three generations and the tenure of which had lifted them into the ranks of the minor gentry. Indeed, Richard may have been the first member of the family to have regarded it as a home rather than as just a source of income. The first major building operations at Compton Verney are usually credited to Richard Verney the elder, based on a much later statement, in 1656, by William Dugdale. But the evidence Dugdale cites, the sequence of heraldic glass to be found in his day in the windows of the great hall (Plate 3), suggests, in fact, a date towards the end of Richard's long life, if not later.[20] It was around this time that Compton Murdak came to be known as Compton Verney, another indication of a growing association between the family and its estates. Richard's enlargement of the church for his (and his successors') place of burial was the next and conclusive step in establishing Compton Verney as an ancestral home.

20. Dugdale, *Antiquities*, i, 565. The glass includes his son Edmund's arms, and those of the Danvers family, into which his grandson, Richard, married.

Richard's son, Thomas, head of the family from 1526 until 1557, illustrates, albeit in a modest way, how a family could advance its prospects by means of an advantageous marriage. His wife was Alice Tame, joint heiress to the estates of her brother Edmund, lying principally in Gloucestershire. There was an element of luck involved here, for at the time of Verney's marriage, Tame was still alive and well. On his untimely death, however, without direct heirs, his lands were partitioned, in 1547, between his three sisters, one of whom was Verney's wife. Her share comprised estates in Eastleach Turville, Coln St Aldwyn, Tetbury Upton and Nympesfield, all in Gloucestershire, with an annual value of about £72.[21] He also acquired further estates in and around Compton Verney, building up the family's local dominance.[22] Sheep farming continued to form the bedrock of the family's estate management. On Richard's death in 1557, his Warwickshire estates alone were said to include 1,200 acres of pasture spread through the adjoining manors of Kingston (in

21. SBTRO, DR 98/141, 141b, 877, 1277.

22. SBTRO, DR 98/137, 607a,608-10

Chesterton), Compton Verney, Lighthorne, Combrook and Brookhampton.[23] These figures need to be treated with some caution but there can be little doubt, over the sixty years since the death of Richard Verney in 1490, when only 400 acres of pasture were recorded, that the family's landholdings had increased very considerably.

23. SBTRO, DR 98/141a.

His son, Richard, inherited in 1557 at the age, it was said, of thirty-two thus placing his birth at around 1525. If true, he must have been very young, only fourteen or so, when married in 1539 to Frances the daughter of George Raleigh, lord of the manor of Farnborough.[24] Whilst his father was alive, Richard and his young bride lived at Eastleach, one of the newly-acquired Gloucestershire estates, moving to Compton Verney on Thomas's death in 1557.[25] Richard's career affords an example of advancement through social contact. In 1550, even before his father's death, he had entered the service of John Dudley, earl of Warwick, as deputy constable of Warwick Castle.[26] Dudley was executed three years later for trying to put Lady Jane Grey onto the throne, but Verney survived the downfall of his master, and in 1559 was still Master of Game of Wedgnock Park, a post linked with the constableship of the castle.[27] He was well placed, therefore, to take advantage of the resurgence of the Dudley family in the late 1550s. In particular, he attracted the patronage of the young Robert Dudley, who, with his brother Ambrose, was rapidly re-establishing the family's power base in the west midlands.[28] Dudley was appointed Lord Lieutenant of Warwickshire in 1559, jointly with Ambrose Cave, and in July that year received a letter from his colleague advising him on a suitable candidate as deputy, in place of John Fisher: 'in whose stede, Sir Richard Varney, a gentilman mete to serve in that behalf wolde willingly endevor himself for Warwicksheir yf it please you to appointe or require him by your letters to take the chardge upon him.'[29] Dudley needed no persuading, no doubt aware of Verney's service in his father's household, and a close master/servant relationship soon established itself in a way obvious to contemporaries. There is no better proof of this than a libellous pamphlet, published in 1584, in which Verney was actually named as a leading accomplice in Dudley's alleged murder of his wife, Amy Robsart, in September 1560. 'Sir Richard Verney, who by commandment remained with her that day alone, with one man only, and had sent away perforce all her servants from her... he... can tell how she died.... It is not also unlike that he [Dudley] prescribed unto Sir Richard Verney.... that he should first attempt to kill her by poison'. This story used to be dismissed out of hand, and there is little doubt that it was a gross libel. But, from recent research, we do now know that Amy was staying at Compton Verney in September 1569, and that one of Verney's servants took two pair of hose down to her there.[30] Contact between the two men is also to be found in a letter from Verney to Dudley in April 1560, in which he apologises 'that I can not, according to your Lordshippes expectacion and my dutie, make my repaire presently towards you for two

24. SBTRO, DR 98/578.

25. SBTRO, DR 98/594, 596.

26. SBTRO, DR 98/141.

27. SBTRO, DR 98/1268-9.

28. For Dudley's career, see Simon Adams, '"Because I am of that countrye & mynde to plant myself there": Robert Dudley, Earl of Leicester and the West Midlands', *Midland History* xx, 1995, 21-74.

29. *HMC, Bath*, v, 142.

30. *Household Accounts and Disbursement Books of Robert Dudley, Earl of Leicester, 1558-1561, 1584-1586*, ed. Simon Adams, Camden Society, 5th series, vi, 1995.

PLATE 4
Brass marking the tomb of George Verney (died 1574) in the church at Compton Verney; from a drawing in Dugdale's *Antiquities of Warwickshire*.

principall causes. Thone health, whiche I possesse not as I could wissh. Thother wealth, which doth not habond in me as perhappes is thought. But as it is both I and althinges els myn are and alweis shalbe to my best power advaunced inany your affaire or commaundement when oportunytie offereth'.[31] His letter goes on to make another apology, this time for his cousin Danvers, for whom Verney had secured a post in Dudley's service but who had then proceded to lose two of Dudley's hawks. Two years later, Dudley's influence secured Verney the post of sheriff of the county and from 1562 to 1564 he also served as a Justice of the Peace. In short, there is more than enough evidence to establish a close relationship between the two men at around the time of Amy's death, which would have been obvious to contemporaries, and which Dudley's enemies later exploited to the full.

31. *HMC, Bath*, v, 156.

Richard died in 1567, aged about forty, and was buried at Compton Verney, leaving as son and heir George, aged twenty-two. George, like his father, had been married, or at least betrothed, young. His bride was Jane, one of the daughters of William Lucy of Charlecote, whom he married at the age of fourteen.[32] This inter-marriage, and his father's before him, into the Raleigh family of Farnborough, are exactly what we would expect of families which had achieved minor gentry status within the county. The tender age of the bridegrooms (both he and his father had been only fourteen) also reveals the family's anxiety to ensure the succession in the male line without the disruption of a minority. In George's case, this paid off: even though his father was only forty years old on his death, his son, George had just come of age. At one time, George seemed inclined to offer up his own son, Richard, at an even younger age, reaching an agreement, in 1568, that Richard, then no more than three years old, should marry Ann, daughter of Ludovic Greville of Milcote.[33] In fact, within months the marriage was called off, quite why is not known. There is some evidence that Ludovic, who was to become notorious for his financial dealings and infamous for his murder of one of his servants, may have entered into the arrangement as a means of satisfying debts incurred by George's father, Richard. However, even if the marriage had taken place, it would not have averted a minority. George was to live for only six years more. He died in 1574, and was buried at Compton Verney (Plate 4), leaving his son Richard, aged nine, to succeed him.

32. SBTRO, DR 98/878-9,1412.

33. SBTRO, DR 98/881,883.

Up to this point, the family could congratulate itself on a steady consolidation of its position. Since the death of Edmund Verney, a combination of good luck, shrewd estate management, fortunate marriage alliances and wise choice of patrons had produced a significant advance in status for its leaders. It had also been lucky enough to produce a succession of male heirs over four generations. But minorities of the sort which now arose could cause serious problems, as the wardship of an heir in most cases did not remain within the family but could instead be sold to the highest bidder. However, the family's luck held. There is no evidence of Robert Dudley, the Verneys patron in the 1560s, doing much for George, generally a shadowy figure[34]; but he had clearly not lost interest in the family and now, as earl of Leicester, showed concern for the young Richard's future. Three months after George's death, he was writing to Lord Burghley, one of the most powerful men in the country, about the poor state of the Verney lands. The following year he wrote again, this time about a possible marriage between 'the young Verney', as he called him, and Burghley's niece. In 1579, Dudley took over the wardship himself, guaranteeing to spend £20 a year on Richard's education on his reaching the age of twelve.[35] Whilst still a minor, Richard also made what turned out to be a fairly profitable marriage, in 1582, to Margaret Greville, daughter of Sir Fulke Greville of Beauchamps Court, though, as we shall see, not as spectacularly successful as it might have been. All the same, on the death of her brother, another Fulke, unmarried, forty-six years later, in 1628, Verney obtained a number of estates in Somerset, Hertfordshire, Cambridgeshire, Lincolnshire, Staffordshire, and Gloucestershire which had been entailed in that branch of the family. It is unlikely that this could have been predicted at the time of the marriage, in 1582, though the elder Fulke's wife did die at around that time and the younger, aged 28, was still unmarried. In any event, it was Dudley's influence which had been all important, as the Grevilles were another family which owed much to his patronage and were therefore under an obligation to accede to his wishes. Margaret also brought with her a claim to the barony of Willoughby de Broke, though this may not have been appreciated at the time: as we shall see, it was not until the end of the century that the family tried to make anything of this, and then only as a second option.

34. He was, however, appointed Marshal of the King's Bench, maybe through Dudley's influence (*CSPD, 1547-80*, 506).

35. *History of Parliament, 1558-1603*, 3 vols, London 1981, iii, 558-9; *CSPD, 1547-80*, 498; *Cal.Pat. Rolls, 1578-80*, 1220.

Dudley died in 1588, but not before he had set the young Richard on his career. Having completed his education with a spell at Gray's Inn, Richard sat regularly as a Justice of the Peace from 1586, was returned as Member of Parliament for the county in 1589, and served as sheriff of Warwickshire in 1590-1. From that point on, until his death in 1630, he remained pre-eminent in the ranks of the gentry of south Warwickshire, being returned to Parliament on at least two further occasions, serving as sheriff again in 1604/05, and as Deputy Lieutenant in 1623. These appointments were not without incident: in his first term as sheriff, he was faced with a massive fine of £1,000 for allowing an important prisoner, Thomas Wheatman, to escape.[36] He was also sheriff at the time the news of the Gunpowder Plot broke: amongst his letters to the Privy Council is an anxious one, of 13 November 1605, to the effect that 'when in this tumultuous business you shall here of, or deserne any wantes or defectes in performinge those dewtyes which appertain to my place and office, you will rather favourably pass over than suffer them to undergo the censure of your judgment'.[37] He was, in fact, having serious trouble keeping safe the prisoners he had taken, scribbling a note to Burghley in the early hours of 15

36. *Acts of the Privy Council*, xxii, 132.

37. PRO, SP 14/216, fol. 139.

PLATE 5
Richard Verney, died 1630; from a painting in the possession of Lord Willoughby de Broke, artist unknown.

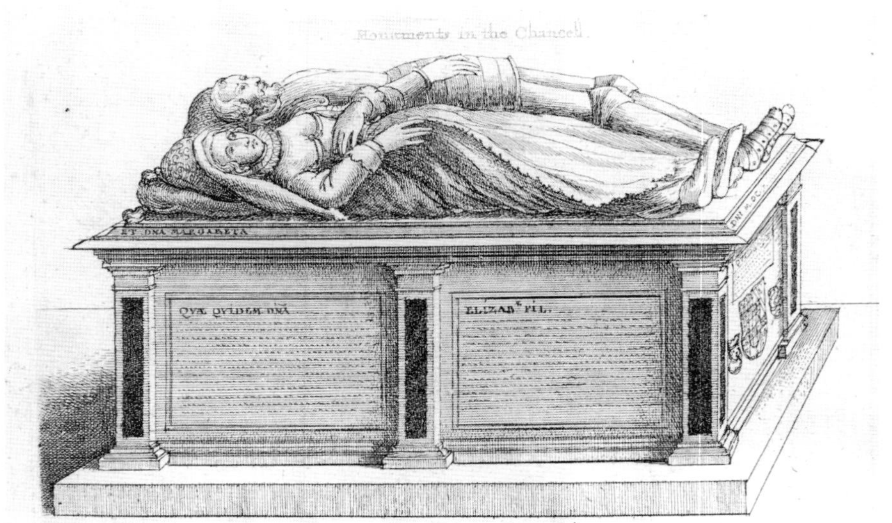

PLATE 6
Tomb of Richard Verney, died 1630, and Margaret his wife, in the church at Compton Verney; from a drawing in Dugdale's *Antiquities of Warwickshire*.

November that his lodgings in Warwick had been set on fire for a second time, though whether by a mob intent on rescuing or lynching the prisoners is not clear. Two days later, it was with some relief that he despatched some at least of them to London.[38]

Richard died in 1630, still active in government service, this time as chief commissioner for fining those who had not attended Charles I's coronation, one of the king's expedients for raising revenues without having recourse to Parliament.[39] This would not have made Verney popular with his fellow landholders, although there is no evidence that he pursued this, or any other royal policy, with much enthusiasm. He also died a disappointed man; for although he had lived long enough to see his wife inherit the entailed Greville estates on the death of her childless brother, Fulke, two years earlier, in fact he had expected much more. But in February 1628, Fulke, now Lord Brooke, and a man of vast wealth, made his will leaving all his other property, far exceeding the entailed estates in value, to Robert Greville, a distant cousin, in order to keep the bulk of his inheritance within the Greville family. Ever since his marriage to Fulke's sister in 1582, Richard had nurtured the relationship with the Grevilles. He had, for instance, named his eldest son Greville, whom, as we shall see, Fulke treated with some favour. In 1601, we know that Fulke bore the expense of keeping Verney's children at his house at Deptford and then 'for one week's diet at London'.[40] As the years passed and Fulke remained unmarried, expectations were clearly raised. This is established from a letter written in 1632 in which Fulke, in a volume of his poems about to be published, was accused of making claims which would somehow clear his name of accusations that he had treated the Verneys badly ('take off the charge of the world for what injury he hath otherwise done').[41] The Verneys brought a Star Chamber case against Robert Greville, whom Fulke had made his heir, as a result of which they were awarded £2,200 as a down payment and a grant of land of an annual value of £500.[42] Whether the Verneys knew before Fulke made his will in 1628 that they were not to inherit everything is uncertain. But Fulke's death itself shows he had a way of upsetting people: for he was stabbed by a disgruntled servant, who was commonly believed to have been aggrieved by news of how Fulke was intending to dispose of his estate. A letter from Lord Brudenell to the earl of Westmoreland, written a day or two after Brooke's death, also implies that the disposition of his estates was newsworthy, rather than a matter settled years before.[43] The unfairness of the settlement, and the resentment of other Warwickshire gentry that an interloper had been introduced into their midst, is also to be found in a letter by the antiquarian, William Dugdale, written in 1637, who was anxious to investigate the Brooke pedigree 'for that worthy Sir Greville Verney's sake', i.e. Richard's son.[44]

Despite his disappointments (the Greville estates he acquired with his wife were valued in 1634 at less than £100 a year), Richard Verney had made an important

38. PRO, SP 14/216, fol. 149 (and see fol. 120); *HMC, Salisbury*, xvii, 493, 529, 532.

39. *CSPD, 1629-31*, 333.

40. *HMC, Cowper* i, 32.

41. *HMC, Cowper*, i, 483-4.

42. Ann Hughes, *Politics, Society and Civil War in Warwickshire, 1620-1660*, Cambridge 1987, 25. It is far from clear, however, that this compensation was ever made.

43. *HMC, Rutland*, i, 487.

44. William Hamper, ed., *The Life, Diary and Correspondence of Sir William Dugdale*, London 1827, 164.

PLATE 7
Sir Greville Verney in 1639, aged 51; from a painting in the possession of Lord Willoughby de Broke, artist unknown.

PLATE 8
Sir Greville Verney, died 1648; from a painting in the possession of Lord Willoughby de Broke, artist unknown.

contribution to the family fortunes. He was clearly the most able head of the family since his namesake, Richard, who had first established the family in Warwickshire; and he had given it solid respectability and the prospect of further advancement through his efficient discharge of those political and administrative duties expected of the local landed gentleman. His legacy was to give the family an unquestioned authority in the south of the county; and if the additions to the family estates were not quite what he may initially have dreamt of, the inscription on his tomb (Plate 6), tracing his ancestry back four generations, reflects the importance which the family later attached to his career.

His heir, as we have seen, was his son, Greville, by then aged about forty-four, the choice of name, of course, intended to emphasise a relationship to a family out of which the Verneys had hoped they might one day profit. In 1600, Greville was admitted, like his father, to Gray's Inn. A year or two later we find him under the tutelage of Robert Naunton at Cambridge University. A friend wrote to him: 'I assure you the care and pains you take to encourage and direct Mr Greville Verney's studies are most kindly accepted and much valued by all his friends . You sow in a plentiful and well tilled ground which must needs yield an abundant harvest if the heart thereof through too much heat be not smothered and spent'.[45] His father was well pleased with his progress, writing in 1604: 'Grevyll and Jack [his brother John] are well grown and with good shape. It seemeth Grevyll will grow to be nimble limbed which I did much doubt of. I think his heart is inclined to follow his books seriously.'[46] In 1607 he was granted a licence to travel abroad for four years and we learn, according to his father, that at Christmas 1609 he 'avoided the expense of Paris and went to Orleans and Blois'.[47] A letter from his uncle, however, Fulke Lord Brooke, is a little more revealing. In October Greville had clearly written to Brooke begging for money, and in November £30 had been forthcoming. Brooke also sent him a long and pious homily which the young man may not have been quite so pleased to receive, ending: 'Not to spend your spirits, and the precious time of your travaile, in a captious prejudice, and censuring of all things, nor in an infectious collection of base vices and fashions of men and women, and generall corruptions of these times; which will be of use only among humourists for jests and table-talke; but rather straine your wits and industry soundly to instruct yourself in all things betweene heaven and earth which may tend to vertue, wisedome and honour and which may make your life more profitable to your countrey, and yourselfe more comfortable to your friends and acceptable to God'.[48] As Brooke was still unmarried, and Greville's inheritance prospects therefore brightening, the young man may have thought such advice as just something he had to put up with.

Soon after his return to England, he married, in 1618, Katherine the daughter of Sir Robert Southwell and was returned to Parliament in 1620. On his father's death in

45. *HMC, Cowper*, i, 38.

46. *HMC, Cowper*, i, 47.

47. *CSPD, 1603-10*, 379; *HMC, Cowper*, i, 68.

48. The whole letter was published in 1633 as pp. 295-8 of *Certaine Learned and Elegant Workes of the Right Honorable Fulke Lord Brooke*, London.

PLATE 9
Sir Richard Verney (later Lord Willoughby de Broke) as a young man;
from a painting in the possession of Lord Willoughby de Broke, artist unknown.

1630, he stepped into his shoes as a leading member of the local gentry, serving continuously as a Justice of the Peace from 1630, and as sheriff in 1635/36. His father's years as sheriff, as we have seen, were far from trouble-free, and Greville's was also to coincide with another crisis, the collection of the controversial Ship Money, another of Charles I's revenue-raising expedients and deeply unpopular, especially in inland counties. By June 1636 Greville was in trouble with his political masters over the delay in getting the money in: his record, it seems, was the worst in the country. Verney attributed this to various tax evasion techniques, concluding, in a letter to the Privy Council: 'In general, it groweth to be a piece of cunning in the country not to agree of any levies or assessments but leave me to be puzzled'. He then wrote to his old friend, Sir John Coke, to thank him 'for answering heartily in my behalf at the [Privy] council concerning the neglect objected of not returning with more speed the ship money'. He ended his term of office still £400 in arrears, and a letter of 1639 implies that his estate was still encumbered with debts.[49]

The Civil War appears generally almost to have passed the Verney family by. They are usually regarded as neutral, and this may have been the case, given that they feature very little in the records of the time. On the other hand, Greville's unexpected death in May 1642, before the Civil War had entered its serious phase, and the inheritance of the family estates by his son, another Greville, only twenty-two or so, and still completing his education at the Middle Temple, may have discouraged active participation. In November, Greville the younger received a Royalist command to supply provisions for Banbury, held for the king by his near neighbour, the earl of Northampton of Compton Wynyates.[50] But we do not know that the young man responded. Certainly he did nothing to put himself out of favour with the Parliamentarians. His father's tax assessment of 1642 for £2,500 had gone unpaid during his lifetime and his son had still not paid anything by April 1648. Yet 1647-8 was the year Greville the younger was asked to serve as sheriff of the county. Clearly, then, such an omission had not been held against him, nor by implication anything else he or his family had done over the previous five or six years.[51] At this point, however, the family's luck ran out. Greville died at the end of 1648, aged twenty-nine, leaving a widow, Elizabeth, who herself died just over a month later, giving birth to their only son, Greville III.

Before moving on, it is worth considering what effect, if any, the events of the previous forty years might have had on the evolution of the house. It is often said that the Greville inheritance would have injected sufficient capital into the Verney coffers to fund major rebuilding work. There is, however, very little documentary evidence to substantiate such a claim. The inheritance in any case did not amount to very much (worth less than £100 a year[52]). Moreover, if it was a factor, then it would not have come

49. Hughes, *Politics and Society*, 107; *HMC, Cowper*, ii, 119, 226. See also *CPSD, 1635-6*, 278, 446, 452, 454, 551.

50. Alfred Beesley, *The History of Banbury*, London 1841, 330.

51. *Calendar of the Proceedings of the Committee for the Advancement of Money*, HMSO 1888, 683. For other evidence of the neutrality of many other Warwickshire gentry at this time, see Hughes, *Politics and Society*, 158-65.

52. Above, p.31.

into the equation until Lord Brooke's death in 1628, when these estates eventually came into the family's possession. This in turn raises the question, if there had been any rebuilding after that date, why William Dugdale made no mention of it in his *Antiquities*, published soon after, in 1656, especially in view of the fact that he paid generous tribute to a member of the Verney family for helping him with the section on Compton Verney.[53] Dugdale was interested in the fabric of the house as he knew it: indeed, as we have seen, he attributed most of it to the first Richard, who died in 1490. This interest would surely make a failure to mention recent rebuilding work unlikely. An inventory of 1642, taken on Greville Verney's death, does reveal a man of considerable wealth. His house comprised thirty rooms, furnished with velvet, tapestry, pictures and musical instruments, with a total value of nearly £900. His clothes were valued at £100, as was his cupboard of plate, with a study of books worth 100s.[54] But amongst the rooms there is mention of only 'a new parlour' and 'a new chamber', implying that most of the other twenty-eight were existing. Some small additions, then, may perhaps have been made in the recent past but not enough to warrant Dugdale drawing attention to them.

53. Dugdale, *Antiquities of Warwickshire*, i, 565.

54. SBTRO, DR 98/898.

We return now to the poor orphaned Greville who, indeed, never even knew his parents. There was a dispute as to who should bring him up (and control his estates during his minority) between his paternal grandmother, Katherine Lady Verney, and his maternal grandfather, Thomas Viscount Wenman.[55] In the meantime, the young Greville was sent to Oxford, where he graduated in 1663. Four years later, at the age of eighteen, he married Diana, the daughter of the earl of Bedford, who was to bring with her the very tidy sum of £7,000.[56] Tragedy was to strike again, however, for Verney died eleven months later, a year before coming of age, leaving a son and heir, William, barely a month old. More legal wrangling then ensued, this time between the earl of Bedford, representing his daughter (she was still under age) and representatives of the Verney family, and mainly revolving round the £7,000 marriage portion.[57] A final blow was to follow with the death of young William in Paris, at the age of fifteen. Lord Preston, Envoy Extraordinary in France, wrote: 'Master Verney, son to Sir Greville Verney, and grandson to my lord of Bedford and I think the only son of his family, is just now in the agonies of death; he was very hopeful and seemed to be of a very good and loyal principle'.[58]

55. SBTRO, DR 98/1653.

56. SBTRO, DR 98/1311.

57. SBTRO, DR 98/1653.

58. *HMC vii*, app. 289.

After ten generations, then, the direct male line failed, and the estates passed, perhaps to his considerable surprise, to William's great-uncle, Richard Verney, then aged sixty-three. Richard, since his marriage, in 1651, to the daughter of Sir John Pretyman, had established himself as a minor country gentleman at Allexton, in Leicestershire, moving to Belton in 1672. He was a cultured and intelligent man: Dugdale described him as 'a gentleman accomplished with singular endowments, and of a noble and courteous disposition'. Samuel Wright, the historian of Rutland, was later to describe him as 'a true lover of antiquities and a worthy Maecenas'. He also had a generous streak: on his arrival in Allexton, he had granted the parish 'a silver plate for the carriage of the consecrated bread in the time of the administration of the Lord's Supper'. He was evidently a sporting man too, advertising in a newspaper in 1660 that he had lost a falcon. 'She hath neither bells nor varvels; she is a white hawk, and her long feathers and sarcels are both in blood. If anyone give tidings thereof to Mr. Lambert, at the Golden Key in Fleet Street, they shall have 40s for their pains'.[59]

59. John Nichols, *The History and Antiquities of the County of Leicester*, 4 vols in 8, London 1795-1811, iii, pt.1, 9.

In 1683, on inheriting his great-nephew's estates, Richard moved to Compton Verney. The following year he was appointed sheriff of Warwickshire, was elected to Parliament for Warwickshire in 1685 (and again in 1689), representing, in what became a family tradition, the Tory interest, and served as Deputy Lieutenant from 1686. In short, he resumed the mantle last worn by his father Greville some forty years before as head of the leading gentry family in south Warwickshire. The intervening period of early deaths and minorities had caused some anxieties but had not caused any lasting damage. As if to crown his success, he managed, after a two-year struggle, to secure a peerage. He first laid claim to the title of Lord Brooke through his grandfather's marriage to Margaret Greville; and, when this failed, to the older title of Lord Willoughby de Broke. The argument hinged on whether the title had passed down in the female line (that is, through Elizabeth Willoughby and then through her grand-daughter, Margaret). Initially, the Lords, having debated the matter, ruled against his claim: then, a year later, on the realisation by some of their number that their own titles might become suspect, this decision was reversed.[60] Verney took his seat in the House of Lords as the eleventh baron on 13 February 1696, the third to the tenth having been assumed to have held the title without realising it.

60. *HMC, Lords*, ns i, 403-10; ii, 213; *Complete Peerage*, iv, 742-4.

Richard lived to the great age of eighty-nine, outliving his son, John, a Tory Member of Parliament for Leicestershire from 1685, who lived at Allexton all his life and died in 1707, and his two grandsons, John and Greville. On his death, in 1711, the estates and his newly-acquired title therefore passed to his second son, George Verney, then aged fifty.

George, like his father before him, could hardly have expected to have been heir, the succession depending as it had done on the deaths of his elder brother and his two nephews. He had therefore gone into the church and his powerful family connections had assured him rapid promotion. By the time of his succession he had twice been in the running for a bishopric, first Chichester, in 1709, and then Bristol in 1710. Even after his succession, he retained his close connection with the church, in 1712 preaching vigorously in St Sepulchre's Church, London, before a congregation assembled on behalf of a local foundling charity, on the benefits of giving,[61] and accepting the position of dean of Windsor in 1714. He it was, as we shall see, who began the rebuilding work at Compton Verney, and laid out extensive formal gardens. It might seem odd that his father, who had put the family back on its feet after a series of minorities and who had been so anxious to become a peer of the realm, had not taken the initiative in this; but he may have thought

61. There is a printed copy of this sermon at SBTRO, DR 98/1729.

PLATE 10
John Peyto Verney, 14th Lord Willoughby de Broke, and his family in the Breakfast Room at Compton Verney, c.1766; from a painting in the J. Paul Getty Museum, Los Angeles.

himself too old, when he inherited at the age of sixty-three, to take on such a task. George, however, at fifty, clearly had no such misgivings; and we can imagine the condition into which the house may have fallen during the aged Richard's final years.

However, all was not well in the dean's family. His eldest son, Thomas, had died of smallpox in 1710. His second son, Richard, was a great trial to his father. He left Oxford without a degree, and in July 1718, after a violent quarrel, George disinherited him, arranging for all his estates to pass instead to his younger son, John. An unwise marriage (or marriages) seems to have been the cause of the trouble. Richard's first love, it seems, was Penelope, daughter of Clifton Packe of Prestwold Hall in Leicestershire. The actual marriage has not been traced but she was buried at Prestwold in September 1718, still aged only eighteen,[62] only two months after Richard had quarrelled with his father. This suggests that he may by then already have deserted his teenage bride, as does a grudging agreement made two years later whereby his father, George, allowed Richard an annuity of £300, but only on condition that he and his new wife, Elizabeth (her surname is uncertain but she was, it was later alleged, a sempstress from Bristol) never darken the doors of Compton Verney again. He also provided £500 for paying Richard's debts, but again only if they had not been contracted by his wife either before or after the marriage.[63]

George, the father, died in 1728, like his father before him, a sad and lonely man. As might have been expected, his eldest son challenged the will and several witnesses reported the common local gossip that George 'was very ill and saw no company' and 'was believed to be incapable or unfit to make a will'.[64] This was to no avail, however, and, as originally arranged, the estates did indeed pass to his younger son, John: but nothing could be done about the title which therefore descended to the landless Richard, who was at least able to call himself a peer for the rest of his life, and indeed is known to have taken his seat from time to time in the House of Lords. His marital adventures were far from over. On 6 January 1736, Lord Egmont noted in his diary: 'I learned this day that Lord Willoughby de Brook has carried off the wife of one Stiff, a stocking weaver. My lord had separated some time before from his lady, a sempstress of Bristol'.[65] The date of separation, apparently, was 1732, by which time Richard was seriously in debt. He had taken a lease of Farewell Hall, near Lichfield, but his wife refused to join him there and he failed to pay his rent. The only way he could manage to keep afloat (even his Parliament robes had been seized by a creditor) was to agree to make over his annuity to his landlord, John Wightwick. When he failed to keep to his word on this, Wightwick wrote angrily: 'this is so unworthy a behaviour that I am amazed a man of his rank can be guilty of it'. In 1734, in recognition of a permanent separation from his wife, he made arrangements for a third of his annuity to go to her.[66] In 1736, as we have seen, he made off with Mrs

62. Nichols, *History of Leicestershire*, iii, pt 1, 361. The marriage must have post-dated 1714 (SBTRO, DR 98/1440).

63. SBTRO 98/1326a-1327a.

64. SBTRO, DR 98/1658.

65. *HMC, Egmont Diary*, ii, 218.

66. SBTRO, DR 98/1649/22-31,42.

Stiff and disappears from view. He is said to have married again, but his only child died before him and on his death, in 1752, the title reverted to the descendants of his younger brother and was thus reunited with the estates.[67]

67. *Complete Peerage*, xii, part 2, 696-7; *Collins's Peerage*, vi, 702.

John, as third son of the dean, would normally have had to make his own way in life, and to prepare for this he had been trained in the law. His brother-in-law, Anthony Duncombe, also gave him a helping hand, nominating him as Member of Parliament for his pocket borough of Downton, in Wiltshire, at the age of twenty-one. He sat as a Tory, in the process gaining the hand of the daughter of Edward Harley, cousin of the earl of Oxford, who seems to have taken steps to give his career a further boost. It was apparently through his influence that he was appointed a justice of the Brecon circuit, although there had been a problem, as we learn from a letter to the earl from a political friend: 'I had almost forgot to give your lordship joy of the promotion of Mr Verney; but it looks as though there was some rub in the way: I hope he has not managed like some indiscreet ladies to have scandals without joy'. Whatever the problem, it was resolved and John went on to fill the offices of Attorney General for Queen Caroline, from 1729, and Master of the Rolls from 1738 until the year of his death in 1741. He also continued to sit as Member of Parliament for Downton. His contributions to various debates were noted by contemporaries from time to time, but not always flatteringly: on one occasion even his friends were said to have felt 'he spoke very ridiculously and of that which it was plain he was utterly ignorant'.[68]

68. *History of Parliament, 1715-1754*, ii, 495; *HMC, Portland*, vii, 382,412,445,457-8.

John, it is fairly clear, spent much of his time in London. No doubt, he was also worried that his reprobate brother might be successful in overturning the family settlement; indeed, he had been involved in a legal dispute on just that issue from 1728 to 1732, with problems re-occurring as late as 1737, only four years before his death.[69] He also died young, aged only forty-two. As a result, little seems to have been done to improve the house and grounds which he had rather unexpectedly inherited. In 1736, some thought had been given to laying out a park, and by 1738, a stable block had been built. His death, however, in 1741, put paid to further schemes.

69. SBTRO, DR 98/1658.

His heir was a son John, only three years' old, but only to the estates, as his reprobate uncle, Richard, the thirteenth baron, was still alive. This was resolved in 1752, on Richard's death, without a male heir, whereupon the title reverted to his young nephew. John the younger also had a great stroke of luck for he was made heir to the estates of the neighbouring Peyto family of Chesterton. The last of that family was a spinster, Margaret Peyto, whose father, Edward, had married the only daughter of Greville Verney (died 1642). She had produced six children, three boys and three girls, one of whom, Margaret, eventually became sole heir. She lived to the great age of eighty-nine, dying in 1746. Under her will, made in 1742, all her estates, principally in

Chesterton, but including considerable property elsewhere, were left to her distant cousin, John Verney, provided he and his heirs adopted the additional name of Peyto.[70] On his reaching his majority, in 1759, there thus dawned a new age in the family's history. John was both a peer (which his father had not been) and the possessor of considerably more in the way of land. The Chesterton rents, for instance, appear to have more than doubled his income, and his mother's death in 1760 ensured that the income from land reserved to her as dower became available to him too. Almost immediately plans were made to improve the estate and it was in his time that contemporaries were to witness a complete remodelling of the house and grounds.

70. SBTRO, DR 98/1525-3.

John showed great enterprise in the management of his estates. He sold off, in 1772, some of the more distant parts, using the money to buy up extensive estates in Chesterton, Kineton and Brookhampton in 1772 and 1773, thus consolidating his dominance in south Warwickshire.[71] Later, in 1806, he bought the manor of Great Kineton, and land in Lighthorne and elsewhere as late as 1814, just two years before he died at the age of seventy-seven.[72]

71. SBTRO, DR 98/1779-80,1872-3.

72. SBTRO, DR 622/238,241-6; DR98/1959.

One sadness, however, was the fate of his eldest born, John, who was declared a lunatic in 1788. He had been sent to Oxford in 1780, but never completed his studies. In an effort to disguise his incipient condition, he was sent abroad with a young tutor, Robert Barnard, a graduate from Cambridge, for four years, but his condition failed to improve and his father therefore bought a house for him at a safe distance, in Castle Carey, where he was placed in the care of another clergyman. In 1788, his behaviour had deteriorated to such an extent that he was officially declared a lunatic, placed first in the custody of his father, until his death in 1816, and then of his younger brother, Henry, for another four years until his own death in 1820.[73] His father's final years may have been rather unhappy ones. His wife had died in 1798, as had seven of his ten children. Of those who had survived, his elder son was a lunatic, and his daughter, Louisa, as we shall see, had made an unfortunate marriage. Henry, his second son, had remained single and so when John fell ill, he appears to have gone to live with Louisa, at Lighthorne, where he was later buried. Compton Verney must have been a dull and lonely place during this period.

73. SBTRO, DR 98/1675.

Following John's death in 1816, the administration of the estates therefore fell to his second son, Henry Verney, who became the sixteenth baron on the death of his unfortunate brother in 1820. His reign was to see a steady rise in the family's prosperity. Further significant purchases of lands were made in Little Kineton, Combrook and Brookhampton in 1823, and in Burton Dassett and Radway in 1829.[74] To some extent, economic conditions favoured such expansion but there are plenty of examples of spectacular excesses on the part of the aristocracy to show that some degree of careful

74. SBTRO, DR 622/230,269(11-15).

stewardship was required. The Verneys' purchase of the manor of Kineton had only become possible as the result of the extravagances of the previous owner, George Earl Brooke who, despite his vast estates, spent his last years in 'penury, mortification and wretchedness'. Henry's later acquisitions in Burton Dassett and Radway were likewise the result of the spectacular debts of the duke of Buckingham and Chandos. So, while the accumulation of wealth during this period may not have been particularly difficult, there was some requirement for a family's chief representative to show a degree of caution.

Henry had this quality in ample measure; indeed, it appears that during his father's final years he had been entrusted with the administration of the family estates. This we may deduce from the fact that it was he, in 1810 (six years before his father's death), who conceived the idea of extending the lower lake and building the huge dam above Combrook.[75] The contractor he engaged was William Whitmore, but it took five years to agree on a price. After the work began, Verney's anxious interfering (not entirely unwarranted as the work was dogged with problems) eventually led to a complete breakdown in the relationship between the two men. At the end of eighteen months, a very angry Whitmore wrote: 'I ... conclude it right to let your work stand till you are in a better humour ... I will not go on longer without money. You ought to have paid as the work proceeded ... I wish neither to see you or your work any more.' Verney replied that he would have had no objection to paying as the work proceeded: what he objected to was advancing money 'as it fell down'. His purchase of the Burton Dassett estate was another venture plagued with delays.[76] Negotiations began in 1828, on an asking price of £125,000. Henry began by offering £114,000 as the absolute maximum, though he eventually allowed himself to be forced up to £120,000. It took a further eight years, however, to clinch the deal, after tortuous procedures, which involved, at one time, Henry threatening to seize goods from the duke's London home in Pall Mall.

Henry did have a passion though, sailing, which, in fact, may have been the reason for extending the lake. In the 1820s he went on several voyages in his yacht Antelope: around the coast of Scotland in 1822 and to St Petersburg in 1825. And in the early 1830s, he had a small frigate built which was brought up to Compton Verney and in which, apparently, he enjoyed himself on his new lake.[77]

At this time, Henry had no wife with whom to share these pleasures. He did not marry until 1829, when he was fifty-six, and then almost as an afterthought. His bride was Margaret, daughter of John Williams of Bodelwyddan, twenty-seven years his junior, a frequent visitor to Charlecote Park since her sister Mary's marriage to George Lucy in 1823. Mary describes the courtship in her memoirs:[78]

75. For the details which follow, see Robin Chaplin, 'The "Landscape" Lakes at Compton Verney', *Warwickshire History*, i, no. 1 (1969), 20-3.

76. For what follows, see J.V. Beckett, 'The Land Market in Nineteenth-century England: the Sale of Burton Dassett, 1828-1836', *Warwickshire History*, ix, no. 1, 1993, 2-11.

77. SBTRO, DR 98/1655,1724-5.

78. *Mistress of Charlecote: the Memoirs of Mary Elizabeth Lucy*, ed. Alice Fairfax-Lucy, London 1983, 48-9; and see 33-4,37.

PLATE 11
Robert John Barnard/Verney, 17th Lord Willoughby de Broke; from an etching published in *The Passing Years.*

PLATE 12
Henry Verney, 18th Lord Willoughby de Broke; from an early photograph published in *The Passing Years.*

PLATE 13
Richard Greville Verney, 19th Lord Willoughby de Broke, in 1919; from a photograph published in *The Passing Years*.

> In mid-January Lord Willoughby came to Charlecote for the hunt ball at Stratford. At the ball he sat by me and, our conversation turning on matrimony, I said to him: 'Why don't you take a wife?' 'Oh, no nice girl would take such an old fellow as me'. I said: 'Faint heart never won a fair lady. Take my advice and try.' The next day he left Charlecote and I got the most ridiculous letter from him, asking if I thought he had any chance of winning my sister. I showed Miggy [Margaret] the letter and said 'What answer shall I send? Remember he is old enough to be your father and you cannot be in love with him. It may be all very fine to be Lady Willoughby de Broke but a coronet will not ensure your happiness.' George, too [her husband] spoke very seriously to her but all cautioning was vain. She determined to be mistress of Compton Verney, so my answer to him was: 'You had better come and ask her yourself.'

This he did but prompting more comments from Mary:

> Lord Willoughby, it struck me, was rather afraid of entering the Holy Estate of matrimony. He stayed at Charlecote till the end of January, his love-making was very mild: no lover's vows 'sweet in every whisper'd word.'

The marriage caused great consternation in the family. Henry's heir at the time was the son of his only surviving sister, Louisa Barnard. She had herself caused a great stir in 1793 when she married Robert Barnard, the companion or tutor, as already explained, of the unfortunate John, prior to his committal as a lunatic. In recognition, perhaps, of Barnard's four-year effort to keep his charge within the bounds of respectable behaviour, he had been made rector of Lighthorne in 1787; but then, six years later and to the family's general alarm, he managed to persuade Louisa to become his bride. By 1829, her son, Robert John Barnard was heir to the Compton Verney estate; hence her fury at the news of the marriage.[79] However, she need not have worried. Henry may have tried (though the description of his courtship leaves this in some doubt), but he failed to produce any offspring. What he may have lacked in romantic ardour, however, he made up for in his hatred of 'all change with the deadly hatred of a true Eldonian Tory. He was never tired of voting against the Reform Bill, and died many a silent death in the last ditch, or in the last lobby, in defence of the existing order'.[80] He died in 1852, aged eighty.

79. Or so Mary Lucy alleges (*Memoirs*, 49).

80. Richard Greville Verney, *The Passing Years*, London 1924, 9.

On his death, the family estates passed more or less intact to his nephew, Robert John Barnard, who took the name of Verney. Educated at Eton and Christchurch, Oxford, he is soon found settling into the life of a country gentleman, following in the footsteps of his father, the archetypal hunting parson. 'Prebendary Barnard', it was later recorded, 'was in many respects a remarkable man. An active magistrate, a respected country clergyman of the old school, a noted partridge shot and walker, and a keen, bold rider –

he represented an ideal which is fast passing away. Many tales are still told in Lighthorne [where he was rector] of his prowess in the saddle .... No day was too long for him, and no task too hard , till the time when, stricken down by an attack of paralysis..., he had to spend the rest of his days in a Bath chair'.[81] With such an example before him, the young Robert's life followed a predictable course. At Eton, he developed a passion for shooting and fishing, and at Oxford for the 'road', that is, the art of a coach and four. His father died in 1834 and, as the years ticked by, he must have become increasingly confident that his uncle would remain childless and that he would therefore eventually succeed to Compton Verney. In 1839, he became Master of the Warwickshire Foxhounds, running up debts in this and other sporting pastimes totalling nearly £5,000 in anticipation of his inheritance.[82] In his grandson's words, 'he had no taste for county or Parliamentary business, nor indeed for any other business except the business of being a country gentleman'.[83] Nevertheless, it was during his tenure of the estates, though only for some ten years (1852-1862), that they assumed their largest extent. Throughout the 1850s, Robert continued his uncle's policy of buying up small properties in the Compton Verney area, as and when they came onto the market, on one occasion raising the capital through the sale of distant estates in Lincolnshire.[84]

81. Carles Mordaunt and W.R. Verney, *Annals of the Warwickshire Hunt*, 1795-1895, London, 2 vols, 1896, i, 139.

82. SBTRO, DR 622/272/11.

83. Verney, *Passing Years*, 9. See also Mordaunt and Verney, *Annals*, 1, 139-41.

84. SBTRO, DR 98/1962, 1969-2017; DR 622/ 8,255(4), 256 (6), 257(7), 59 (10); DR 636/28.

When Robert died, in 1862, his son Henry was only eighteen, in the process of transition from Eton to Oxford. According to his son, he found the prospects of instant wealth a serious distraction to his studies, and left college without a degree. Henry later claimed that he had enough brains to have taken a degree 'on his head'.[85] Be this as it may, he turned out to be another member of the family with little interest in anything but sporting pursuits. In these, he was said to be pre-eminent and, to his sporting contemporaries, his achievements here made him a far more impressive figure than any amount of academic success would have done.

85. Verney, *Passing Years*, 26.

> He had served a continuous apprenticeship in the saddle ever since he could remember anything and he was not at Oxford for very long before he became one of the best, if not the very best, of steeplechase riders among the undergraduates... Riding over a country was not the only art my father acquired at Oxford. As his father before him, so was he a first-rate shot. He brought to Oxford a considerable proficiency with the gun, and by constant practice at the traps he quickly became a first-rate pigeon shot, and subsequently one of the best game shots of his day... second to none at rocketing pheasants or driven patridges.[86]

86. Verney, *Passing Years*, 26-7, where there is also a long discourse on his other sporting achievements.

It is no coincidence that his most significant addition to the house is the freize of hunting scenes still to be seen in the great hall.

Such a man, however, was not best equipped to deal with the challenges which faced the land-owning classes in the second half of the nineteenth century. The Verneys' wealth was largely dependent on the land they owned. Yet as the agricultural depression of the late 1870s and '80s began to bite, and their rent rolls dwindled, it proved impossible to maintain the appearance of fabulous wealth without mortgaging their estates. The nineteenth baron's description of family life at Compton Verney around this time is well known:

> The remembrance of a full-blown Victorian establishment in full swing is .. a very great treasure...At one time a big leathern black-jack was filled to the brim with the good stuff [home-brewed beer] four times every day, over and above what was drunk at table. What was not poured down the throats of the retainers .. was poured down the sink. .... In the same frank style did they burn a ton of coal in the kitchen every day. I have had the privilege of seeing the sirloin hanging by a chain, slowly turning round and round and being basted by the stout kitchen wench as hot as the huge open fire in front of her.[87]

87. Verney, *Passing Years*, 3-5.

These sentimental recollections, however, conceal the fact that the family had begun to mortgage their estates from 1872, and then to sell the outlying ones in 1893.[88] Nor is there any mention of the fact that the family let the mansion in 1887, and went to live in Kineton, where they remained until shortly before the First World War.[89] Personal tragedy also struck: in 1893, Henry lost a younger son, in 1894, his wife, and in 1897 his daughter. He last went hunting early in 1899, and spent his last three years an invalid and a broken man. He died at sea, near Colombo, whilst on what was supposed to have been a curative voyage.

88. SBTRO, DR 98/1889,1893-6; DR 622/14,17,19.

89. See especially, *Stratford-upon-Avon Herald*, 16 September 1887.

His son, Richard Greville Verney, succeeded in 1902. His book, *The Passing Years*, shows he had some understanding of the economic factors behind the decline in his family's fortunes, but this did not alter his conviction that any changes to the established order would only cause further damage and should therefore be resisted. Ironically, it is he, the last and possibly most impoverished head of the family, who has achieved some lasting political fame. An extreme right-winger in politics, he led a group called the 'Ditchers', after their last-ditch attempt to resist reform of the House of Lords. A passionate Unionist, he was an implacable opponent of Irish home rule and did what he could to bolster up Ulster opposition once the principle of home rule had been conceded.[90] But the First World War dealt the final blow to any hope that the family could regain its old ascendancy. In 1921 Richard sold Compton Verney house and two years later was dead.

90. His career is dealt with in detail in Chapter 6 below.

Nearly 500 years after the acquisition of the estate and sixteen generations later, the house thus passed to new owners, particularly ironic in view of the fact that only seventy years before the family estates had reached their greatest extent. This itself was the culmination of a fairly rapid period of growth over the previous 150 years, during which the house and grounds had been reconstructed out of all recognition. Earlier, that is before 1700, the impression is of a family which, though it had established itself in dramatic enough fashion in the middle years of the fifteenth century, had found progress up the social ladder painfully slow; active in local affairs (when the succession was not disrupted by minorities), the family had been unable to break into the upper reaches of society until the early years of the eighteenth century. That it did so may have been partly psychological (the successful claim to a peerage in 1696), but was also due to the generally favourable economic climate and, above all, to the Peyto inheritance which gave such a boost to the family's income in the middle years of the eighteenth century. Thereafter, the family's position must have appeared unassailable and remained so, at least superficially, until the 1860s. But within twenty years the writing was clearly on the wall, and within sixty, the whole edifice had collapsed like a pack of cards.

CHAPTER TWO

Compton Verney:
LANDSCAPE AND PEOPLE IN THE MIDDLE AGES

❦

CHRISTOPHER DYER

This book is mainly about a great country house and its owners. The Verneys created buildings and parkland in a style appropriate for aristocratic living. This chapter is concerned with the people of Compton Verney (or Compton Murdak as it was called for most of the middle ages), both the lords of the manor and the numerous peasant tenants, and the landscape that they inherited and adapted to their needs before the sixteenth century. Anyone visiting Compton Verney now is bound to be impressed by the impact of landscape gardening in the eighteenth century, and more recent changes, but we will see that there were other equally radical upheavals long before 1700. The central question must be how and why these transformations occurred. If we can add to our understanding of changes in landscape and society in one village we can throw light on parallel developments over a much wider area. Compton lies at the centre of the Feldon district of south and east Warwickshire, which like much of midland England is dominated by nucleated villages and open fields (Figure 2). Firstly a brief account will be given of previous research into the village's pre-modern past; then the settlement and landscape of the parish over two millennia will be reconstructed; and finally we will turn to the inhabitants and investigate their role in the development and decay of the village and its fields.

~ ~ ~

A succession of historians have contributed to the history of Compton Verney, each reflecting the different approaches and preoccupations of the period in which they wrote. The earliest comments were made by Warwickshire's first local historian, John

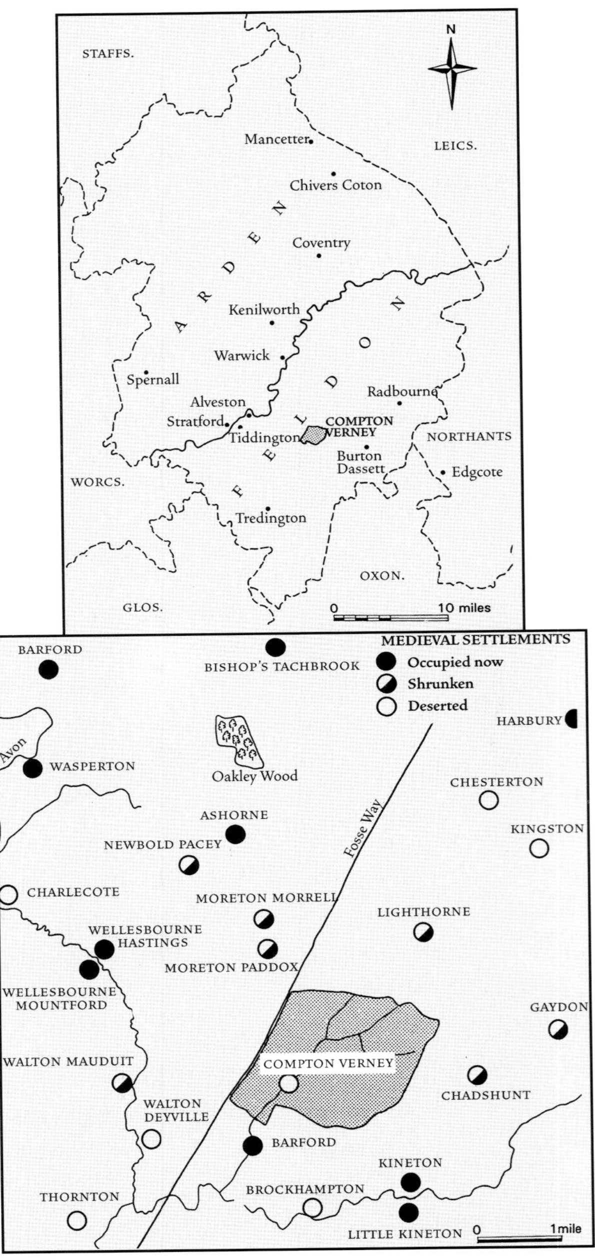

FIGURE 2
Compton Verney's location in Warwickshire, showing places and features mentioned in the text.

Rous, a priest who is best known for his interest in the Beauchamp family. He is also famous for his list of sixty deserted villages in the locality of Warwick, which was compiled in about 1486, and inserted as an aside in his chronicle history of the kings of England. He said that 'Compton Mordak' was 'now only a manor and church, once of free and servile twenty-seven tenures, and besides a good rectory with its mansion'. Rous was a historian as well as a contemporary witness. He based his information partly on his observation of the place, and perhaps conversations with the clergy of St Mary's church at Warwick to which Compton Verney church was attached. But his crucial reference to the previous size of the village came from the Hundred Rolls of 1279-80, which he mentions explicitly when giving numbers of tenants in other villages, though he miscounted the number of tenants at Compton Verney (there were forty-four, making it one of the larger villages in the county). The cause of the abandonment of villages was clear to Rous who was drawing a moral lesson in typical medieval style: they had been destroyed by avaricious men.[1]

Sir William Dugdale, writing in the mid-seventeenth century, knew that Compton Verney had once been a village, and also used the Hundred Rolls as evidence for the size of the settlement, arriving at the figure of thirty-four tenants – again the wrong number. He included in the *Antiquities of Warwickshire* Hollar's print showing the house, with a pool in the foreground. The site of the village to the north of the house is labelled as 'The elms in the town' (Plate 35). Dugdale accepted that villages had disappeared and unlike Rous made no moral comment, which was appropriate as his book celebrated the gentry families who had often profited from the exploitation of the sites of former villages.[2]

Interest in deserted villages lapsed among local historians, so that the author of the *Victoria County History*'s article on Compton Verney, published in 1949, could write about the manor, house, church and parish without noticing the absence of a village or recalling its former existence.[3] Like many historians in the first half of the twentieth century, he was primarily concerned with institutions and with the activities of the aristocracy. At precisely that time Maurice Beresford was listing the deserted villages in Warwickshire, and included Compton Verney among his hundred examples. He noted the comments of Rous and Dugdale, and found in a seventeenth-century will a reference to fields called the 'Townes' lying 'on both sides of the pools'. When he visited he saw the field a hundred yards north-east of the house 'pitted and abundantly covered with nettles'. Beresford argued that Compton Verney, like most of the Warwickshire 'lost' villages, had fallen victim to deliberate depopulation in the fifteenth century, caused by the calculation among landowners that enclosed pastures stocked with sheep gave better profits than peasants practising mixed farming.[4] Beresford, an economic

1. Joannis Rossi, *Historia Regum Angliae*, ed. T. Hearne, Oxford 1745, 122-4; *The Warwickshire Hundred Rolls of 1279-80*, ed. Trevor John, British Academy Records of Social and Economic History, new series, xix,1992, 248-50 (henceforth cited as *Hundred Rolls*).

2. W. Dugdale, *Antiquities of Warwickshire*, London 1656, 433-9; Jan Broadway, *William Dugdale and the Significance of County History in Early Stuart England*, Dugdale Society Occasional Paper xxxix, 1999, 3-6. Dr Broadway points out to me that Dugdale regarded the enclosure of Burton Dassett as a benefit to the public.

3. *Victoria County History, Warwickshire*, v, 58-60.

4. M.W. Beresford, 'The Deserted Villages of Warwickshire', *Transactions of the Birmingham Archaeological Society* lxvi, 1945-6, 89-90. (This was published in 1950.) For the background to his work see M.W. Beresford, 'A Draft Chronology of Deserted Village Studies', *Medieval Settlement Research Group Annual Report*, 1986, 18-23. Compton Verney also appears in M.W. Beresford, *The Lost Villages of England*, London 1954, and in M. Beresford and J. Hurst, *Deserted Medieval Villages*, London 1971, 41, 45-6.

historian, had been influenced by the writings of R.H.Tawney about the agrarian problem of the sixteenth century, and shared Tawney's sympathy for the injustices suffered by the common man. He was also anxious to show that maps and the physical remains in the countryside could extend our understanding of the past.

A few years later Rodney Hilton discovered that the Willoughby de Broke archive contained a great deal of evidence for the decay of the village of Compton Murdak around 1400. He used this example, with others, to emphasize that disruption in the agrarian economy preceded enclosure and depopulation. He was concerned to shift the explanation for deserted villages away from avaricious individuals towards the overall social and economic troubles in the later middle ages, which he saw as symptomatic of the general crisis of the feudal order during the transition to capitalism. This important revision of Beresford's interpretation of village desertions had a rather slow impact because it was published in Italy in 1957, and did not appear in a more accessible place until 1975.[5] Meanwhile Dorothy Styles edited the fifteenth-century financial accounts of the collegiate church of St Mary at Warwick, which contained a good deal of information about Compton Verney as the parish church provided St Mary's with one of its prebends. In 1466 an auditor's note added to an account states that tenants had been expelled by Richard Verney, in explanation of the non-payment of a fine (imposed annually on the tenants for the previous eighteen years) for failing to attend a court in Warwick. This led Dr Styles to suggest that the depopulation of the village had begun in the 1440s. However, the auditor was referring to the three tenants of the rectory, not the whole village. Dr Styles noticed that the site of the village was recalled in the 'Old Town' field-name marked on the 1736 estate map of Compton Verney.[6]

This author's involvement with Compton Verney began in the late 1970s with research for the *Agrarian History of England and Wales*. The results were published in 1982 and 1991, in which evidence from dozens of villages, including Compton, was used to extend Hilton's argument that desertion was a symptom of the widespread changes in the countryside in the century and a half after the Black Death of 1348-9.[7] Having seen the 1738 estate map with its 'Old Townes' field to the south-east of the lakes, in 1979 the author took students and colleagues on a field course to Compton, and the group found medieval pottery in the plough soil along the edge of the lake.[8] When it was proposed to build an opera house at Compton Verney, this field was chosen as its site, and in consequence in 1991 an archaeological evaluation was made which revealed building foundations, post-holes, pits and other evidence of an extensive medieval settlement.[9] In preparation for the public enquiry of 1994 into the application for planning permission for the opera house a report was commissioned from James Bond and the author on the deserted village site in its regional context.[10] The account of

5. R.H. Hilton, 'A Study in the Pre-history of English Enclosure in the Fifteenth Century', in *Studi in Onore di Armando Sapori*, Milan 1957, i, 647-85, reprinted in R.H. Hilton, *The English Peasantry in the Later Middle Ages*, Oxford 1975, 161-73.

6. *Ministers' Accounts of the Collegiate Church of St Mary, Warwick 1432-85*, ed. D. Styles, Dugdale Society xxvi, 1969, 77.

7. C. Dyer, 'Deserted Medieval Villages in the West Midlands', *Economic History Review*, 2nd series, xxxv, 1982, 19-34, reprinted in C. Dyer, *Everyday Life in Medieval England*, London 1994, 27-45; *Agrarian History of England and Wales*, iii, 1348-1500, ed. E. Miller, Cambridge 1991, 85-92.

8. *Medieval Village Research Group Annual Report 27*, 1979, 10.

9. *Compton Verney Opera House Archaeological Evaluation 1991*, Warwickshire Museum.

10. C.C. Dyer and C.J. Bond, *Compton Murdak Deserted Medieval Settlement and its Historical and Archaeological Context*, Warwickshire Museum, 1994.

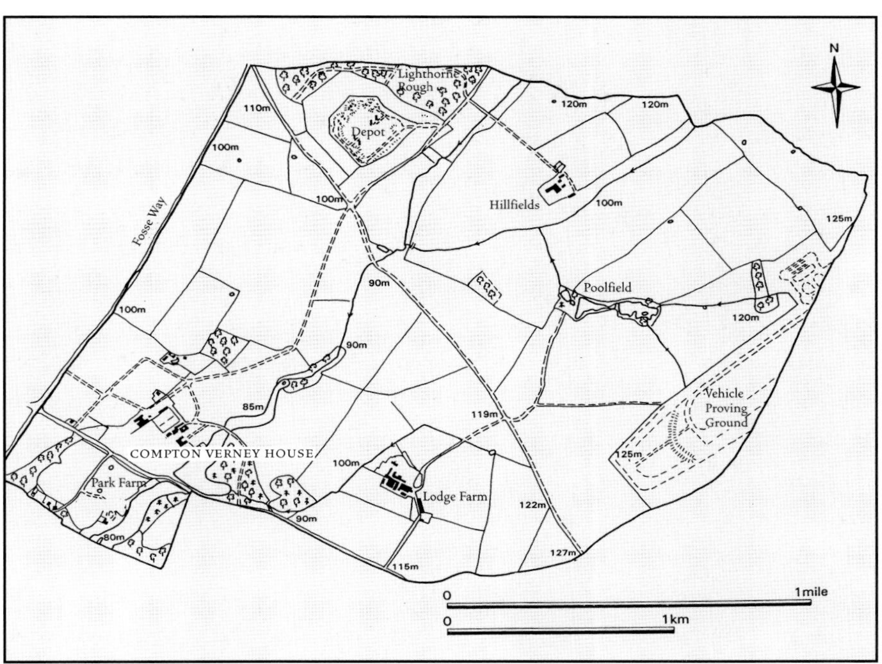

FIGURE 3
Compton Verney in 1999, showing buildings, field boundaries, water courses, marl-pits and heights above sea level.

Compton which follows is based on the documentary research done for the report, and on field work before and after the conference held at the house in 1998. It reflects the changing approaches to local history at the end of the twentieth century by combining more than one discipline, by drawing on the techniques of landscape history, and by attempting to reconstruct the ideas and attitudes of the people involved.

The starting point for investigating the history of a landscape is its modern pattern of roads, hedges and buildings, recorded in large scale maps, aerial photographs and direct observation. In common with many other Feldon villages in south-east Warwickshire, Compton Verney presents us with a challenge for enquiring into earlier periods, because so much has been destroyed by modern developments. The landscaping of the park has removed all visible traces of the village and its immediate surroundings. Modern arable farming has led to the flattening of the ridge and furrow and the grubbing out of hedges. The construction of Gaydon airfield has removed all features on the eastern edge of the parish, and a 'depot', originally built as a store for nuclear weapons, has obliterated a large area in the north-west (Figure 3).

The main elements of the pre-modern landscape can nonetheless be reconstructed by using early maps and illustrations, documents which contain field-names and other topographical information, aerial photographs of the late 1940s, which give a useful indication of the extent and form of the ridge and furrow, field work on surviving earthworks, systematic field walking to collect artefacts from the plough soil, and small-scale excavations.[11]

Although the research proceeds backwards from modern to earlier times, the results can be reported here in chronological order, beginning with the period before the middle ages, and then examining the origins of the medieval village and its fields, the exploitation of the land in the thirteenth and fourteenth centuries, and the transformation of the village into a pasture in the fifteenth. The parish measures about 2.5 miles by 1.5 miles (3.5 by 2.5 km), with land falling from a height of 420 ft to 260 ft (130m to 80m) into the valley of a brook and its tributaries (Figure 3). The soils are mainly heavy clays, those in the south and west consisting of the sticky Jurassic clay known to soil scientists as 'Evesham 1' and 'Evesham 2', while there is more 'loam over clay' in the east.[12] The assumption would once have been made that such inhospitable soils supported little early settlement, but field walking in Compton Verney shows that the land was cleared for agriculture and settled long before the middle ages. A thin scatter of flint flakes over nine fields in the parish provides us with no specific information about the date or nature of the earliest settlements, but the finds

11. The maps are the 1736 and 1738 estate maps: SBTRO, DR 98/1819,1820. The aerial photographs have been analysed by Warwickshire Museum. For the excavations see note 10 above and *Archaeological Evaluation at Compton Verney House, Warwickshire*, Warwickshire Museum, 1995, and *Archaeological Observation at the Art Gallery Extension, Compton Verney House, Warwickshire*, Warwickshire Museum, 1998. The field walking was carried out between February 1998 and February 1999, based on transects at 10 metre intervals.

12. *Soils and their Use in Midland and Western England*, ed. J.M. Ragg and others, Soil Survey of England and Wales, Bulletin no. 12, Harpenden 1984, 95-7, 189-92.

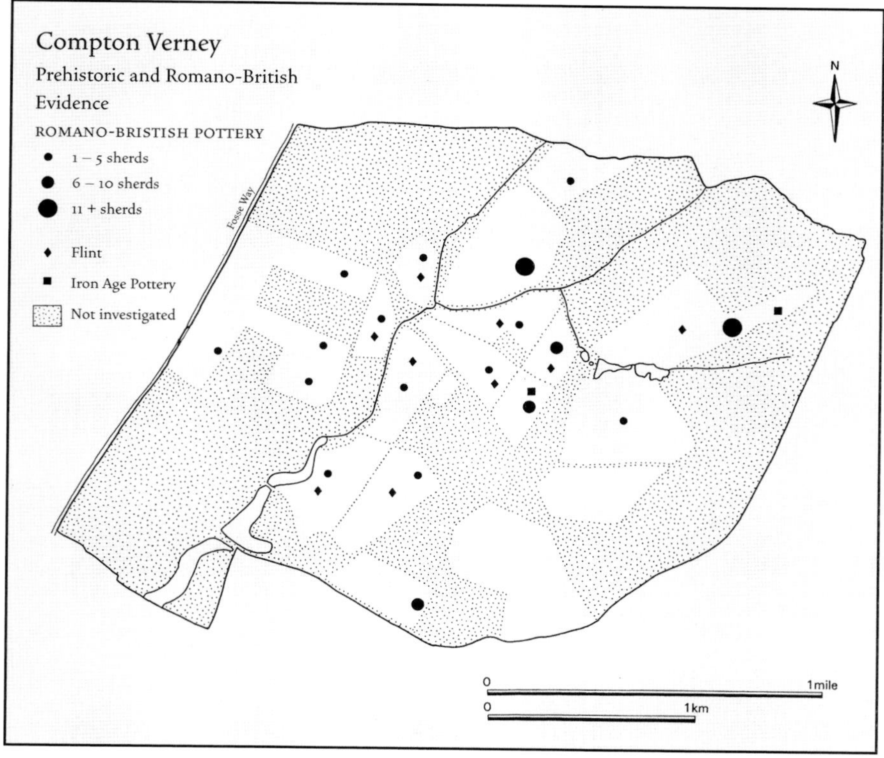

FIGURE 4
Compton Verney, prehistoric and Romano-British evidence.
These are the results of systematic field walking in 1998-9.
The stippled areas were not walked, mostly because they
were covered with grass or fast growing crops.

presumably reflect prehistoric activity, either by mesolithic hunter gatherers or by seasonal visitors or more stable communities in the neolithic or bronze age (Figure 4). In Warwickshire most of the known sites of the neolithic and bronze age, including an impressive number of monuments used for religious ceremonies and burials, are concentrated in the Avon valley, but this is partly because features in light, gravelly soils are more likely to produce crop marks which are visible from the air. Finds of neolithic stone axes have been made on a number of sites on the higher clay lands of the Feldon, suggesting that the district supported a population of some kind. It must, however, be said that the Compton Verney flints are smaller in number than in field-walking programmes elsewhere in south Warwickshire, and, compared with the Cotswolds, prehistoric finds are very scarce indeed.[13] Only two isolated finds of Iron Age pottery have been made in the parish, but occupation at this time could have been extensive as the rather fragile pottery of the period does not survive well in the plough soil, and is often missed in field walking.

13. R. Hingley, 'Prehistoric Warwickshire: a Review of the Evidence', *Transactions of the Birmingham and Warwickshire Archaeological Society* c, 1996, 1-24. The basis of the comparisons are provided by field walking by the author at Admington (Warwickshire) and Hawling, Hazleton and Hidcote (Gloucestershire). Each field, with flint finds marked, produced between one and six flints only.

The field-walking evidence becomes more abundant and coherent from the Roman period (Figure 4). Two small concentrations of Romano-British pottery covering areas no more than 300 ft (100 m) across have been found in the north of the parish, which are likely to mark the sites of single farmsteads. They are on high ground, in one case on a rather bleak plateau, but both lie within 600 ft of small water courses. The finds consist mainly of fragments of utilitarian grey pottery, the products of local kilns, with a few pieces of Severn valley ware brought a short distance from the west, suggesting that the inhabitants were low in status and with limited resources. Other sites in south Warwickshire have produced a greater variety of pottery, including fine wares from other parts of Britain and from the continent. A piece of hand mill made from Millstone Grit (perhaps from Derbyshire) and a fragment of black-burnished ware manufactured in Dorset from the eastern Compton site, and a sherd of Samian ware from the western, are the only objects carried from any distance. A few sherds of Romano-British pottery have been found on almost all of the fields investigated, and the most likely explanation for their presence is that the land was under cultivation at some time in the Roman period, and that pieces of pottery, thrown with domestic rubbish on to middens, were carried onto the fields in loads of manure. Only one part of the parish, the south-eastern corner, has consistently failed to produce any finds. We must conclude that most of the territory was cultivated at some time between the first and fourth centuries – the finds are not closely datable but include pieces which belong to the first or second centuries, and, from the later part of the period, a fragment of mortarium made at Mancetter in north Warwickshire. The fields were likely to have been worked from a number of farms, of which two have been located, but others may lie undiscovered in fields that have not yet been investigated. Clusters of finds from the centre and south of the parish, near Poolfields and Lodge Farm, while not sufficiently concentrated to be identified as settlements, nonetheless hint that such sites lie nearby. No trace of a villa has been found, although such relatively high status sites are scattered over this part of south Warwickshire, including two in parishes adjacent to Compton.[14]

The Romano-British settlements and farming in Compton Verney did not just form 'background' to the later landscape, but had a direct influence on its development in the medieval centuries. The Fosse Way, a new road of the first century, did not merely give Compton parish a convenient western boundary mark, but provided an alignment for fields laid out beside it. The ridges and headlands of the medieval field system up to a half mile (1km) from the Fosse lay either at right angles to, or in parallel with, the Roman road (Figure 5). Perhaps medieval people when fixing the boundaries of their fields took advantage of an existing line as a surveying point, but another possibility is that Roman fields survived in use, and were perpetuated as a framework for subsequent cultivation.[15] A stretch of the northern boundary of the parish follows a minor Roman road probably ran east from Tiddington near Stratford-upon-Avon towards another small town at Duston in Northamptonshire, though this does not seem to have had much influence on later field patterns in the northern part of Compton. On the other hand, the road which runs along the southern edge of the parish, now linking Kineton and Wellesbourne, which is another likely early route, has furlong boundaries and ridge and furrow lying in parallel. The medieval fields in the centre and east of the parish follow more irregular patterns, apparently determined mainly by the stream valleys and slopes.

The medieval villagers were conscious that they were living in an old landscape, as they used earlier features in describing boundaries. A thirteenth-century deed mentions an 'old ditch', and a division in the East Field was called Badelowe, referring to a burial mound which could have had prehistoric or pagan Saxon origins. The field-name Tunstall (meaning the site of a settlement), which lay towards the Fosse Way in the north-west of the parish, might also have been coined by medieval ploughmen who found traces of earlier occupation.[16]

Compton's inhabitants in the middle ages are likely to have worked within a framework of boundaries and field divisions some of which were based on alignments established in the Roman period. Most of the land that was cultivated in the middle ages had also been under the plough in Roman times, judging from the scatters of pottery reflecting manuring in both periods. This could be a matter of coincidence – when a new settlement was established in the middle ages the incomers made the same judgement as their predecessors that the land was suitable for arable. They could have

14. P. Booth, 'Warwickshire in the Roman period: a Review of Recent Work', *Transactions of the Birmingham and Warwickshire Archaeological Society* c, 1996, 25-57. The two sites produced thirty-two and thirty-seven sherds respectively, which, while small in number, were closely concentrated.

15. For examples, *Early Land Allotment*, ed. H.C. Bowen and P. Fowler, British Archaeological Reports xlviii, 1978.

16. SBTRO, DR 98/12, 13, 31a.

discovered the old roads and derelict field boundaries and reused them. But it is more likely that at least part of the land was cultivated continuously after the fourth century, so there would have been no need for much medieval clearance of woodland or waste. The descendants of the Romano-British population may have continued to occupy the territory, albeit with some addition of migrants speaking a Germanic language in the fifth or sixth centuries.[17] The incorporation into the place-name of the adjacent parish of Chadshunt of the Latin word *fons* ('Ceadel's well' – an early form is Chedelesfont) can only be explained by the survival of a native population who kept at least some words of Latin in their speech. Compton's name is an Old English description of its location: the estate or settlement (*tun*) in the valley or combe.[18] Like Chadshunt there was probably a British or Latin name coined in the Roman period for the area in which Compton lay, which continued to be employed in the fifth century, but was replaced by an English name as that language became dominant among the local population in the following two or three hundred years.

When was the territory of Compton Verney formed? The modern parish, which perpetuates the medieval boundaries, has a topographical coherence (Figure 3). In the northern part three small watercourses join to form a brook which runs through the valley (the combe of the place name) in which the modern house, lakes and park now lie. The brook flows through Combrook ('brook in the valley') to join the Dene, a tributary of the Avon. Compton's northern and eastern boundaries run on ridges which separate the combe from the adjoining valleys containing Kineton, Chadshunt and Lighthorne. On the western side the Fosse Way, though a man-made boundary, runs partly on high ground which marks the eastern limits of Walton and Moreton Morrell.

The eastern edge of Compton's territory could have been defined by 969, because a (rather enigmatic) boundary clause attached to a charter for Kineton of that date seems to exclude our village.[19] Kineton, which as its name implies was a royal estate, was likely to have been very large, and Compton probably once formed part of that expanse of land. Wellesbourne, though it was described by Domesday as a berewick of Kineton, which implies a minor appendage, is known to have been a royal residence in the ninth century, and may always have been part of this estate or may have constituted another royal centre to which Compton belonged.[20] The estate was no doubt split up in the ninth and tenth centuries as happened in the case of the similar estates of Stratford and Tredington immediately to the west. The great estates had a federal structure in the seventh and eighth centuries, when for example Shottery, part of the Stratford estate, appears to have had its own identity. Compton may well have been recognized as a distinct unit within the Kineton estate, but was set completely apart, perhaps in the tenth century, when it was granted to a layman, probably a thegn. The process of

17. The debate is summarized in H. Hamerow, 'Migration Theory and the Migration Period', in *Building on the Past*, ed. B. Vyner, Royal Archaeological Institute, 1994, 164-77. The local evidence is discussed in W.J.Ford, 'Anglo-Saxon Cemeteries along the Avon Valley', *Transactions of the Birmingham and Warwickshire Archaeological Society* c, 1996, 59-98. Important evidence for the continuous use of the same site, albeit with some migration over short distances, has come from Wasperton, only four miles from Compton Verney: P. Wise, 'Wasperton', *Current Archaeology* 126, 1991, 256-9.

18. J.E.B. Gover, A. Mawer and F.M. Stenton, *The Place-Names of Warwickshire*, English Place-Name Society xiii, 1936, 249-50, 252; M. Gelling, *The West Midlands in the Early Middle Ages*, Leicester 1992, 55-9. There is a slight possibility that Walton and Wellesbourne to the west of Compton have names referring to British (Welsh) inhabitants : A.D. Mills, 'Three Difficult English Place-Names Reconsidered', in *Names, Places and People*, ed. A.R. Rumble and A.D. Mills, Stamford 1997, 243-4.

19. Gover, Mawer and Stenton, 282.

20. H.P.R. Finberg, *The Early Charters of the West Midlands*, Leicester 1961, 46, 153. The link between Kineton and Wellesbourne: *Domesday Book*, ed. A. Farley, London 1783, 238. (henceforth *DB*)

endowing a lesser aristocracy with land is found throughout England at this time. At first Compton would have become a separate estate or manor, and was later further subdivided, to be exploited for the benefit of its new lay owners. In addition, and certainly by 1086, when a priest is recorded, the lord of Compton built a church for his household and his tenants, which would initially have been attached to a mother church at Kineton or Wellesbourne, but which would have eventually gained its independence as a parish church.[21] The new parish served the secular estate, and so shared its boundaries, which means that the modern parish preserves the outline of a unit of pre-Conquest landholding.

What can be said about early medieval settlement in Compton? It was heavily populated by the eleventh century, when forty-eight tenants and slaves are listed, many of them heads of household, so we must think in terms of a total of at least two hundred people. They are unlikely all to have arrived recently, as the basis for the creation of the separate estate in the tenth century would have been a sufficient number of tenants and slaves or servants. It would have been rated at ten hides for purposes of assessing taxes and services only if it was regarded as a valuable asset, which presumes that the land was supplied with labour. Presumably people were living at Compton in the seventh century, when two people were buried there with high quality jewellery, and we have already suggested that the settlement and cultivation of the first to fourth centuries is unlikely to have ceased in the year 400.[22] We do not find scatters of pottery datable to the sixth to ninth centuries like those found in neighbouring Northamptonshire and Gloucestershire, but this may reflect the different pottery-making and pottery-using traditions in Warwickshire, rather than the lack of settlements in that period. In those other counties the settlements were small and scattered, and not necessarily sited near to the later nucleated villages.[23] Our expectation would therefore be that Compton was populated from the fifth to eleventh centuries, but that in the early centuries of that period the inhabitants would have lived in dispersed hamlets and farmsteads rather than a single large village. The late medieval field-name Tunstall, already mentioned as evidence of an early settlement, could refer to a hamlet of this period.

The first large-scale innovation in the landscape of Compton Verney seems to have come when the inhabitants abandoned their dispersed settlements and gathered together in a single compact village in the valley. The precise date of this movement is not known, but the earliest pottery from the village site belongs to the eleventh century. Modern readers of Domesday often imagine that the people listed in that survey under the name of a place which is now a village were also then living in a nucleated settlement, but this may not have been the case for the forty-eight households of Compton. They could in the eleventh century have still been in the process of uprooting

21. D. Hooke, 'Reconstructing Anglo-Saxon Landscapes in Warwickshire', *Transactions of the Birmingham and Warwickshire Archaeological Society* c, 1996, 99-116; *DB*, 239, 241. There are a number of Compton entries in the Warwickshire Domesday, and I have followed the consensus among Domesday editors in identifying the two entries which refer to Compton Verney.

22. A. Meaney, *A Gazetteer of English Anglo-Saxon Burial Sites*, London 1964, 260.

23. C. Taylor, *Village and Farmstead*, London 1983, 112-24 ; D. Aldred and C.Dyer, 'A Medieval Cotswold Village: Roel, Gloucestershire', *Transactions of the Bristol and Gloucestershire Archaeological Society* cix, 1991, 139-70, especially 141-2.

themselves from their scattered hamlets and moving alongside their neighbours near the church and lord's house. If the village had been fully formed by 1086, it would have been a relatively recent development.

Villages were being created at this time through much of the midlands, and some of those in south and east Warwickshire, judging from pottery finds, began a little before Compton, but mostly their first phase of occupation seems to belong to the eleventh or twelfth centuries.[24] From the middle ages and into the eighteenth century the compact villages of the Feldon were associated with extensive cultivation, organized in great open fields in which the villagers held many quarter- and half-acre strips mingled with those of their neighbours. These champion landscapes contrasted with the wooded Arden of north Warwickshire, where the fields were small and enclosed, more land was used as pasture and wood, and the settlements were small and scattered[25] (Figure 2).

In the Feldon village of Alveston in the late tenth century, a land grant consisted of acres (long strips of land, later called selions or ridges) lying in a complex and extensive field system just like those found in later centuries.[26] Compton's large open fields with their hundreds of scattered strips, though not documented in detail until the thirteenth century, probably developed before the Conquest. We know that the cultivated area was large enough to keep fifteen ploughs working in 1086, which can conservatively be estimated to mean a thousand acres of arable, or about 60 per cent of the territory (the parish covers 1,668 acres or 676 ha). Indeed, as Compton seems to have supported as many people in 1086 as in 1279-80, cultivation may already have reached the level of more than 1,500 acres. No wood is mentioned in Domesday, which cannot be regarded as conclusive evidence of its absence as the survey omitted small 'groves' which provided villagers with fuel without profit to the lord.[27] However, there is no later medieval reference to woods at Compton either, nor any mention of clearances or assarts. The field-name Walde or wold, which is often taken to refer to former woodland, may indicate that trees had at some remote time occupied part of the parish, probably in the south-east corner which was a common pasture in the later middle ages.[28] Ploughed fields extending to the edge of the village territory were normal in the later medieval Feldon, and in many cases these large areas of arable had a very early origin. Tenth-century charters, for example at Longdon in Tredington, mention such features as a furrow and a headland as boundary marks, and, in the case of Compton's neighbour Walton, arable land lay next to its eastern boundary, the Fosse Way, by the 1160s.[29] Not just the large area under the plough, but also the division of the land into two fields subject to alternate cropping and fallow, are likely to have been established before the thirteenth century, but again the precise date is not known. We may suspect a connection between the systematic organization of the fields and the formation of the village.[30]

24. C. Dyer, 'Rural Settlement in Medieval Warwickshire', *Transactions of the Birmingham and Warwickshire Archaeological Society* c, 1996, 118. Since this was published Stephanie Ratkai has revised her dates of the pottery tempered with oolite from the Compton Verney excavations, and would date the beginning of the sequence of medieval pottery to the eleventh century.

25. Dyer, 'Medieval Warwickshire', 117-32, and many works cited there on this theme.

26. *Anglo-Saxon Charters*, ed. A.J. Robertson, Cambridge 1956, 88-9.

27. S.J. Wager, *Woods, Wolds and Groves: the Woods of Medieval Warwickshire*, British Archaeological Reports, British Series, 269, 1998, 12.

28. SBTRO, DR 98/6 (Letlewolde); 12 (le Wolde); 31a (Walde).

29. D.Hooke, 'Village Development in the West Midlands', in *Medieval Villages*, ed. D. Hooke, Oxford 1985, 127-31; SBTRO, DR 98/3.

30. H.S.A. Fox, 'Approaches to the Adoption of the Midland System', in *The Origins of Open-Field Agriculture*, ed. T. Rowley, London 1981, 64-111.

The village and its fields can be reconstructed with more precise and secure evidence for the thirteenth and fourteenth centuries. To begin with the fields, the ridge and furrow recorded in the aerial photographs of the 1940s has fossilized the field patterns of the middle ages (Figure 5). In many parishes, where enclosure was delayed until the eighteenth century, the ridge and furrow could have been subject to post-medieval modification, but much of the arable in Compton had been turned over to grass by 1400, and was not ploughed again until the 1960s. Field work helps to fill any gaps in the aerial evidence, for example in modern woods where the trees concealed the earthworks from the camera. In addition the documents describe the location of selions within the system with much detail.

We can firstly conclude, as has already been proposed for an earlier period, that a very high proportion of the territory was ploughed in the thirteenth and early fourteenth centuries. Cultivation went up to the parish boundaries, included a good deal of the low-lying land beside brooks and water courses, and extended on to the higher ground. A notable gap on the plateau in the south-east corner, which has already been noted as an area without evidence of pre-medieval occupation, was apparently used as a pasture. Another area without ridge and furrow lay in the bottom of the valley of the main water course in the north-east of the parish, which was presumably meadow. Of course, the area around the modern house lacks ridge and furrow because it was removed when the park was laid out, though this area also includes the land occupied by the village and manor house. Otherwise there are a number of narrow strips of land without ridge and furrow, which are mainly where hedges have obscured the earthworks. Some of them would have served as roads and paths along the headlands to give access to the fields. This physical evidence agrees with the survey of 1279-80, which tells us that there were 35½ yardlands, each of which we believe contained 40 acres (16 ha) of arable, and two ploughlands in the lord's demesne, near to 200 acres (80 ha), making a total of about 1,600 acres (648 ha) under the plough, or around 95 per cent of the parish.[31] This calculation exaggerates somewhat the proportion of arable, no doubt because of inconsistencies in the size of yardlands and acres, but the topographical evidence, after allowing for the pasture, meadow and the village itself, would still suggest that about 90 per cent of the parish was under the plough at the peak of its development around 1300.

31. *Hundred Rolls*, 248-50; SBTRO, DR 98/6 (gives the yardland acreage as 40).

A late thirteenth-century deed reveals the details of the organization of the land, in recording the grant of a messuage (house) and 10 acres (4 ha) by Robert Durvassal to John, son of Geoffrey Smith of Compton.[32] The 10 acres consisted of eighteen parcels or selions, varying in size from a rood (quarter-acre) to an acre and a half, which lay distributed over sections of the field called furlongs (Smetheforlong, Ruggeforlong) or

32. SBTRO, DR 98/13.

'lands' (Banlond, Hongynglande), or subdivisions which took their names from topographical features such as Hale and Hornput. The fields had clearly been laid out in a very orderly fashion, because, in describing the location of each selion in relation to its neighbour, in no less than eleven examples the adjoining tenant was named as Gilbert le Grys. One might expect that a regular sequence in which each tenant had the same neighbour would break down after some generations, so this regular arrangement may well have been the result of a recent reallocation of parcels. The parcels or selions can be seen on the aerial photographs as ridges, and the furlongs and other subdivisions appear as groups of between twenty and fifty ridges lying in parallel. The limits of the parcels were defined partly by the furrows, and by boundary markers (merestones) at the junction of the ridges and the headlands. The deed describes half of the land, in fact 5¾ acres (the acres had evidently not been precisely measured), as lying in the East Field, and the other 5¾ acres in the West Field. We do not know where the boundary between the two fields lay, but the most likely division would have run in a northerly direction up the brook from the village, and then to the north-east following the stream that flowed in the Northslade near the modern Hillfields Farm (Figure 6).

Compton had two fields, divided firstly into about seventy furlongs, and then into 2,000 or 3,000 selions, altogether occupying a high proportion of the available land. There were obvious dangers in devoting too much land to arable, and it might be alleged that the eventual decline and desertion of the village was almost predestined because of the extreme specialization, the shortages of manure from the limited numbers of animals, and the rigidities of the system of husbandry. Indeed the whole medieval economy is said to have ceased to expand in c.1300, and went into a general crisis in the fourteenth century, because of the ecological problems created by excessive growth.[33]

33. This idea, developed in M.M. Postan, *Medieval Economy and Society*, London 1973, has been much criticized, for example in *Medieval Farming and Technology. The Impact of Agricultural Change in Northwest Europe*, ed. G. Astill and J. Langdon, Leiden 1997, especially 2-9, 225-49.

The division of Compton's land, like that of many other villages, into two fields maintained some balance in agriculture, because in theory one field was fallowed each year, the land was rested from continuous cropping, and some grazing was provided for the animals which gave the necessary pulling power and manure. Each 40-acre yardland would have been made up of sixty to eighty scattered selions, which ensured that everyone had equal involvement in the system, with good soil and bad, some land situated near to their homes, some at a distance. Every yardland also had sources of fodder and grazing for livestock, including shares in meadow in Northmede in Northslade, and in the south near Combrook. Permanent pasture could be found on the verges of 'the roads between the lands', and 'in the several of the vill', which might refer to an area of common, or more likely to grazing land adjoining the village or enclosed within it, perhaps along the brook.[34] We have seen that there was no wood at Compton, and the trees growing in hedges round the houses, gardens and crofts in the village, and

34. SBTRO, DR 98/13, 31a, 6.

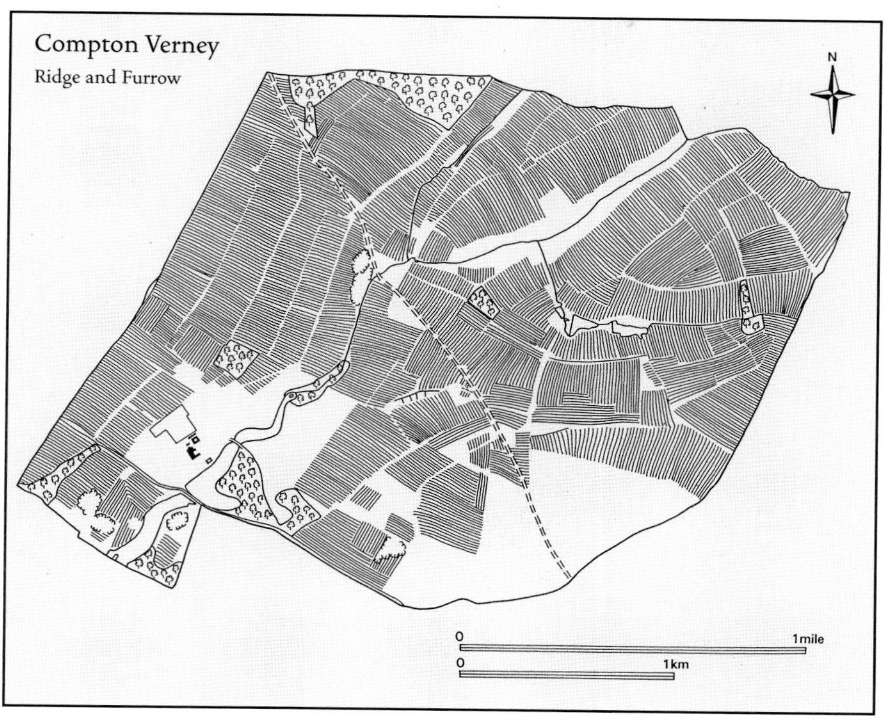

FIGURE 5
Ridge and furrow in Compton Verney parish, transcribed from the vertical R.A.F. photographs of the late 1940s. (A. Isham and N. Palmer of Warwickshire Museum, for the Royal Commission on Historical Monuments, England).

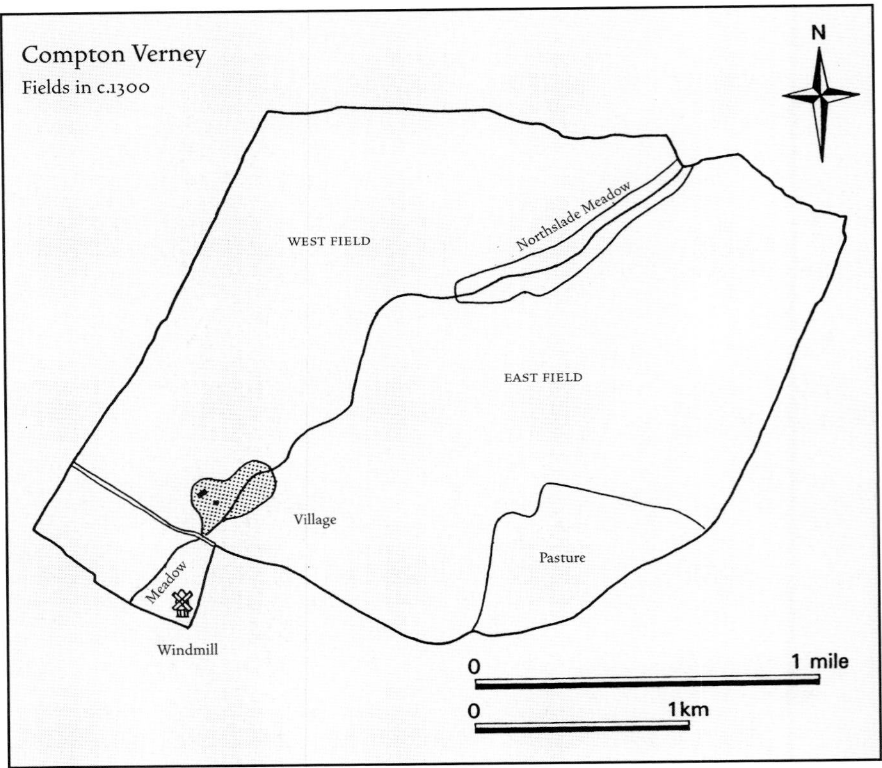

FIGURE 6
Compton Verney fields in c.1300. Based on the air photographs and documentary evidence.

along boundaries in the common fields, would have been inadequate sources of fuel and timber. Perhaps the inhabitants shared woods with their neighbours in Lighthorne or Walton, or they could have had access to distant woods in the Arden, like their neighbours at Chadshunt who in 1297 were expected to cut fuel for their lord in Kenilworth Wood (12 miles or 19 km away), and probably could collect their own supplies there as well. But if this were the case it is not recorded, and it remains possible that the villagers of Compton bought their wood and timber at Stratford or Warwick, or from the owners of local woods such as Oakley Wood.[35]

In the late thirteenth century, as well as the twenty-two yardlanders and four other tenants sharing two other yardlands, who between them accounted for three-quarters of the land in the fields, the three largest holdings of land were those of the Murdaks, the lords of the manor, with about 200 acres, and a similar amount in the hands of the Durvassals, who held a sub-manor. The parson's glebe accounted for another 80 acres. Sometimes demesnes were gathered into a consolidated block, but a reference to a tenant's individual selion lying next to the land of William Murdak might suggest that at least part of the demesne was scattered over the fields alongside the peasant holdings.[36] The field system served a variety of interests – those of the lords of the two manors and the parson, but also those of the peasants. The regulation of the system depended on the villagers acting collectively, and there would always have been some tension between individual peasants and the village as a whole, particularly over such matters as the numbers of animals grazing on the commons, and the time and place when animals could be brought on to the common arable after the harvest. All of this was clearly designed for sustainable agriculture, in which the equilibrium between pastoral and arable farming was kept, and the yields of grain could be maintained at a level which would allow the population of the manor to be fed, and in addition to provide a marketable surplus.[37] The fact that the peasant population remained at much the same size between 1086 and 1279-80, and that most of the standard holdings of a yardland were not broken down into fractions, suggests that over a long period the lords and people of Compton had arrived at a balance, between the interests of lords and peasants, and between arable and pasture, that worked. This generalization can be made about a number of Feldon villages,where populations increased only modestly in the two centuries after 1086.[38]

The farming methods were not as rigid and mechanical as the formal descriptions of the two fields and the crop rotations might suggest. Peasants could maximize their returns by using their strips in the best way, which can be deduced from the names given to furlongs – Banlond suggests that it was well suited to bean crops and Stoulamore refers to low-lying and wet land. Awareness of these limitations would have helped

35. Staffordshire Record Office, D1734/J2268, fos 8-9 (survey of the estates of the bishopric of Coventry and Lichfield); Wager, *Woods*, 210, 241.

36. *Hundred Rolls*, 248-50; SBTRO, DR 98/12.

37. J.N Pretty, 'Sustainable Agriculture in the Middle Ages', *Agricultural History Review* xxxviii, 1990, 1-19.

38. Trevor John, 'Population Change in Medieval Warwickshire: Domesday Book to the Hundred Rolls of 1279-80', *Local Population Studies* lix, 1997, 41-53.

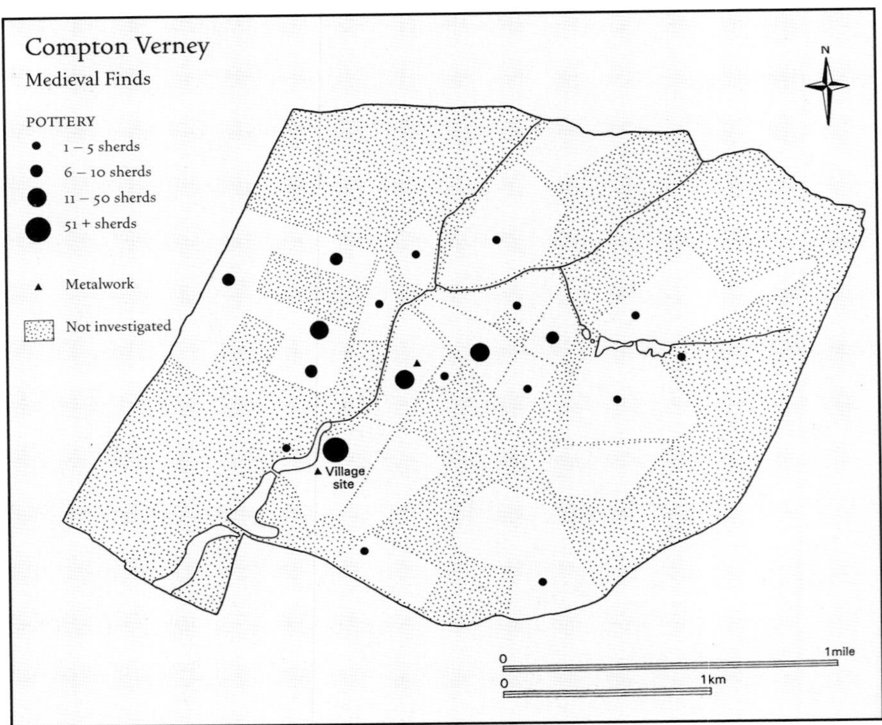

FIGURE 7
Compton Verney, medieval finds from field walking.

peasants to use them to the best advantage, though from other manors with more documents there is specific evidence for the application of accumulated wisdom in cultivation. 'Water furrows' are named in boundary descriptions: these refer to drainage channels at the end of furlongs, which were especially necessary on the heavy clays which are found in the west of the parish.[39]

Archaeological evidence shows that there were variations and flexibility in husbandry practices, again warning us against exaggerating the formality of the field system. Considerable quantities of medieval pottery have been found by field walking throughout the parish, showing that household refuse, placed on the same muck hills as animal manure, was carted out to fertilize the fields.[40] One would expect a pattern in which the densest concentrations occurred on the fields nearest to the village, as the dung carts would economize on time and labour by travelling short distances, and the outer furlongs would be dunged by sheep folded on them, leaving no trace of archaeological evidence. The results are more complicated than this (see Figure 7), so that while land immediately to the north and north-east of the village has quite a high density of pottery, little has been found on other fields which were just as close, while the finds are quite numerous, three-quarters of a mile (1 km-1.3 km) from the settlement. This relatively intense manuring seems to have been practised quite persistently over time, judging from the pottery from a field to the west of Poolfields which dates from the twelfth to the fifteenth centuries. It seems that certain furlongs in both of the large open fields (the high densities of finds come from both the West Field and the East Field) were chosen to receive quantities of carted manure. They were perhaps thought to be the best land that would repay this effort. Compton peasants grew a good deal of wheat – it is mentioned as being paid in rent, and accounted for a high proportion of the crops, along with barley, oats, peas and dredge (a mixture of barley and oats) at neighbouring Lighthorne and Chadshunt.[41] They could have concentrated their wheat on the land that had been manured in this way, so as to produce as much as possible of that most highly priced cash crop. Records from some west midland villages of 'inhoks', that is land that was taken out of the fallow field and cropped in successive years, may be connected with the carting of manure. There might have been at Compton some 'every years' land', which was manured and cropped continuously while the rest of the fields followed the orthodox two-course rotation.[42] Marl pits were also dug to improve the quality of the soil, especially in the outer furlongs. The dozen marl pits which are still visible are of course undated, and may have been dug in recent times, but some belong to the middle ages. One figures in a court case in 1335, when a man who killed another with an arrow in the fields of Compton claimed that he acted in self defence, because as he ran a marl pit barred his way and his only means of escape was to shoot his assailant[43] (Plate 14).

39. SBTRO, DR 98/13, 35*.

40. A parallel result from similar evidence is A. Davison, *The Evolution of Settlement in Three Parishes in South-East Norfolk*, East Anglian Archaeology xlix, 1990, 19-23, 62-3.

41. Payments of wheat are recorded in SBTRO, DR 98/10 (1 quarter 1 bushel); 11 (16 bushels); 12 (2 quarters); 17 (4 quarters); 22 (9 bushels). For crops at Lighthorne in the late fourteenth century, SBTRO, DR 98/674; and at Chadshunt in 1306-7, Lichfield Record Office, D30/N9 (accounts of manors of the bishopric of Coventry and Lichfield).

42. C. Dyer, *Warwickshire Farming*, Dugdale Society Occasional Paper xxvii 1981, 28.

43. PRO, C 260/47, no. 207.

PLATE 14
Marl pit in north-east Compton Verney (1998). This is likely to be of medieval date because of the post-medieval use of the fields as pasture.

It would be difficult to argue that Compton Murdak was doomed to fail as a settlement because of its system of agriculture. The large population supported itself for more than two centuries, and seems not to have been held in the grip of some inflexible system of husbandry heading for ecological disaster, but instead they practised sustainable agriculture. The villagers used a variety of methods to maintain the fertility of the soil, and may not have been rigidly confined within the two-course rotation. Other villages with similar agrarian economies have survived, even if often in rather shrunken form.

Between the two fields, in the valley of the brook towards the south of the parish, lay the village (Figure 8). Discovering its location is not difficult, in spite of the removal of all visible traces by the landscape gardeners. Reconstructing its plan, however, might seem foolhardy, but there is so much evidence, both written and material, that it seems appropriate to sketch its possible appearance, even though a considerable amount of speculation is involved. The likely boundaries of the village can be established by locating the edge of the ridge and furrow, which leaves us with the area under the middle and northern lake, the grounds of the house, including the site of the medieval church, and the fields called Old Town and The Town to the north-east of the house. Negative evidence in the form of excavations and field walking which have produced no sign of occupation help to narrow the likely area of settlement down to about 10 hectares (25 acres), within which we have precise knowledge of the church, remains of five buildings, and paved surfaces, including a road [44](Figure 9). The documents mention various features which can still be located – the church and its cemetery, now indicated by an obelisk, and the nearby rectory. The bridge by which the Kineton to Wellesbourne road crossed the brook is now a causeway along the edge of the middle lake, and this marked the end of the village, where a tenant's house stood near the bridge.[45] The manor house and its associated buildings, which is called 'the site of the manor' in 1405 and 'the close of the manor' in 1406, presumably lay on the site of the present house, which incorporates masonry from the mid-fifteenth century residence of the Verney family.[46] Other parts of the village fabric which cannot be placed precisely on the modern map include a cross, and a well or spring, which probably lay in the valley now occupied by the northern lake. A landmark called the 'corner' refers to a road junction near the cemetery.[47] By analogy with other villages sited in stream valleys nearby, such as Combrook and Lighthorne, which are likely to preserve at the present day elements of their medieval plan, roads led up the valley on either side of the brook, with houses along them. One house was described in the thirteenth century as having 'an orchard adjacent, up to the running water', which suggests buildings with gardens backing on to the stream, as they do now at Combrook.[48] A green may also have formed part of the village plan, judging from a reference in 1630 to Grimston Green.[49]

44. In addition to the archaeological excavations of which reports are cited in notes 9 and 11 above, a pipe trench observed to the north of the northern lake produced no evidence of settlement, and there are very few field-walking finds on the south-east side of Boathouse Coppice.

45. SBTRO, DR 98/24. A deed of 1315 refers to a messuage which 'lies between the bridge of Compton and the messuage of Alice at the Bridge'. Leticia atte Bregge is mentioned in the *Hundred Rolls*, 250. The bridge may have been built in the mid thirteenth century, as a deed dated before 1242 mentions 'Compton Wade', implying a ford across the brook.

46. SBTRO, DR 98/79, 31a. See p. 98 below.

47. The surnames de la Croyx and atte Welle appear in *Hundred Rolls*, 248-9. A tenement in 1438 was 'near the cemetery, on the corner', and another was 'near the church there, on the corner': SBTRO, DR 98/110, 111.

48. SBTRO, DR 98/13.

49. SBTRO, DR 98 /1657.

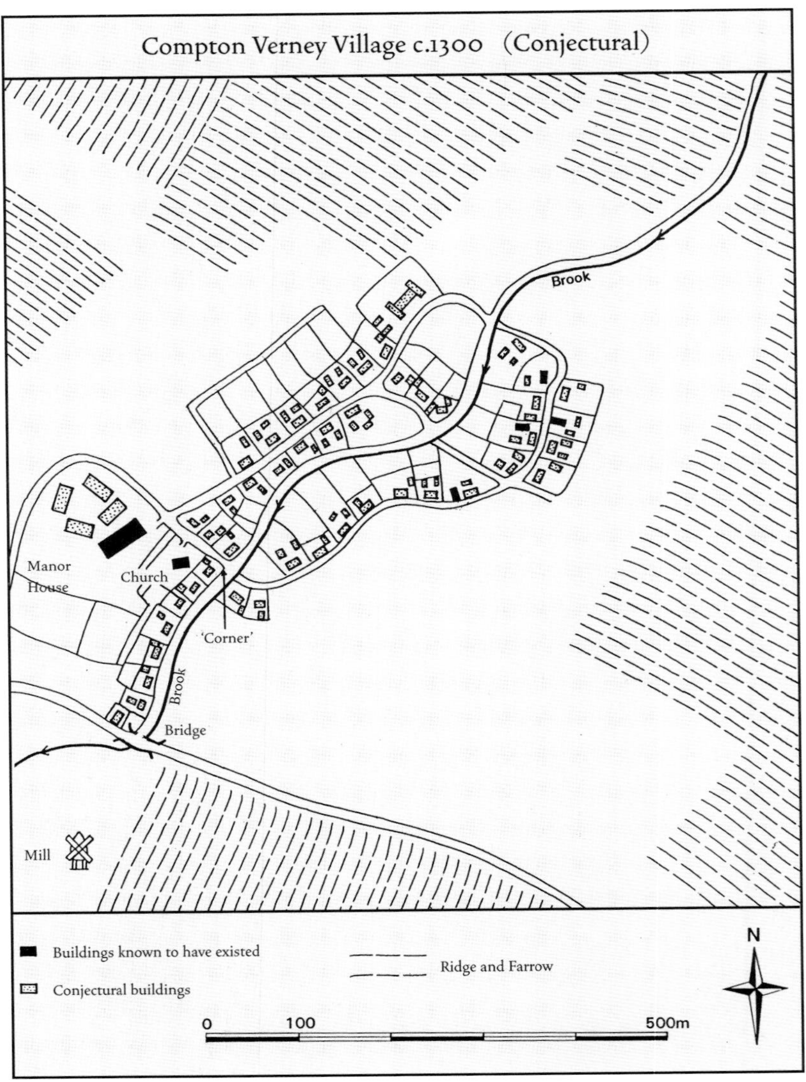

FIGURE 8

Conjectural reconstruction of Compton Verney, as it might have looked c.1300. The location of a few buildings are known from excavation and documents, and some use of analogies has been made, but the bulk of the information derives from guesswork and speculation, and will no doubt be disproved by future research.

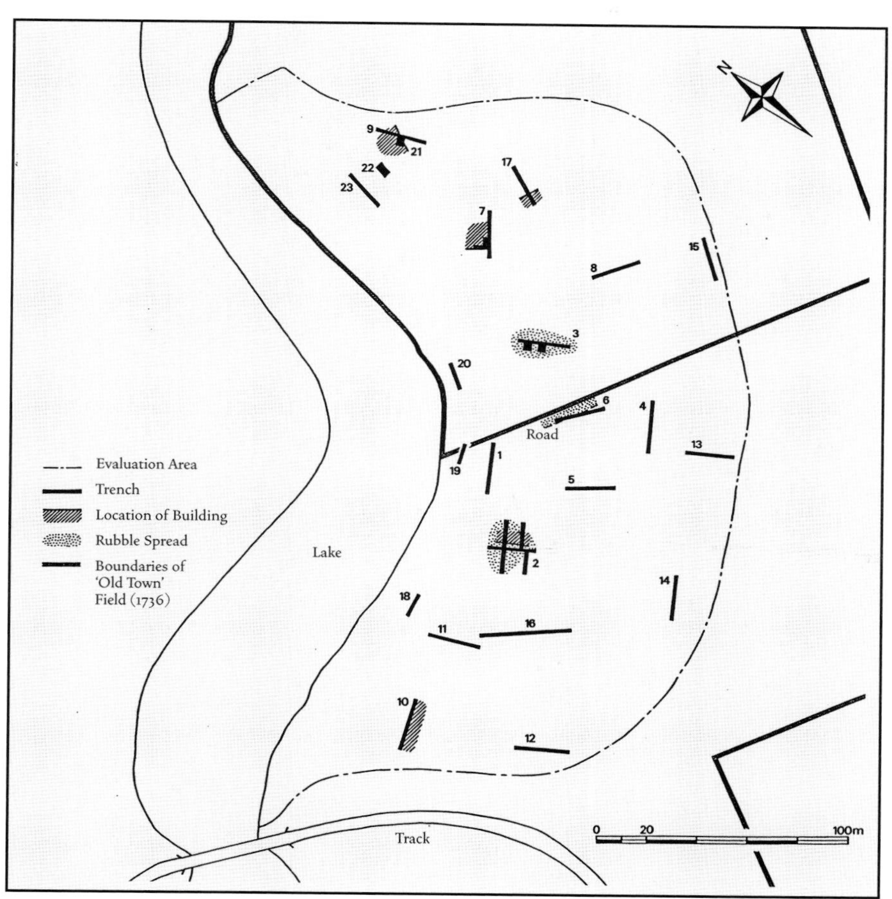

FIGURE 9
Excavations in 1991 – location of trenches
(for more details see Appendix). (Warwickshire Museum).

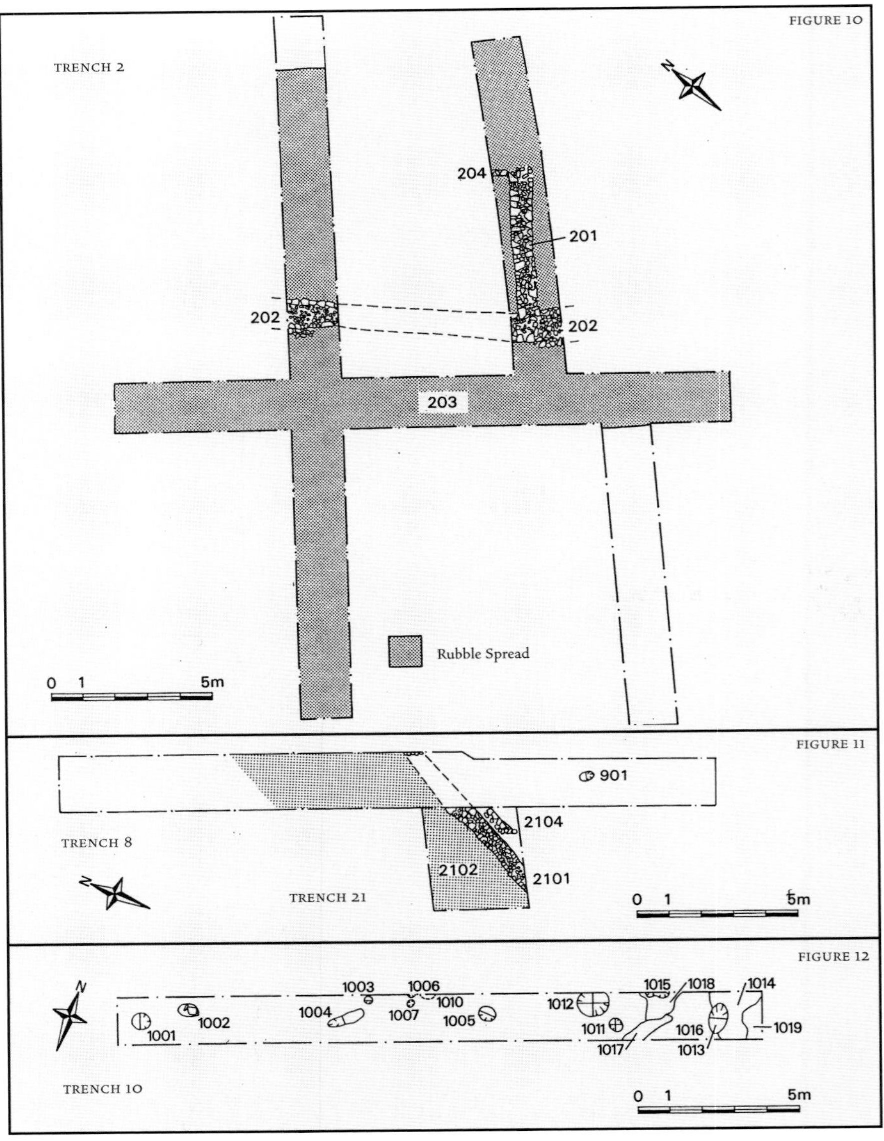

FIGURE 10

Excavations in 1991 – plan of Trench 2, showing stone walls of a medieval building. (Warwickshire Museum).

FIGURE 11

Excavations in 1991 – plan of Trench 21, showing stone paving and walls. (Warwickshire Museum).

FIGURE 12

Excavations in 1991 – plan and sections of Trench 10, showing post sockets from timber buildings. (Warwickshire Museum).

Elements in Compton's plan can be reconstructed by comparison with other villages, and especially nearby deserted sites with well-preserved earthworks such as Westcote in Tysoe, and excavated evidence, such as that from Dassett Southend. They are useful for estimating the likely size and shape of the tofts (plots of land within which houses and other buildings stood), and the layout of streets and lanes. The general impression is, around 1300, of a tight cluster of about forty-five houses in a relatively restricted area, with numerous gardens, orchards, crofts and closes, even a vineyard. There are more indications of horticulture than one would normally expect to encounter in a Warwickshire village. The documents occasionally indicate the size of these enclosures. A croft containing six selions which is mentioned in 1361 would have been unusually large, and in the next year two parcels (*particulas*) described as 'near the cemetery' measuring 41 ft by 18 ft and 29 ft by 33 ft (12.5m by 5.5m, 9m by 10m) suggest both by their small size and by the exactness of their dimensions that space was limited. A messuage (house and its plot) attached to a free yardland was described, also in 1362, as having 'a chamber with a curtilage' and a 'cottage and curtilage' adjacent as if they had been carved out of the larger holding, again implying that houses were closely packed.[50] A number of cottages are recorded between the church and the bridge, which might place the houses of the more substantial peasants, those with yardlands, to the north-east. The buildings, from those partly excavated, had stone foundations (Figures 10, 11 and Plate 15). Some had low stone walls supporting a timber-framed superstructure, while in others the stone walls may have risen to the eaves of the building. At an earlier period, probably going back to the twelfth century, post holes remain from buildings entirely of timber (Figure 12). Roofs were of thatch, with a few tiles, of which fragments have been found, probably placed around the smoke hole to protect the straw from sparks. A piece of daub baked hard from heat could belong to a smoke hood built over a hearth as an internal chimney. Floors and external yard surfaces were paved with stone. The documents of the early fifteenth century mention barns and stables, and in one case a 'yard door', suggesting that, as in other villages, houses and farm buildings were grouped around a yard with a gated entrance on to the street.[51] The church, which survived until 1772, is shown in prints and maps as quite a small structure for such a populous village, about 60 ft (18m) long and 15 ft (4.5m) wide internally, with a chapel or aisle in the south-west, and the burial chapel of the Verneys to the north-east (see Plate 42). It had a bell cote near the western end of the nave. The monuments and stained glass were moved to the new chapel attached to the house when the medieval church was demolished.[52]

We can be quite confident that there was no mill pond or pool in the medieval village, simply a brook running through the settlement. If there had been a water mill it

50. SBTRO, DR 98/35*, 39*, 37*.

51. SBTRO, DR 98/120.

52. The detailed plan is in *Notebook of George Vertue*, Walpole Society xxiv, 1958, 75. The depiction of the church labelled Compton Murdak in the Aylesford Collection, reproduced in *VCH, Warwickshire*, v, facing 58, is clearly not the same building.

PLATE 15
Excavations in 1991 – photograph of Trench 21, showing stone paving and walls. (Warwickshire Museum).

would have been mentioned in a document. Instead, a windmill, which stood on high ground to the south of the village, was leased by the lord of the manor to John Jones in 1323.[53] Often windmills were built in places lacking a water mill, and at Compton the mill pool and water mill are not recorded until the seventeenth century. The puzzle is why the lord did not take advantage of the water resources earlier, as they were apparently adequate to power a mill. As well as the road to Kineton which is still in use, roads led from the village northwards to Lighthorne and eastwards to Chadshunt.[54] For some features we have tantalizing details from the documents, but no clue as to where they fit in the village plan. A notable example is the important house of the Durvassals, which is described in 1324 as having a house and byre (and no doubt other agricultural buildings) in a gated yard, but as we do not know where it stood, on the reconstruction map it is guessed that it lay to the north-west, away from the Murdak's manor house.[55] Nor do we know the site of the common oven. In spite of the gaps in our knowledge, we can be certain that the village that is glimpsed from documents and archaeology was large, compact and complicated.

53. SBTRO, DR 98/28.

54. SBTRO, DR 98/23.

55. SBTRO, DR 98/29.

The village and its open fields were a product of a radical reorganization of the landscape in the early middle ages. Another upheaval overtook Compton in the fifteenth century. The village survived the epidemic of 1349, but the overall decline in population was having its effect around 1400, when houses were decaying and land was being abandoned. In the thirteenth and fourteenth centuries the holdings had been coherent units, often complete yardlands of 40 acres, but with some halves and quarters, attached to houses in the village. In the period 1396-1410 holdings were being amalgamated. For example, John Stacy, who 'withdrew from his tenure' in 1402, had held a messuage and 3 acres, a messuage and a yardland, and a toft. Often the buildings had fallen down leaving only an empty toft, as with Walter Vykers's holding of a messuage and half yardland and two tofts acquired in 1401.[56] A tenant only needed one house and set of buildings, so could allow the others in his collection of holdings to decay. If the tenant lived outside Compton he needed no house at all, like the Lighthorne man who acquired in 1390 a barn, with a curtilage and a quarter yardland, or the tenant from Brookhampton who acquired two tofts and two yardlands in 1403.[57] The lord had difficulty in persuading tenants to take on holdings that were 'lying' in his hands, but conversely tenants were putting together parcels and other fragments of holdings which had formerly belonged to a number of different tenants, sometimes unofficially. Robert Cele's holding in 1406 contained land that had belonged to five previous tenants, none of which coincided with a former yardland or fraction under the orthodox structure of tenancy. John Cumpton was reported to the lord's court in 1402 for occupying and cultivating twenty selions without licence.[58] Out in the fields the rules were being

56. SBTRO, DR 98/64a.

57. SBTRO, DR 98/50, 71.

58. SBTRO, DR 98/31a, 64a; Hilton, 'English Enclosure', 167.

broken in other ways. Boundaries were being ignored and abused, as when Richard Wylkyn and John Copcote alleged in 1402 that William Felisson moved merestones, presumably marking the boundary between selions, at Horsputsiche. Another tenant left gaps in her orchard fence in order to gain access to the lord's meadow. The village's boundaries with its neighbours were being ignored; Compton's territory must have been seen by outsiders as under-used and not rigorously policed. Trespasses by animals from Combrook and Walton were reported, and an alleged (and perhaps exaggerated) mass invasion by the people of Lighthorne with 200 mares in 1402.[59]

59. SBTRO, DR 98/64a, 67.

In Compton's records around 1400 we see a village that had once been committed to extensive corn growing retreating from its arable fields, and converting land to pasture, but not coping adequately with the difficult transition. Tenants paid rents for groups of selions or ridges which were being used as pasture. For example, Henry Coly in 1406 was paying 12d. for the pasture of twenty selions at Moreforlong.[60] Such records suggest a combination of changes, not just in the use of land, but also in the consolidation of groups of ridges which would previously have been intermingled. But why was the rent so low? The advantage of pasture lay in the greater profits from the sale of animals and wool compared with the poor return from low-priced grain, and also in the reduced costs of labour. Good pasture should have commanded rents above the 1d. or 2d. per acre that Coly was paying, and the explanation may lie in the lack of fencing. In some villages at the time, the change to pasture was being managed in such a way that the surviving peasants could retain some common field arable while benefitting from the profits of pastoral husbandry by enclosing groups of selions or by agreeing to turn parts of the field into leys.[61] At Compton it appears that the outer furlongs (for example, at Northslade in the north and Moreforlong in the south) were being used for grazing, and land near the village was kept as arable; but if old boundaries were breaking down and the grassed-over arable was not being enclosed the changes may not have brought much advantage.

60. SBTRO, DR 98/31a.

61. *Agrarian History*, iii, 225-7.

The last phase of the village is recorded in the court rolls of 1449-51, when a jury of only a half-dozen men were left to report to the court that fellow tenants were leaving and dying but that no-one wished to take up their holdings. The village community was still able to issue bye laws, to attempt to stop pigs rooting in the corn, and to control horses tethered in the harvest field lest they damage the uncut corn. Oxen, cows and geese were not allowed into the cornfield. Nor had the lord at this point given up hope of preventing the decay of the tenants' buildings, because orders were made through the court for the repair of a dwelling (an *insetehous*), various barns, and a stable.[62]

62. SBTRO, DR 98/120

The end was near by 1461, when Richard Verney drew up a rental which showed Compton divided into eight units (Figure 13). Three of them had names familiar to us

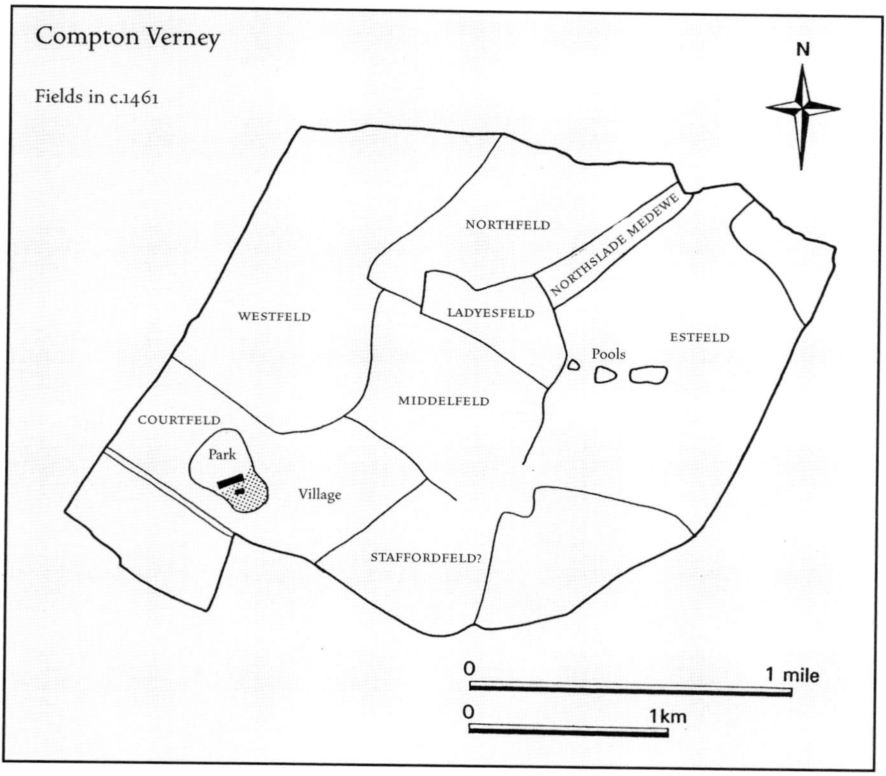

FIGURE 13
Compton Verney fields in c.1461. This is based on some guesswork.
The precise locations and boundaries of some of the fields are not known.

from the heydays of the open fields – Westfeld, Estfeld and Northeslade medewe – but the two former arable fields were called pastures, and they had been reduced in size as new fields were carved out of them – Courtfeld, Ladyesfeld, Middelfeld, Northfeld and Staffordfeld. They were also mostly described as pastures, and rented for large sums. Middelfeld was leased for £13 6s. 8d. per annum, and the total annual rental of the whole manor came to £60, which must represent an average rent per acre of about a shilling. These changes had more than trebled the value of the manor. Such a drastic increase in the profits from land has been observed elsewhere in this period of declining rents, and can be linked with the benefits of enclosure.[63] The word 'field' had been transformed in meaning from an open expanse of hundreds of acres of subdivided strips to the modern sense of an enclosed block of land, varying at this time between 50 and 250 acres. The rental records that the 'Farms and rents in the vill of Compton' contributed a mere £4, the rump of the villagers occupying land presumably confined to the south-west of the parish. The Verneys still kept a demesne in their hands, described in an inquisition in 1491 as 100 acres of arable, 200 acres of pasture, and 40 acres of meadow, much of the produce presumably being used to supply the lord's household.[64] The other 1,300 acres in the parish, including the glebe which they held from the church at Warwick, was now mainly leased as enclosed pastures to farmers producing meat, cheese and wool for the market. A territory which had been 90 per cent arable in 1279-80 had become 90 per cent grassland two centuries later. The peasant tenants had been virtually eliminated.

63. SBTRO, DR 98/504a. For parallels see Dyer, *Warwickshire Farming*, 21.

64. *Calendar of Inquisitions Post Mortem, Henry VII*, i, 268-9.

The landscape of Compton Murdak was apparently transformed into pasture closes soon after the arrival of the Verneys in the late 1430s. In two repects this change seems less revolutionary than initially might appear. Firstly, the trend towards the conversion of arable to pasture, the breakdown of the old yardlands, and the consolidation of selions into blocks of land was already far advanced by 1406, apparently on the initiative of the peasants, long before the Verney family took over the manor. Secondly, echoes of the former pattern of fields, furlongs and selions persisted in the new enclosed landscape, because the hedged boundaries of the new pastures, rather than cutting across the redundant ridge and furrow, as happened in some modern enclosures, tended to follow the headlands of the open fields[65] (Plate 16). This would have seemed an obvious way to lay out the new fields at the time, because trees and bushes, and even some hedges, may already have been growing on some of the old headlands; also, if the enclosures were gradually encroaching on the open field, groups of furlongs were being taken out of common use and fenced, while the adjoining furlongs were still being cultivated.

65. Techniques of enclosure are discussed in C.C. Taylor, *Fields in the English Landscape*, London 1975, 113-17; C. Dyer, 'Peasants and Farmers: Rural Settlements and Landscapes in an Age of Transition', in *The Age of Transition*, ed. D. Gaimster and P. Stamper, Oxford 1997, 71-3.

At Compton as in other fifteenth-century village desertions the landlords evidently responded to a demand from graziers for large enclosures, and it was not until later that

PLATE 16
Hedge in north-east Compton Verney. This multi-specied hedge planted on a bank with a substantial ditch, following the line of a headland in the open fields, is typical of the early enclosure hedges of the parish.

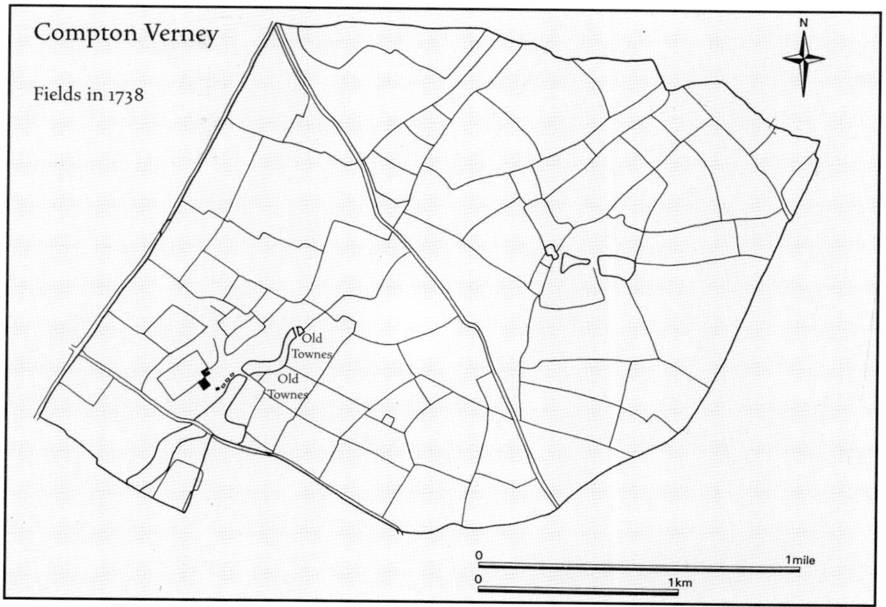

FIGURE 14
Compton Verney fields in 1738 (from the estate map, see note 11).

they were subdivided into smaller modern fields. By 1738 the eight great closes had been replaced by fifty fields, averaging about 30 acres, some with hedges ignoring the redundant ridge and furrow. In the eighteenth century the framework of the old landscape was being eroded as the park with its lakes obliterated the village site, and a new road was driven through the parish from south-east to north-west, which cut across the grain of the old field system[66] (Figure 14).

66. SBTRO, DR 98/1819. The organization of the fields is discussed in Beresford and Hurst, *Deserted Medieval Villages*, 41.

The Verneys found a new use for part of the old east field by damming one of the smaller tributaries of the brook to make a line of pools at Poolfields. Their precise date of construction is not known, but they may be linked with the stalls (shambles) for selling fish which the Verneys held in Northampton in the late fifteenth and early sixteenth centuries.[67] Next to their house they seem to have created a small park, of perhaps 20 acres, the boundary of which was marked in the seventeenth century by a line of mature trees to the west of the house.[68] The early park might have been larger – the evidence comes from later centuries after a number of changes to the areas of parkland.

67. 'Poole fields' are mentioned in 1630 : SBTRO, DR 98/1657; for the fish shambles, SBTRO, DR 98/504a; Northamptonshire Record Office, Northampton Borough Records, section 1, royal charters no. 29 (I owe this last reference to Dr Jane Laughton).

68. Dugdale, *Warwickshire*, 435; SBTRO, DR 98/1657; the size of the Park is suggested by its value in 1630, at £10, compared with £30 for the Towne.

The agrarian landscape which was created out of the decaying fields of the village and which was recorded in the estate maps of 1736 and 1738 remained essentially in place until the late twentieth century. The third great landscape upheaval (the formation and dissolution of the village and the open fields being the first two) overtook Compton Verney in the post-war changes in agricultural practice, when the ridge and furrow, which had remained largely intact in the late 1940s, was destroyed by ploughing over most of the parish, a number of hedges were removed and some fields remodelled. Farms extended their arable until most of the parish was once more under the plough to an extent that had not been seen since the fourteenth century. Two farms were built on entirely new sites, and a group of residential houses were built to the west of the great house. Substantial parts of the parish in the north-west and east were taken over by the military, with total removal of traces of previous human activity. In spite of all these alterations to the historic landscape, hedge lines can still be seen which were planted on the headlands of the open fields, and which therefore are following boundaries drawn in the twelfth century at the latest. Indeed, they are likely to date back before the Conquest.

Having traced the physical developments in Compton's landscape, we need to examine the people who brought about these changes. This means looking at the full social range of those who held and worked the land. The lords had more power than anyone else, but in a complex society their decisions were only one factor among many. In tracing the origins of Compton as a separate unit of land holding, we have already seen that it became a distinct manor on which lordship was likely to be focussed intensively when it was divided from Kineton or Wellesbourne before the Conquest. Under a royal lord, as part of a huge estate, the dues demanded from the local population would not have been very oppressive. But even under successive lay aristocrats from the eleventh to the fifteenth century the peasants were not ruled by especially demanding lords. At the time of Domesday, Compton was divided into two manors, one held by the count of Meulan and the other by Alwin, a tenant of Turchill of Arden. Their Compton manors were just small parts of larger estates. Their primary concern was that Compton would generate regular annual revenue (£6 for the count, £4 for Alwin) and the details of management would have been left to the local reeves or farmers. The surplus extracted from Compton averaged exactly £1 for each hide of fiscal assessment, a common valuation in Domesday. The demesnes of the two manors, one with three ploughs, the other with two, were not very large, so the fairly numerous tenants would not as individuals have had to contribute great quantities of labour. The only sign of a rather harsh regime comes from the unusual number of slaves, eleven, who carried out much of the work on the demesnes.[69]

69. *DB*, 239, 241.

The division of the village between two manors was perpetuated in the thirteenth and fourteenth centuries when the lordship of the manor was controlled by the Murdak family, with the Durvassals holding about a third of the land in a sub-manor. A third influence was the church of St Mary at Warwick, which acquired Compton parish church as the endowment of one of its prebends in the late 1150s.[70] This division of lordship must always have been to the advantage of the peasant tenants, who were not subject to a single authority, and the community represented the unity of the village. The lords of Compton had other lands – the Murdaks held a manor just across the county boundary at Edgcote in Northamptonshire, and the Durvassals' main property lay in west Warwickshire, at Spernall – but unlike their magnate predecessors their revenues from Compton provided a high proportion of their wealth.[71] So they had good reason to squeeze as much as they could from their lands. As relatively minor gentry lords, however, they had limited power. They do not seem to have been very enterprising in their management of Compton, judging from their failure to invest in a water mill, though the Murdaks founded a common oven which gave a small profit from the villagers paying to bake their bread.

70. *English Episcopal* Acta, 14. *Coventry and Lichfield, 1072-1159*, ed. M.J. Franklin, Oxford 1997, 74-5.

71. *VCH Warwickshire*, iii, 172-3; Edgcote often figures in the deeds in the Willoughby de Broke collection.

By 1279-80 the most important tenants were the twenty-two yardlanders, each with 40 acres of arable, the descendants of the twenty-three villeins in 1086.[72] There were also four tenants who shared two yardlands, and so presumably held a half-yardland each, and two tenants who held more than a yardland. The successors of the

72. *Hundred Rolls*, 248-50.

thirteen smallholders (bordars) at the time of Domesday, together with some of the eleven slaves who had subsequently been granted smallholdings, account for the eighteen cottagers in 1279-80. Only seven of the peasant tenants held their land by free tenure, and the lords of Compton exercised strong lordship over the yardland tenants. Most of them were servile, and owed tallage 'at the will of the lord', which was a test of villein (unfree) status in the thirteenth and fourteenth centuries. Their rents and services do not seem to have been exceptionally burdensome, as, like many south Warwickshire peasants in the late thirteenth century, they did not owe works in every week of the year, but instead paid a good deal in cash, and performed seasonal services only.[73] A standard of comparison is the work load on one of the large church estates in west Warwickshire, like Tredington, where the yardlanders were expected to labour for the lord for four days each week throughout the year.[74] Henry le Provost (or Reeve, as he would presumably have been known to his neighbours), who was chosen by the compilers of the survey as typical of the Compton servile yardlanders, owed 6s.3d. per annum in rent, with an obligation to provide labour on the lord's demesne of one man every day between 29 June and 29 September, the period of the hay and corn harvests. He would not work on saints' days, but was to provide the labour of two men when harvesting the lord's corn. In the whole of the rest of the year he was expected to plough the demesne on only six days.

73. R. H. Hilton, 'Social Structure of Rural Warwickshire in the Middle Ages', in R.H. Hilton, *The English Peasantry in the Later Middle Ages*, Oxford 1975, 128-9.

74. *Red Book of Worcester*, ed. M. Hollings, Worcestershire Historical Society, 1934-50, 282.

We can detect in the obligations at Compton evidence of a process of bargaining between the lord and his tenants in the century before 1279. The rent of 6s. 3d. was probably the result of the conversion into cash of labour service once owed. The lord would have found it convenient to receive revenues in money, but the tenants also preferred that arrangement because it left them in control of their labour to use on their own land. A proportion of the services owed in the summer and autumn were no doubt 'sold' for cash in the late thirteenth and early fourteenth centuries, bringing a yardlander's money rent to 10s.0d. or more.[75] A brief description of the hay-making customs in which Henry le Reeve and his fellow yardlanders participated reveals a relationship in which the lord felt the need to soften the burden of labour services by giving the peasants reciprocal benefits.[76] The lord allowed each tenant to take away as much grass as he could lift on his scythe, which must have ended a hard day's forced labour with a note of collective festivity as the peasants gathered to compete in this trial of strength and skill. The lord also provided the hay makers with a sheep, a cheese and some salt, the basis for a collective meal. The tenants no doubt resented the work that they were required to do, but the contest in the meadow and the feast linked the service with a celebration. Henry le Reeve's name was gained by him or his forbears through serving the lord by managing the manor as one of their obligations as customary

75. For example, at Chadshunt in 1306-7, works were sold for 29s.6d.: Lichfield Record Office, D30/N9.

76. A. Jones, 'Harvest Customs and Labourers' Perquisites in Southern England, 1150-1350; the Hay Harvest', *Agricultural History Review* 25, 1977, 98-107.

tenants. The lords depended on peasant officials, especially for the conduct of business in the manorial court. The courts passed bye laws and helped to enforce the regulations on which the fair and efficient management of the fields depended. The rules often came from the community, and peasant officials reported offenders. Perhaps in some earlier, undocumented era the lord was more dictatorial, but our suspicion must be that a field system which was managed by peasants in conjunction with the lord in the later middle ages, was also devised and created by the same combination before the Norman Conquest. The gathering of the inhabitants into the central village, which is closely associated with the laying out of the fields, is another change in the landscape which must have been ordered by the lord, it is often assumed. He certainly promoted the process by building the church as a focal point for the village, and by settling slaves around his manor house on parcels of demesne; but again the peasants are likely to have made a contribution, as such matters as equal access to the fields, and the new balance between private and collective rights, were matters which would have been difficult to settle by dictates from the lord. The village and its fields performed useful functions in aiding the efficiency of production and providing a disciplined framework for cooperation, but they also reflect contemporary ideas about the regulation and order in settlements and landscapes.[77]

77. C. Lewis, P. Mitchell-Fox and C. Dyer, *Village, Hamlet and Field*, Manchester 1997, 202-44.

Our documents come from the lords, or from the state investigating the resources of lords, but we can still glimpse the society of the village which had some degree of independence. We have already noted the village's dimension of self-government, in which the yardlanders played a leading role. As a social group, the village seems divided in status, between the free and unfree, and stratified in wealth from the yardlanders with their 40-acre holdings, to the almost landless cottagers. In the deeds through which the free tenants conveyed their land in the late thirteenth and early fourteenth centuries we note an élite of freeholders acting as witnesses, from the Eyton, Lucas and Smith families for example.[78] They were not especially wealthy, but their free status gave them both privileges and important legal responsibilities.

78. SBTRO, DR 98/12, 19, 21b, 23, 24, 26, 28.

In terms of material goods, the top rank of Compton Murdak villagers were the yardlanders, most of them holding by customary or villein tenures. Their low legal status meant that the lord could demand tallage and marriage fines from them, and in theory restrict their movement from the manor. Nonetheless they were not desperately poor, as they cropped at least 20 acres of arable each year, and owned cattle, sheep, pigs and poultry which produced more than they needed to feed their families and pay their rents. As the opportunity to sell agricultural produce expanded in the thirteenth century, the yardlanders carried their grain, cheese and wool to the nearest markets at Kineton and Wellesbourne, or perhaps to the rather larger venues at Stratford or

Warwick.[79] Yardlanders on a two-course rotation could have sold 10 quarters of grain in a normal year, for at least £2. Compton yardlanders had the benefit of the high proportion of wheat that they grew, which around 1300 often sold for 6s. 0d. per quarter (2s. 0d. more than barley): this was the price of a quarter of wheat sold in June 1347 to the sheriff of Warwickshire by John Jones of Compton.[80] Another advantage lay in their rents, which were not very high, probably not much more than 13s.4d. per annum if they paid cash in lieu of labour services, or on average 16s.0d. taking into account tallage, amercements charged in the manor court, and other extra and occasional charges such as entry fines paid when a new tenant took up a holding. Many contemporaries owed more than 20s.0d. A remarkable demonstration of their relative good fortune comes from the two free yardlanders at Compton in 1279-80 who paid annually 20s.0d. in one case and 21s.0d. in another, which must have been near to the economic rent for the land, at a rate of about 6d. per acre. These apparently expensive free holdings must still have been quite attractive propositions for their tenants, because in 1322 John and Alice Shepherd were prepared to pay 30s. 0d. for one of them when it came on to the market.[81] The servile yardlanders had apparently had their rents and services fixed at a rather low level, probably before some of the thirteenth-century inflation, and they were protected by customary law from increases which would have reflected the full value of the land. Accordingly their rent payments would have swallowed up less than half of their income from the sale of produce.

The resources of the better-off peasants are reflected in the tax list of 1327, when the Compton Murdak contributors numbered twenty-two, that is almost half of the households in the village, and most of them yardlanders.[82] Indeed seven have the same surnames as tenants of yardlands in 1279-80. The assessments reflect the overall wealth of the Compton tenants, so that the village contributed more to the king's taxes than most of its neighbours: of the eighty villages in Kineton Hundred in 1327, Compton Murdak lay in the top twelve with an assessment of 71s.6d., and not much less than Kineton itself. The individual payments display the disparity in possessions between tenants of theoretically standard yardland holdings, so that the atte Garden, atte Welle, Bole, Jones, Page, Felice, Reeve and Monks households paid 4s.0d. or 5s.0d., while others possessed such a small quantity of goods that they contributed only 1s.0d. or 1s. 6d. This might reflect the life cycle of the peasants at the time of the tax, some of whom were declining in prosperity in their old age, or struggling at the beginning of their land-holding careers, but must also show that some were better than their neighbours at managing their land and profiting from the market. The taxes, theoretically based on a valuation of a wide range of moveable goods, were mainly assessed on livestock, so the more successful peasants would be those with perhaps six cattle and thirty sheep.[83]

79. W Barker, 'Warwickshire Markets', *Warwickshire History* vi, 1986, 161-75.

80. PRO, E 213/382.

81. SBTRO, DR 98/26.

82. W.B. Bickley, 'Lay Subsidy Roll, Warwickshire, 1327', *Transactions of the Midland Record Society* vi, 1902, 19.

83. J.F. Willard, *Parliamentary Taxes on Personal Property, c.1290-1334* Cambridge, Mass. 1934.

The yardlanders would have had surplus cash to spend on their own consumption requirements. Their houses would have been built by craftsmen, seen in the quality of the walling in the excavated buildings, and the estimated costs when tenants were ordered to repair them – for example in 1450 a dwelling house was said to need work valued at 13s.4d. The expense would have been less around 1300, but the work would have been done by specialists in the same way[84] (Figure 11 and Plate 15). The most substantial goods acquired by peasants were sometimes listed in court records because the lord wished to retain them on the holdings in order to maintain the attractiveness of the property for new tenants. For example, in 1396, when John atte Welle surrendered a yardland holding, he was ordered to leave behind a cart bound with iron, a plough with its iron share and coulter, a brass cooking pot and pan, a vat (for brewing ale) and a kneading trough.[85] The peasants also bought cloth and foodstuffs, which has left no evidence, but finds of a copper alloy dress fastener and iron horse shoes show that manufactured goods were acquired in markets. A whetstone made from non-local stone, and hand-mill stones of German origin, reflect the long-distance links of the local towns. The abundant pottery indicates the complexity of local trading patterns, whereby wares made at kilns twenty miles and more from Compton were available to the peasants of the village. In the twelfth and thirteenth centuries much of the pottery came from centres of manufacture in the east midlands, in Northamptonshire or Bedfordshire. Later the eastern link continued with some sherds from Potterspury in Northamptonshire, but the bulk of the pottery came from Warwickshire kilns, including those at Chilvers Coton, Coventry, and other centres in north Warwickshire. A few pieces came from Hanley Castle in Worcestershire and Brill in Buckinghamshire. By drawing on a variety of wares, and buying non-utilitarian items such as decorative jugs, the villagers seem to have been exercising choices as consumers.[86]

The cottagers, though much poorer than the yardlanders, were still bound closely into the village community, because they supplied vital labour. There was much opportunity for employment on the two demesnes and the glebe. The Murdak demesne, which as we have seen was inadequately supplied with labour services, would have needed both full-time farm servants as ploughmen, a shepherd and a carter, and short-term workers for such tasks as threshing and ditching. The yardlanders also employed the cottagers. For example, the obligation to work every weekday in the harvest season would in many cases have been discharged by sending an employee as a substitute. But even leaving aside the services, a yardlander without a son would have hired a full-time servant or a succession of labourers thoughout the year to work his 40 acres and look after the animals.[87] We can see an unusual opportunity for wage work in the village in 1279-80, when there were eighteen female tenants (six of them called 'widow')

84. SBTRO, DR 98/120. On the employment of specialist builders by peasants, and the cost of peasant buildings, C. Dyer, 'English Peasant Buildings in the Later Middle Ages, 1200-1500', in Dyer, *Everyday Life*, 133-65.

85. SBTRO, DR 98/63.

86. The dress fastener was found in the 1991 excavations; two horseshoes, the piece of whetstone and pieces of millstone were found in 1998-9 by field walking on the village site, and a third horseshoe from the field immediately to the north. The main types of pottery from the 1991 excavations are listed in the Appendix.

87. On the labour inputs of peasant agriculture, H.S.A. Fox, 'Exploitation of the Landless by Lords and Tenants in Early Medieval England', in *Medieval Society and the Manor Court*, ed. Z. Razi and R. Smith, Oxford 1996, 518-68.

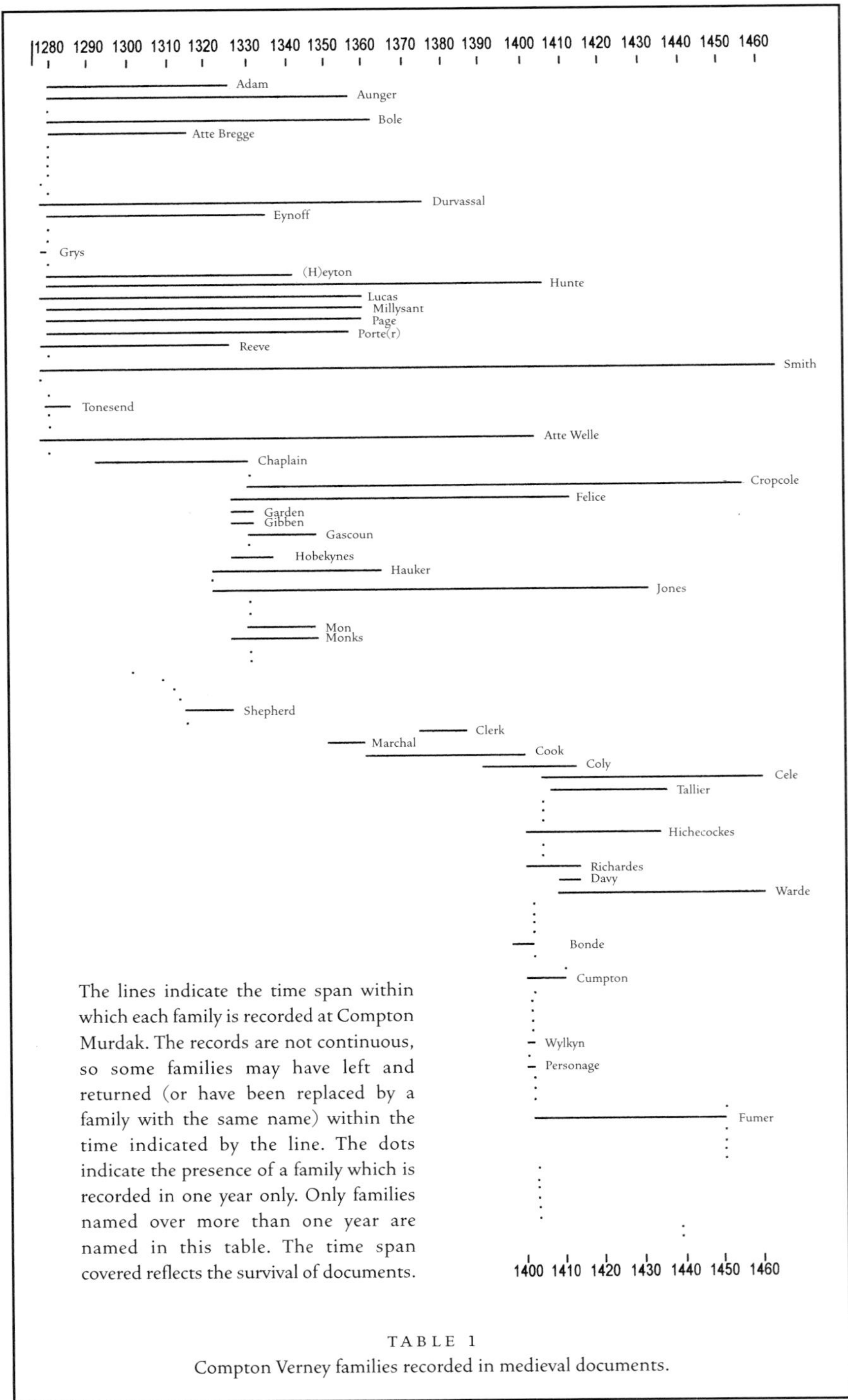

TABLE 1

Compton Verney families recorded in medieval documents.

compared with twenty-seven men, suggesting that an epidemic had affected the village shortly before the survey. The normal proportion of female tenants was in the region of a tenth. The widows were no doubt in many cases well able to manage their holding, but a community which had lost perhaps a dozen adult males in the recent past would be suffering from a severe labour shortage, and the cottagers and their families would have been kept unusually busy. There are few indications – from surnames for example – that the smallholders of Compton took up crafts and trades to make a living, though the common oven was held with a smallholding, so at least one acted as a specialist baker, and some members of the Smith family presumably practised the trade. Work may not always have been very plentiful, and the rates of pay barely covered the cost of basic foodstuffs which became very expensive in many years in the period 1293-1332. Cottagers would have fallen into debt, and become increasingly dependent on loans and charity of their better-off neighbours. This made for a close community, though not one without tensions and resentments. A glimpse of lower-class life in Compton comes from a court case of 1335, already mentioned because the homicide took place beside a marl pit in the fields of Compton. John le Hunte, from a cottage-holding family, quarrelled with John de Huxley of Cheshire, who, judging from the date, 1 August, had come as an itinerant harvest worker. They shot arrows at one another, and Hunte was killed, but his assailant could plead self-defence. Perhaps the source of the dispute lay in competition for work in the harvest season.[88]

88. PRO, C 260/47. On the plight of the poor during bad harvests, P. Schofield, 'Dearth, Debt and the Local Land Market in a Late Thirteenth-Century Village Community', *Agricultural History Review* xlv, 1997, 1-17.

All of this then reveals Compton Murdak as a community of peasants, mutually dependent on one another, not necessarily living in perfect harmony, but clearly having an existence separate from the manors of the Murdaks and the Durvassals. Their involvement in the market as producers, consumers and employers, gave them some confidence and security, which again discourages the belief that they were entirely subordinated to their lords. Above all, Compton, and in particular its score of yardland tenants, gives every appearance of prosperity; yet within a century of 1327, when its wealth was exhibited in the tax list, the village was in terminal decline. Can this reversal of fortunes be explained?

Patterns of migration help us to understand changes in the village's circumstances. The village's population was in constant movement, as was generally the case.[89] This posed no problems so long as the immigrants replaced those leaving. About a half of the family names recorded in 1279-80, fifteen out of a total of thirty-two, do not occur in later records, and another twenty-one names which appear in the period 1280-1335 cannot be traced after the Black Death of 1348-9. But sixty-two new names appear in the records of the village between 1300 and 1410 (Table 1). We are observing here unstable family names, so that some lines may have continued under a new name, but the main

89. L. Poos, 'Population Turnover in Medieval Essex: the Evidence of some Early Fourteenth Century Tithing Lists', in *The World We Have Gained*, ed. L. Bonfield, R.M. Smith and K. Wrightson, Oxford 1986, 1-22.

causes of discontinuity would have been mortality and migration. Most of the families died out in the male line through the normally rather high death rates of the period, which would have been accelerated by occasional epidemics, like that which apparently affected the village just before 1279-80, and harvest failures such as the famine of 1315-17 which killed a tenth or more of tenants in some villages.[90] Peasants were tempted to migrate by opportunities in towns, such as Coventry which was growing at this time, and on a smaller scale there were nearby developments such as Dassett Southend, where an attempt was made to create a market centre at the end of the thirteenth century. Younger sons of yardlanders with no prospect of inheriting the family holding could have moved to other villages where marriage to a widow would have provided access to a holding of land, or where land could be purchased. This might explain the name 'de Compton' at nearby Walton in 1279-80.[91] Cottager families migrated more rapidly than did the yardlanders – they were more vulnerable to mortality, and would hope for better chances elsewhere. Medieval peasants were not confined within narrow local horizons. In the thirteenth century the Fosse Way was known as 'Leicester Way', meaning that it was perceived as leading to a significant town in another county, not the next village. In 1406 one of the tenants was reported to have been on pilgrimage to York.[92] Their movement to local towns and villages, familiar to them from visits to markets or religious festivals, involved no great leap into the unknown. On the other hand, Compton provided opportunities for immigrants, as its 40-acre yardlands offered potential profits, and even the cottagers had a better chance of regular employment than those in many villages.

The Black Death cannot in itself be blamed for Compton's decline, as seventeen family names which appear in documents of the period 1280-1335 still occur after 1350, and indeed the village at the end of the fourteenth century appears to have maintained a good number of inhabitants in spite of the disaster which presumably claimed as many lives (near to a half) in Compton as in other midland villages.[93] Difficulties are apparent in the period 1390-1410, when forty-six family names appear in the records, forty of which were new, and many of these did not stay for long. We have already seen how holdings were amalgamated, broken into fragments or acquired by absentees; buildings were neglected, boundaries ignored, ridges brought into groups, arable converted to grassland, and the fields invaded by animals from neighbouring villages.

The interests of the lords of the manor were threatened by these problems. The Murdaks gave it up in 1370, after which it came into the hands of a succession of absentees, including Alice Perrers, the mistress of Edward III and a notorious accumulator of landed wealth, the bishop of Winchester and groups of feoffees.[94] Did these remote lords, none of whom had any personal commitment to the place, have a

90. R. M. Smith, 'Demographic Developments in Rural England, 1300-48. A Survey', in *Before the Black Death*, ed. B.M.S. Campbell, Manchester 1991, 25-78.

91. *Hundred Rolls*, 229-33.

92. SBTRO, DR 98/6, 31A.

93. Z. Razi, *Life, Marriage and Death in an English Parish: Economy, Society and Demography in Halesowen, 1270-1400*, Cambridge 1980, 99-109.

94. J. Bothwell, 'The Management of Position: Alice Perrers, Edward III, and the Creation of a Landed Estate, 1362-1377', *Journal of Medieval History* xxiv, 1998, 47 ; SBTRO, DR 98/44, 46, 73, 74 ; *Warwickshire Feet of Fines*, vol. III, ed. L. Drucker, Dugdale Society xviii, 1943, nos. 2268, 2276.

damaging effect on Compton? In fact all lords had an interest in attempting to prevent an exodus of tenants and the collapse of buildings. The Catesbys, the earls of Warwick, the nuns of Nuneaton, or the bishops of Coventry and Lichfield, when faced with problems on nearby manors, ordered the tenants to maintain their houses, paid for repairs, or attempted to stem the emigration of their servile tenants.[95] The Murdaks might have had a special concern for a manor which was valued at £24 per annum in the late fourteenth century – a sizeable proportion of their income.[96] But under their successors, even when such a distant figure as the bishop of Salisbury held part of the manor in 1406, a local official was gathering detailed information about peasant holdings and their payments of rent. The courts held at about the same time were pursuing policies designed to remedy the deteriorating situation, ordering a tenant who was departing to leave the 'principal goods' on his holdings to make it easier to attract successors, amercing tenants who neglected their repairs, reporting serfs (*neifs*) who had left the manor, and changing tenancy arrangements so that holdings were let for terms of five, eight, ten or twelve years, presumably because new tenants might be reluctant to commit themselves for a longer time.[97]

95. Dyer, 'Deserted Medieval Villages', 37-8; SBTRO, DR 10/2600-2602.

96. *Feet of Fines*, III, no. 2169.

97. SBTRO, DR 98/31A, 63, 64.

At the beginning of the fifteenth century annual rents were set at the rather unrealistically high figure of 13s.4d. per yardland, though when tenants took on two yardlands together the combined rent was equivalent to 8s.0d. or 9s.0d. per yardland. The tenants were understandably reluctant to pay rents promptly and in full, and arrears built up. These piecemeal and partial payments were recorded in 1406. Robert Cele, for example, who was supposed to pay 12s.2d., firstly contributed 6s.8d., and then 2s.7d. He was let off 4d. but still owed 2s.7d.[98] In 1402 four holdings lay 'in the lord's hands', meaning that they were either completely vacant, or more likely were rented informally from one year to the next for a low rent. The successive lords saw the returns from their manor fall. Its annual value was estimated in 1370-1 at £24, but it was leased in 1405 for £17 6s.8d. per annum.[99]

98. SBTRO, DR 98/31A.

99. SBTRO, DR 98/79.

The Verneys arrived in 1435, when John Verney, dean of Lichfield, who was probably acting on behalf of Richard, his brother, was granted the manor by Robert Skerne, who seems to have held the place for the previous thirty years.[100] The Verneys became prominent in Warwickshire in the service of Richard Beauchamp, earl of Warwick, and were clearly anxious to make their mark, including asserting lordship over the whole of Compton Murdak. In 1437 the Durvassal sub-manor was sold to John Verney, clerk, again on behalf of Richard, and by the late 1440s John Verney was leasing the parsonage of the church from St Mary's at Warwick.[101] This tendency to consolidate control over their territory was a characteristic of gentry land-holding at this time, and was connected with their social and political pretensions, as well as their economic interest.

100. SBTRO, DR 98/97, 109; C. Carpenter, *Locality and Polity. A Study of Warwickshire Landed Society 1401 – 1499*, Cambridge 1992, 126.

101. SBTRO, DR 98/100; *Ministers' Accounts*, ed. Styles, 1, 19.

The Dalby family based at Brookhampton in the next parish acquired land in Compton in the early fifteenth century, and predictably the Verneys came into long-running disputes with these local rivals.[102] Over three generations the family became closely associated with Compton through building work and their choice of burial place. Richard Verney constructed the manor house on a grand scale, and made it his principal residence. Edmund Verney was buried at the friary in Warwick in 1495, but a chantry was founded in the parish church in 1522, after which the Compton church, now virtually their private chapel, became the family's place of burial. The name Compton Murdak was gradually replaced by Compton Verney from 1491.[103] This consolidation of territorial control was of course accompanied by the changes in the landscape of the manor, which by 1461 produced rents of £60 per annum, a threefold increase over the meagre returns of the early fifteenth century. The attitude of the Verneys towards their lands contrasted with that of their predecessors, and they were able to achieve a dramatic increase in revenues during a period of economic 'recession', when most landlords suffered a drop in returns from their manors. They were not unique in this ability to alter their economic circumstances through decisive managerial policies – the Catesby family did much the same on their Warwickshire manor of Radbourne.[104]

102. Carpenter, *Locality and Polity*, 129-30, 184-5.

103. SBTRO, DR 98/127, 135, 136; Carpenter, *Locality and Polity*, 199, 232-3; PRO, PROB 11/10, fol. 168r; PROB 11/22, fol. 210v. It is called Compton Mordak alias Compton Verney in 1491, and Compton Murdak still in 1525 (for the latter reference see note 107 below).

104. Dyer, *Warwickshire Farming*, 21.

The end of Compton was also the result of changing attitudes towards the land and the village by the peasants. They repeatedly opted to live elsewhere – in 1402 Robert Webbe had gone to Tachbrook; Agnes Wilkins, the heiress of the long-established Jones family, married a Stratford man and moved there by 1434; John Webbe in 1449 was reported to be living as a schoolmaster in Warwick.[105] Holdings in Compton continued to be acquired by outsiders, or to fall into the hands of the Verneys. When a Chesterton man conveyed two tofts and a yardland and a half in 1453, the deed described the adjacent plots in the village as belonging to Richard Verney, and in 1461 a yardland that had once belonged to John Warde, a long resident tenant, was granted by a Combrook man to Richard Verney.[106] The precise final date of the village's desertion is not known, but Rous decribed it as having only a church, rectory and manor house in 1486. Among the pottery collected from the village site and its fields, wares normally found at places occupied in the late fifteenth century are absent, supporting the suggestion that the last villagers departed a decade or two after 1461. By 1525 the tax collectors found only Richard Verney esquire, and four men who paid tax on wages, who were probably herdsmen employed on the pastures.[107]

105. SBTRO, DR 98/64A, 120, 90, 93, 96.

106. SBTRO, DR 98/121, 123a.

107. PRO,E 179/192/135. The pottery includes no Cistercian ware or Tudor green, and only a few sherds of Midland purple.

The auditor of St Mary's Warwick, who stated in 1466 that Richard Verney had expelled the tenants in the 1440s, was telling us only about the three tenants of the glebe (see p.52). Did Verney evict the other villagers, as John Rous evidently believed? Such a policy seems entirely in character in view of the decisive and forceful record of Richard

Verney in taking control of the manor and competing with his gentry rivals. On the other hand, the records of the courts held at Compton, 1449-51, show the authority of the lord being used to help the remaining villagers to maintain some discipline in the field system; a serf who had left the manor was required to return; and building repairs were being ordered with some vigour. The court's commands were no doubt flouted, but the lord's aims were still clear. If the lord had an agenda of depopulation at that stage, he kept it well hidden. If at some later date the villagers were removed, it does not seem to have been done suddenly or decisively – rather the village petered out gradually. Verney did not need to take any drastic action as the peasants were leaving of their own accord, and the pasture closes could be created out of land vacated by the retreating open fields. No doubt Richard Verney took advantage of opportunities to acquire vacant holdings, and in the later stages the loss of common pasture from his enclosures made life harder for the remaining tenants, but he cannot be regarded as the single-handed destroyer of the village.

The successive lords of Compton Murdak played some part in its desertion, by neglect in the late fourteenth century, and by enclosure in the mid fifteenth, but it would be too easy to make them the sole agency in the village's desertion. As we have seen, unlike the majority of 'lost' villages, Compton was a large and prosperous community, with its own parish church, not crowded by a nearby rival village, not restricted by its limited size and facilities, and with no obvious disadvantages in terms of its location or resources. Its clay soils, specialization in arable cultivation, and lack of woods were shared with dozens of other Feldon or champion settlements which survived. The symptoms of decay around 1400 are found everywhere, but in most cases ended with the shrinkage of the village rather than its total disappearance.

Deserted villages appear to offer us a model for the origins of English agrarian capitalism. According to a view expressed in the nineteenth century and revived throughout the twentieth, the late medieval and early modern gentry expropriated the land of the peasants in order to build up large productive farms. Compton Verney, which at first seems to offer such a prime example of this process, on closer examination forces us to give a more complicated version of events, in which the desertion of the village can be attributed at least in part to the tenants. They departed for other villages and towns, and developments within the community, hidden from our view, discouraged them from accumulating larger holdings and managing them as mixed farms as happened elsewhere. No doubt some emigrants from Compton were more successful in their new homes. The gentry made profits from deserted villages through the enterprise of lessees, the farmers of the pasture closes, like John Lichfield of Coventry who leased the Verney's pastures at nearby Kingston, or farmers of peasant origin like the Heritage family of

Burton Dassett.[108] The contribution of peasants and farmers to the new methods of managing land at the end of the middle ages should not be underestimated.

108. Hilton, 'English Enclosure', 169; Dyer, *Everyday Life*, 315-22..

APPENDIX

The excavations on the village site of 1991 and 1995-6, and field walking in 1999.

In 1991 archaeological evaluation was carried out by Warwickshire Museum for the Council of the Compton Verney Opera House Project to assess the archaeological implications of the proposed opera house development in advance of a planning application.

The area investigated covered the proposed opera house site, an area of 4 ha (10 acres) on the south-east side of the northern lake, in the field known as 'Old Town' in 1736. A total of twenty-three trial trenches were dug, initially by a mechanical excavator to remove the top soil, and then by hand (Figure 9). Twelve of the trenches produced no archaeological features. Six of these (Trenches 4, 5, 12, 13, 14 and 15) lay on the south-eastern side of the evaluation area, suggesting that medieval occupation was concentrated on the lower ground towards the lake (or brook as it would have been in the middle ages). Six trenches (11, 18, 19, 20, 22 and 23) adjacent to the lake also lacked archaeological features, but this may reflect destruction of medieval occupation layers during eighteenth-century landscaping.

Most excavations on medieval settlements have been conducted on sites with well preserved earthworks, where the tops of walls and floor levels lie within a few centimetres of the modern surface. In the special case of Compton Verney the excavators found that the medieval features were covered with up to 50 cms (20 ins) of soil, consisting partly of soil washed from the hillside on the south-east of the site, and partly of material dumped during the eighteenth-century landscaping, and in particular earth dug from the nearby lake. This meant that the remains of buildings and occupation were not so easily found as on conventional excavations, but once located they were quite well preserved. 'Old Town' field has been cultivated continuously for many years, but much of the village remains have been protected from plough damage by the thick layer of topsoil.

Trench 10 produced evidence for timber buildings, in the form of nine post settings, suggesting the foundations of a building with earth-fast posts (Figure 12). The associated pottery dated from the twelfth and thirteenth centuries. Timber buildings are commonly found on medieval settlement sites from this period, as the thirteenth century marks the transition from earth-fast post built structures to buildings with stone foundations. Evidence of other structures of this period – two ditches and a pit – were found in Trench 16, and ditches in Trenches 2 and 3 had been later covered by paved stone surfaces. Stone building foundations were found in Trenches 7 and 17, and are dated to the thirteenth and fourteenth centuries by associated pottery. The wall in 17 was about 70 cms (28 ins) wide, and that in 7 was 75 cms (30 ins) wide, and the part that was excavated was about 5m (16 ft) long. Both walls were running east-west. Such narrow structures are likely to have served as low foundations supporting timber-framed walls with panels of wattle and daub. Trench 2 contained a limestone paved surface, and a stretch of stone walling (202) that varied in width from 66 cms to 1.18 m. (26 to 46 ins) which was traced for 8.5 m. (28 ft). Another wall (201) ran at right angles for 4.6 m. (15 ft), and a third (204) for a short length in parallel with the longest wall, that is with a north-west to south-east orientation.(Figure 10) The thickness of the wall, and the care with which it was faced with larger stones, suggested a substantial structure which may have been built with stone up to the eaves. In Trench 21 there were two periods of cobbled surfaces and two lengths of good quality walling oriented north-south (Figure 11 and Plate 15).

Stone surfaces were also found in Trenches 3 and 6. In most cases these paved surfaces were floors or external yards, but the edge of the paving in Trench 6 suggested a road or track leading roughly east-west toward the medieval brook. A number of pits were found, including one in Trench 8 with evidence of burning.

The pottery finds included quantities of shelly ware of the twelfth and thirteenth centuries, from kilns in the south-east midlands (Northamptonshire or Bedfordshire). There were also grey/black wares and sandy micacaeous wares which are found in Warwickshire and were probably manufactured there. Some oolitic ware is probably of the eleventh century. There were minor quantities of Potterspury ware, and pottery from kilns at Brill, Chilvers Coton, and Hanley Castle. There was also some Coventry-type ware of the fifteenth century and a few sherds of Midland Purple of the same period, but no Tudor Green or Cistercian ware. The date range was therefore from the eleventh to the fifteenth centuries, but with little from the end of the fifteenth century. The only small find was a copper alloy hooked tag, probably a dress fastening of twelfth-century date. Sufficient animal bones were found to suggest that large-scale excavations in the future would produce a large sample of evidence for animal husbandry and diet.

Excavation in 1995 of two trial trenches in Ice House Coppice produced no evidence of medieval occupation, so this area (which has some ridge and furrow, revealed when vegetation was cleared) lay outside the village. Another trial trench on the extension to the north-west of the house, and subsequent observation of building work when the house was converted into an art gallery, also failed to produce medieval remains, though these may have been removed by the extensive eighteenth-century building foundations.

Field walking of 'Old Town' field in 1999 produced little material from the higher ground to the south-east, confirming that this lay outside the occupied area, but at the northern end of the evaluation area (where no trenches were dug) and for a further 50m. beyond (at the southern end of Boathouse Coppice) a dense concentration of pottery and building stone at the north-west edge of the field showed that here modern cultivation was bringing abundant medieval material to the surface. Medieval pottery was found on the surface in the south-west of the field, but in limited quantity because of the masking effect of the dumped earth. The finds were mainly pottery of the types found in the excavations, a piece of burnt daub, two medieval horse shoes, a whetstone fragment and two pieces of lava millstone.

Field-walking outside the village area produced a similar range of medieval pottery types, except that Chilvers Coton ware, which was rather scarce on the village site, was much more prominent.

I am grateful to those who have helped me with the research for this chapter. James Bond, Andrew Brown, Helen Maclagan and Nicholas Palmer were all involved in the preparation of the 1994 report from which this has developed. At the 1998 conference at Compton Verney I benefited from the formal papers, and from conversations with Nat Alcock, Steven Brindle, Roland Quinault and Geoffrey Tyack. Nicholas Cooper, Anthony Emery, Jane Grenville and Nick Kingsley were kind enough to correspond with me about the architecture of the medieval house and church. I was given permission to walk over the fields, and received much useful information, from the local landowners: C.G.R. Buxton, Dennis Lean, Des Wells, R.F. Wiggin, and Lord Willoughby de Broke. I was assisted in field walking by Jenny Dyer and Paul Hargreaves. Expert advice on various aspects of the history and archaeology of the parish came from Christine Carpenter, Jane Evans, Jane Laughton, Stephanie Ratkai, Penny Upton and Sarah Wager. Margaret Gelling helped with interpretation of place names. Robert Bearman was as patient as ever, and advised and encouraged the work. Nicholas Palmer criticized a draft helpfully. Andrew Isham drew the maps and Cathy Millwood created the table.

CHAPTER THREE

Compton Verney: AN ARCHITECTURAL HISTORY *of* THE HOUSE

STEVEN BRINDLE

Compton Verney today looks like the very model of a grand Georgian house, perfectly complemented by its beautiful park. A discerning visitor, looking at the house, would soon realise that it is the work of at least two building campaigns, of the early eighteenth century and the mid eighteenth century (Plate 17). However, there is more to it than meets the eye. Not only does the eighteenth-century park cloak a much older landscape; the house itself represents the ghost of a much older, fifteenth-century building.

It is clear that there was a medieval manor house at Compton Murdak, even before it was acquired by the Verneys, probably on or near the present site.[1] We know that the medieval church stood just to the south-east of the present house, and it would indeed be normal for a manor house to be close to the church. The manor of Compton Murdak, as explained in Chapter 1 above, was acquired by Richard Verney in the 1430s. Sir William Dugdale, writing his *Antiquities of Warwickshire* in the 1650s, said:

> Richard Verney Esquire (afterward Knight)... built a great part of the House, as it now standeth, wherein, besides his own Armes with matches, he then set up in a fair canton window, towards the upper end of the Hall, the Armes of King Henry the Sixth.[2]

It is characteristic of Dugdale and his interests that descriptive detail here is reserved for Sir Richard's heraldic display in the Hall, which in itself says something about the size and status of the house. However, there does not seem to be any other surviving evidence for the construction of Sir Richard's house. We have a short furniture inventory, made on

1. *The Victoria County History of Warwickshire*, v, London 1949, 58-60. For other general accounts of Compton Verney, see: A.T. Bolton in *Country Life*, 18 October 1913; A.T. Bolton, *The Architecture of Robert and James Adam*, London 1924, i, 216-28; P. Reid, *Burke's and Savill's Guide to Country Houses, II, Herefordshire, Shropshire, Warwickshire and Worcestershire*, London 1980, 138-9; G. Tyack, 'Compton Verney', *Warwickshire History*, iii, No. 1, 1975; G. Tyack, *Warwickshire Country Houses*, Chichester 1994, 64-70.

2. William Dugdale, *Antiquities of Warwickshire*, London 1656, 435: new edition ed. W. Thomas, 2 vols, London 1730, i, 565. The 1656 edition reads 'as it now standeth', the 1730 edition 'lately stood.'

PLATE 17
Compton Verney, from the south-east (photo: Malcolm Davies).

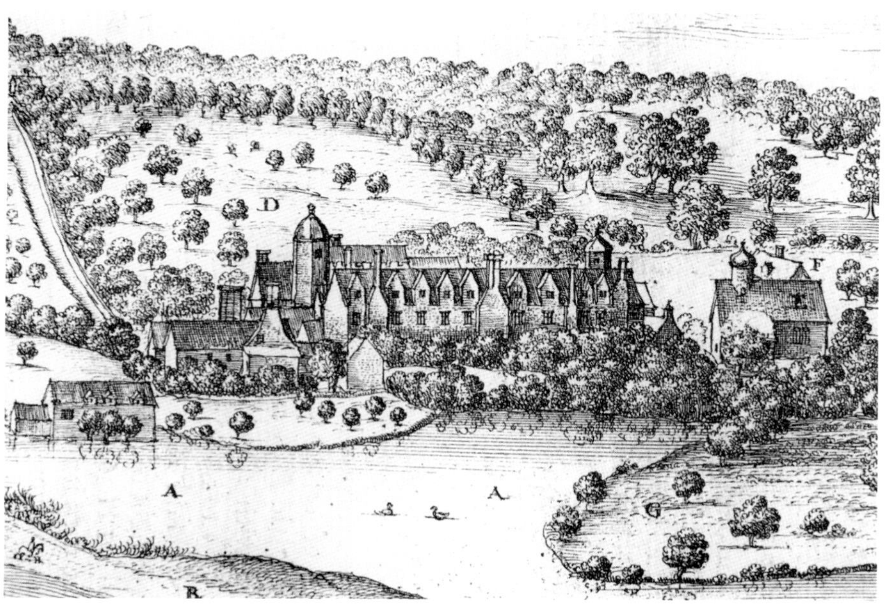

PLATE 18
Compton Verney, c.1655: detail from a drawing by Wenceslas Hollar, published in William Dugdale's *Antiquities of Warwickshire*. (The complete drawing is given as Plate 36).

the death of Sir Greville Verney in 1642, and there is a view by Wenceslas Hollar, made in about 1650 as an illustration for Dugdale's *Antiquities of Warwickshire*[3] (Plates 18 and 36). Hollar's topographical views are known to be fairly reliable, and, as this is by far the most useful document for the early house, it is worth considering at some length.

3. Dugdale (1730 edn) *Antiquities of Warwickshire*, i, 565.

The view shows the house in its setting, in relation to the lake, the Kineton road and the old parish church of Compton Murdak. As Christopher Dyer has shown, medieval Compton Murdak was a village of some size; nevertheless, by the mid seventeenth century, the Verneys had swept it away completely. So far as one can judge, the house is on exactly the site of the present building, and this is very significant. The recent renovation work exposed quite large areas of masonry on internal walls, revealing considerable evidence that the present building contains earlier fabric. The plan of the house embodies further evidence that the Baroque house created in 1714-20 was in fact a remodelling of the previous, fifteenth- and sixteenth-century house, and this is discussed in more detail below. In particular, it seems likely that the present Hall occupies the position of the original Hall referred to by Dugdale.

The first puzzle about the Hollar view is that it is not at all clear where the entrance is. One might expect this to be the west side, towards the road. No drive or entrance courtyard is obvious, though the line of trees crossing from the road towards the house might represent the line of a drive. On the other hand, the stables, marked F, are on the other side of the house beyond the church, towards the site of the lost village. A little further information is given in a survey and valuation document of September 1630, which refers to:

> The manor house with an outer court, 2 stables with other out houses ... £8 per annum.
> One garden on the East side the house two kitchen gardens on the south side and the lardge (sic) orchard on the west side ... £6 per annum.
> Three pidgeon houses & 2 fish ponds ... £6per annum.
> The Parke ... £10 per annum.[4]

4. Shakespeare Birthplace Trust Record Office (SBTRO, DR) 98/1657.

To the left-hand side of the house a low wing is shown, with what appears to be a massive chimney-breast, which could be a kitchen or bakehouse. In 1941, old masonry foundations were found, running west from the present house, which may relate to this building.[5]

5. Public Record Office, WORK 14/1215, a memo by John Harvey dated 22 October 1941: 'During my visit to Compton Verney on 15/10/41, I examined the remains of walls which have been found there. Masonry foundations, running in a S.W. direction from near the S corner of the house, were cut through in making a trench for the new main sewer to the lake. These foundations may have belonged to the outbuildings of the Tudor manor-house, which are shown in approximately this position on the engraving of Compton Verney in Dugdale's *Warwickshire*...' More foundations were noted in between the bridge and the stable building; these were of brick in lime mortar, and were thought by Harvey to be mid seventeenth century.

Behind this, on Hollar's view, rises the main block of the house dominated by a high octagonal tower with an ogee cupola. The tower may well have housed a large spiral stair, but it is imposingly high, and may have been envisaged as a 'Prospect Tower' as well. Just to the right of this, battlements are visible. If the present Hall occupies the site of the fifteenth-century hall, then the battlements would seem to mark its likely place.

Extending to the right, Hollar shows a long range with nine high dormer windows and four chimney-breasts, looking very much like a lodging range. At the far (right hand) end of this is a smaller octagonal turret with an ogee cap, probably a stair turret. It is hard to read what is behind this range, but the two gables flanking the big 'prospect tower' hint at two symmetrical wings. It is evidently a house of some size and pretensions; was it U-shaped, or did it surround a courtyard, as we know the early eighteenth-century house did?

The 1642 inventory does not add very much to Hollar's view. It begins with the Hall, which was almost devoid of furniture. Next was an 'Old Parlour', with twelve leather chairs, a couch and ten pictures. The main rooms were the Great Chamber, hung with arras, and the New Parlour or Drawing Room, also hung with tapestry. There were seventeen bedrooms, a study and an armoury, a bakehouse, a brewhouse and a dairy. In 1663 the house was taxed as having twenty-one hearths.[6]

6. SBTRO, DR 98/898: inventory of the goods of Sir Greville Verney, 1642.

The distinction between the Old and New Parlours is interesting, and indeed some features of the Hollar view, in particular the ogee cupolas, seem to suggest a sixteenth-century, rather than a fifteenth-century house. It is likely that the Verneys had considerably enlarged and extended Sir Richard's original building. Nevertheless, as we have seen, the feature Dugdale singled out for mention was from the house's first building – Sir Richard's heraldic glass in the Hall.

In 1711, on the death of Sir Richard Verney, who had won the right to resume the title of Lord Willoughby de Broke, the title and property passed to his son George Verney, later dean of Windsor. Soon after his succession, he seems to have embarked on a general remodelling of house and grounds. This is dated to 1714 by George Vertue, who visited the house in 1737: he drew a plan of the church and made notes on its glass and monuments, but as to the house, all that he said was:

> Monday Morning sett out for Compton Varney to Lord Willoughbys house – a well built house. 1714.[7]

7. *The Notebooks of George Vertue*, Transactions of the Walpole Society, XXX (Vertue, vol VI), 1955, 75.

No documentary evidence for the rebuilding work seems to survive and we are therefore dependent on a handful of later documents. The most important is a description by the traveller and diarist John Loveday of Caversham, who visited in 1735. This merits quotation in full:

> Just on the right of the road between Little Keinton and Wellsburn is the seat of the Hon. Mr Verney, belonging to his ancestors Lords Willoughby de Broke. It stands low and is built of stone; the front is towards the Garden and has 11 Windows; part of it was

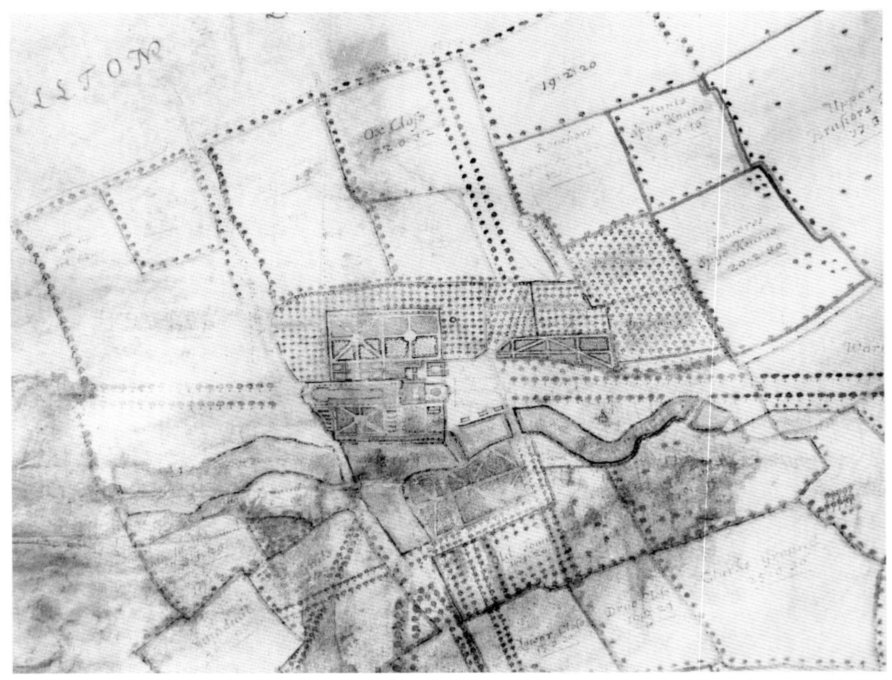

PLATE 19
Detail from estate map by James Fish, 1736,
showing the quadrangular layout of the house at Compton Verney
(SBTRO, DR 98/1819).

built by the late Lord that was Dean of Windsor. Below there is an handsome Gallery or Dancing Room, the Ornaments to it are of the Doric Order. Several family pictures well painted...[here Loveday lists some of the pictures].

There are Chimney-pieces of Derbyshire Marble in this house. The Gardens, with the room taken up by the house contain 20 Acres. The Gardens rise up an hill, and are well-contrived for Use and Convenience. There are Views down to a Pond; of these Ponds there are four in a string, which make a mile in length... The Chappel near the house has Service performed in it when the family is here; and here (and in the Cemitery to it) the Verneys are buryed...[8]

The words 'part of it was built by the late Lord' are ambiguous but suggestive. As has been mentioned, the removal of panelling and plasterwork in the house (in particular in the first floor rooms on the west front) has revealed rubble masonry which looks earlier than that of the early eighteenth-century façade. There is also evidence of a rendered finish to some of the stonework, and of a steeply-pitched roofline, both of them enclosed by the early eighteenth-century roof. There is reason to think, then, that the twelfth lord's work was a remodelling, not a complete rebuild.

The west front and part of the south front of the twelfth lord's work survive. They are in a strong and distinctive Baroque style, consistent with a date of around 1710-20, but their authorship has never been positively identified. A traditional attribution to Vanbrugh, on stylistic grounds, can probably be discounted. Vanbrugh was a Whig supporter with strong connections to the party's leadership, and all of his major patrons seem to have been Whigs, whereas the Verneys were always staunch Tories. The Verneys had a family connection with the Duncombes of north Yorkshire, who were rebuilding Duncombe Park to designs by William Wakefield around the same time; the Baroque front at Compton Verney is close in style to Wakefield's work, but there is no direct evidence of a connection here.[9] The principal local architect-builder of the day was Francis Smith of Warwick. Compton Verney does not look much like any of his known works, but two payments of £200 were made to 'Mr Smith by order' from Lord Willoughby's Staffordshire estate in 1714-15. Smith may, then, have built the new house, but its authorship remains an open question.[10]

In addition to John Loveday's account, we have two block plans of the Baroque house and a little sketch of its south front on a pair of estate maps made in about 1735 by the surveyor James Fish[11] (Plates 37 & 38). These invaluable documents show the elaborate and splendid Baroque landscape, also created by the twelfth lord, and are discussed in more detail by Geoffrey Tyack. They show clearly that the house, as remodelled around 1711-20, was quadrangular (Plate 19). The entrance was on the east,

8. E. Markham, *John Loveday of Caversham*, Salisbury 1984, 190.

9. The twelfth Lord Willoughby de Broke had a daughter Margaret Verney, who in 1716 married Anthony Duncombe. His cousin, Thomas Browne, adopted his mother's name of Duncombe in order to inherit the Duncombe estate near Helmsley and a great fortune (1711), and subsequently built the great house there (c. 1713). Information from Mr. R. Hewlings.

10. SBTRO, DR 98/1811; H.M. Colvin, *Biographical Dictionary of British Architects*, 1600-1864, 3rd edn, New Haven and London, 1995, 887. Andor Gomme has discovered four elevations for a grand country house at the Victoria and Albert Museum, attributed to Smith and known to have come from Compton Verney: A. Gomme, 'The Genesis of Sutton Searsdale', *Architectural History*, 1981, 34-8. None of the drawings looks like the Baroque house at Compton Verney but they help to establish a link between the Verneys and Smith, who is later known to have built the stable block at Compton Verney to James Gibbs's designs, c.1735-6. I am grateful to Professor Gomme for information about these drawings.

11. SBTRO, DR 98/1819.

as it is today. Then as now, this was the side away from the public road. For this reason the drive was brought by an elaborate route around the south side of the pools. There was a final stretch of straight driveway, more or less on the line of the present drive, leading to a forecourt in front of the house with a circular lawn; a little later, the stable block was built overlooking this.

The sketch of the house is puzzling; the façade shown is far from symmetrical (Plate 20). The left hand part, with its two pediments, clearly survives today. To the right of this is a lower wing, five bays wide, with tall windows to the ground floor, but only low square windows to its upper floor. It is not possible to see the lost east (or entrance) front, but it would seem that it, too, was only one and a half storeys high. To the right of the house appears the forecourt and, rising behind it, the stable block, designed by James Gibbs and built around 1735-6 [discussed by Dr Tyack on p.132].

Further information on the Baroque house can be gleaned from two inventories of the house, one made in 1741, the other undated but apparently of the 1720s. The 1741 inventory is the less revealing of the two.[12] It begins with the garrets (entries 1-8). No. 9 was a gallery, and 10-41 were bedrooms, apparently for servants as well as family. No. 42 was the Great Gallery, which had five window-seats, three 'seats for Nitches', twenty-six candle-brackets and a Dutch table, but no pictures. Numbers 43-8 were reception rooms, and no. 49 another bedchamber. No. 50 was a well-furnished parlour with fourteen matted chairs. Then came the Great Hall, housing a dining table and fourteen cane chairs, a Turkey carpet of 16 feet by 6 feet, and a cane mat of 17 feet by 14 feet. A separate list of paintings shows that the Hall housed six full-length, eight three-quarter-length and ten half-length portraits, with a large scene inside a church, two small landscapes, one oval head and twenty-seven prints.

12. SBTRO, DR 98/1742: 'An Inventory of household goods and furniture, linen, china and pictures at Compton Verney, belonging to the Rt. Hon. John Verney late deceased, August 1741.'

The inventory from the 1720s is considerably the more revealing.[13] It starts with the Great Hall, which housed several portraits but little furniture, then the Great Parlour within the Hall, which was well furnished and had two window-seats. There followed a Best Drawing Room, and two Closets within the Drawing Room. Then there was the Old Parlour and the Old Drawing Room, each with two window-seats. There followed a 'Litle Room betwixt the Old Drawing Rome and Velvet Bedchamber', then the Velvet Bedchamber itself with a green velvet bed, then 'the room over the Old Parlour where ye Workt Bed stands': these were presumably the two best bedchambers. Then came a Cedar Closet, the Corner Roome in the New Building, the 'Chince' (ie chintz) Room in the 'New Buildings', and the Dressing Room to the Chince Bedchamber. This had three pieces of verdure tapestry, so presumably it was the bed that was hung with chintz. There followed the First Bedchamber 'on the other side the Great Stairs', where 'My Lady' slept, 'My Lord's Room' and Dressing Room; the latter also had three pieces of

13. SBTRO, DR 98/1743. 'My Lord' and 'My Lady' must refer to the twelfth lord and his wife (died 1728 and 1729 respectively). The reference to the chamber where their son 'Mr. R. Verney used to lie' points to a date after the family quarrel of 1718 (above, p.39).

PLATE 20
Detail from estate map by James Fish, 1736, showing the south front of the house (SBTRO, DR 98/1819).

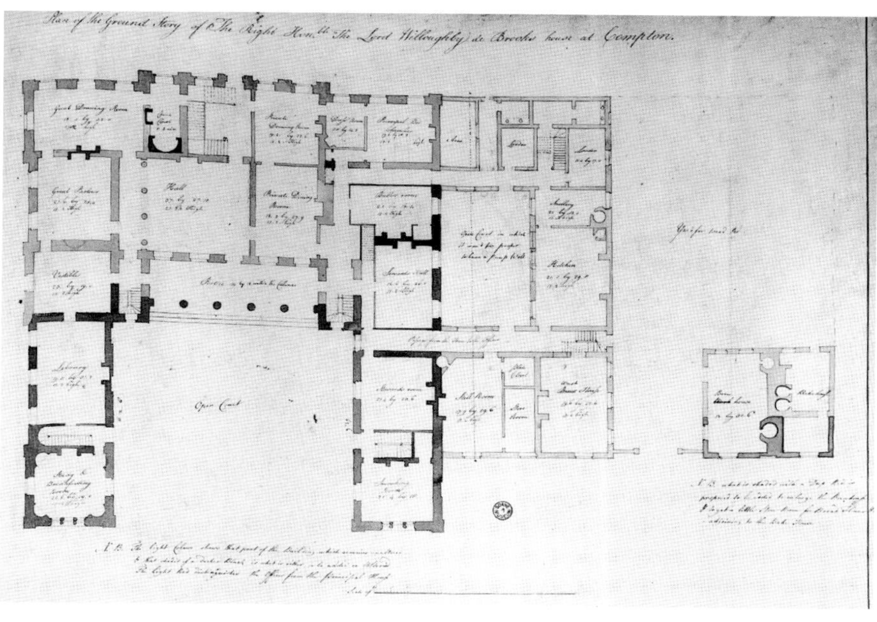

PLATE 21
Robert Adam's plan of the ground floor of the house showing proposed new work in darker shading (By courtesy of the Trustees of Sir John Soane's Museum, Adam Drawings, XLI.19).

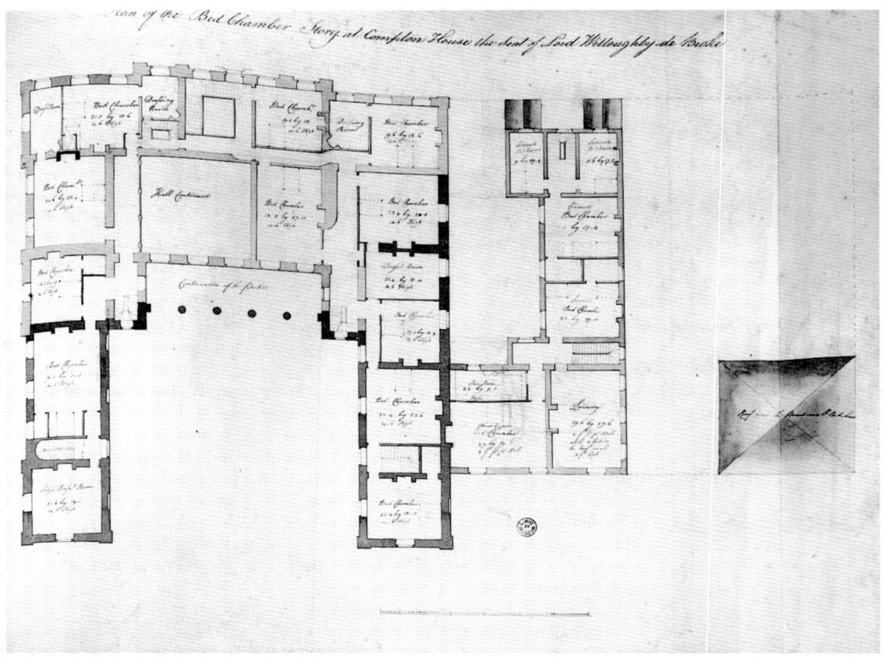

PLATE 22
Robert Adam's plan of the first floor of the house showing proposed new work in darker shading (By courtesy of the Trustees of Sir John Soane's Museum, Adam Drawings, XLI.20).

tapestry with forest scenes. Then came a Gallery, housing a number of portraits. After this came 'Mr Verny's Rooms in ye Old Gallery', another two Closets, and the 'Whight Corner Room where Mrs Bird Lyes', with its closet. Then came 'the Room where My Lord and Lady used to Lye at the end of the Old Gallery'. Then, most intriguingly, comes 'the Room under the Cuplo' and 'the Room next ye Roome under ye Cupolo where Mr R Verney used to lye'. This was followed by two more closets, a room over the Servants' Hall and various servants' bedrooms.

This tells us several things. Most importantly, it seems to provide conclusive evidence that the twelfth lord's work was a partial remodelling and that a number of rooms from the old house remained recognisable after it. It tells us that Compton Verney was grand enough to have three state bedchambers, named for the velvet and chintz and 'workt' (embroidered) upholstery of their beds. These were in addition to my Lord and my Lady's rooms, and were presumably reserved for important guests. The house seems to have had two galleries, an old and a new, neither of which survive today.

The 'cupolo' is a particularly interesting feature; the room beneath it seems just to have been a store-room, for there is a long list of hangings, cushions and curtains which were kept there. The cupola would seem, then, to have been an external feature. One would expect it to be over the centre of a façade, and it is reasonable to think that it may have been over the middle of the lost east façade: in other words, above the main entrance to the house.

More information about the Baroque house can be gleaned from two plans by Robert Adam, now in the Soane Museum[14] (Plates 21, 22). Adam helpfully coloured and marked these plans to show which walls he was retaining from the existing house and which he proposed to build new. This confirms that the two wings of the house were completely rebuilt but that the walls of the main (west) block were retained from the Baroque house. It shows that the 'Great Staircase' referred to in the inventory was on the west or garden front (occupying part of the present Saloon). Most interestingly, the Adam plans show that the hall of the Baroque house was shorter than the present hall, only four bays long. At its north end was another two-bay room, presumably the 'Great Parlour within the Hall' of the inventory. The Hall, though short, was evidently two storeys in height, and at its south (entrance) end the Adam plan shows a screen of four columns supporting a gallery, probably the same columns which survive today.

14. Sir John Soane's Museum, Drawings of Robert Adam, vol. 41, 16-23.

Putting all of this evidence together, we can arrive at a partial picture of the house as rebuilt for the twelfth lord between 1711 and 1728. It had a grand entrance from the east, with a forecourt. The eastern half of the house, including the east or entrance front, seems to have been lower than the western half: to judge by the sketch on the estate map, the façades were severely plain. Despite the lowness of the house (remarked on by

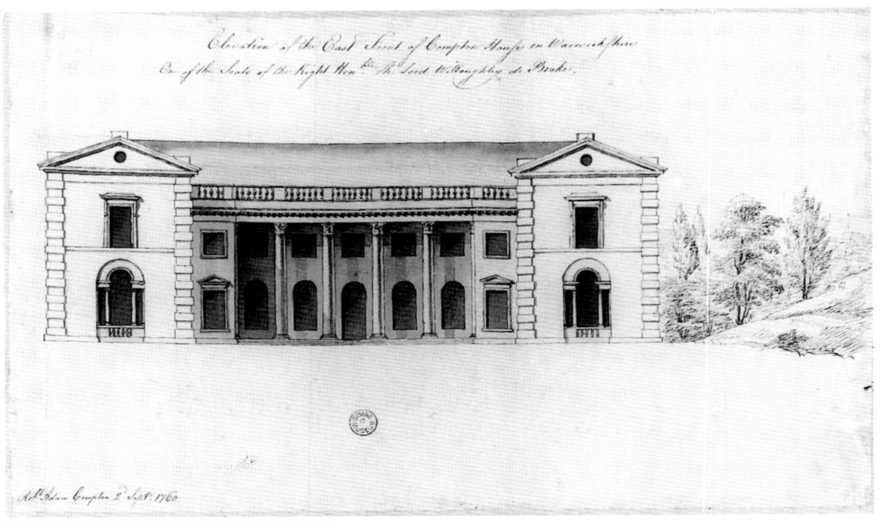

PLATE 23
Elevation of east front of Compton Verney, by Robert Adam
(By courtesy of the Trustees of Sir John Soane's Museum, Adam Drawings, XLI.17).

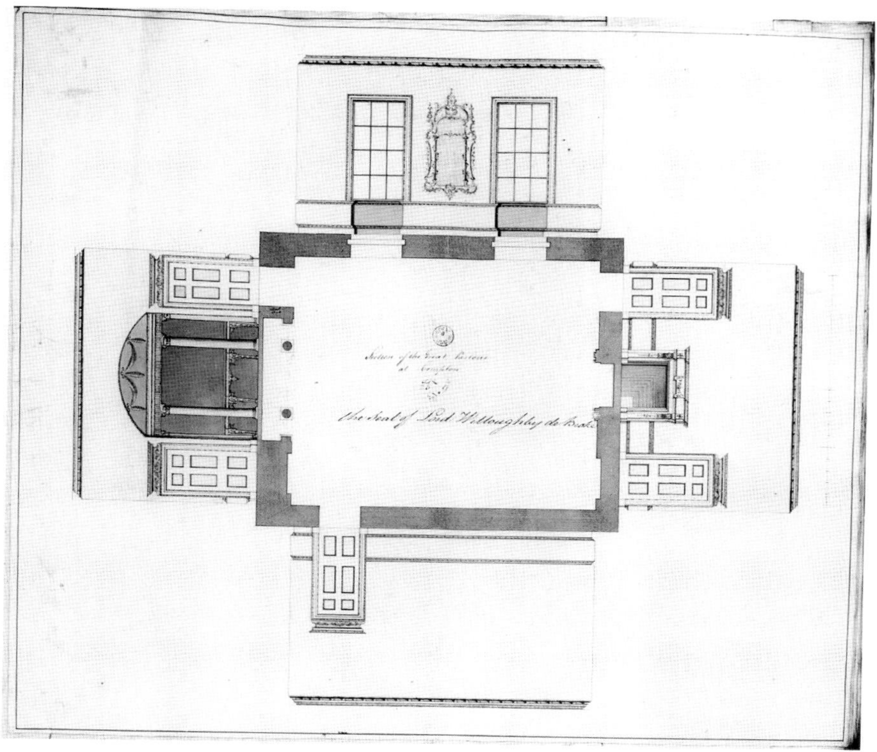

PLATE 24

Design for the great parlour at Compton Verney, by Robert Adam
(By courtesy of the Trustees of Sir John Soane's Museum, Adam Drawings, XLI.18).

John Loveday), the main entrance may have been marked out by a cupola. A gateway or vestibule led through to the square inner courtyard. The visitor would have crossed this to reach the Great Hall on the far side. This was not entered centrally but by a door at the left-hand end. The entrance end of the hall was screened by a row of columns, with a gallery over. Beyond was the Great Staircase on the west front of the house, with a view down the formal gardens with their long pool. To the left and right of the Hall and Great Staircase were the principal reception rooms but it is impossible to be sure how the rooms shown on the Adam plan tally with those named in the inventory.

It is clear that this was not a newly-built house, and indeed the plan does not look like that of a new house of 1711-20. What it does look like is a remodelling of a basically fifteenth- and sixteenth-century courtyard house. This puts Compton Verney into a small but distinct and very important category: late medieval or Tudor courtyard houses which were remodelled in the Baroque age in a way that preserved the essential outlines of their plan. As parallels, one could cite the first duke of Devonshire's rebuilding of Chatsworth in Derbyshire (1686-1707), the earl of Peterborough's renovation of Drayton House, Northamptonshire (c. 1702), the first duke of Manchester's rebuilding of Kimbolton Castle, Cambridgeshire (1707-10), the earl of Scarborough's renovation of Lumley Castle, County Durham (1721-2), the earl of Warrington's renovation of Dunham Massey, Cheshire (1732-40) or the Viscount Gage's renovation of Firle Place, Sussex (undated, probably 1730s)[15]. In all of these cases, the main entrance to the house continued to be through a form of gatehouse, across an open courtyard, and into a remodelled Great Hall.

15. On Chatsworth, see J. Lees-Milne, *English Country Houses: Baroque 1680-1715*, London 1970, 70-84; on Drayton, *ibid.*, 95-101; on Kimbolton Castle, *ibid.*, 102-111; on Lumley Castle, N. Pevsner, *The Buildings of England – Durham*, 2nd edition, revised E. Williamson, London 1983, 357-62; on Dunham Massey, N. Pevsner and E. Hubbard, *The Buildings of England – Cheshire*, London 1971, 203-5; on Firle Place, I. Nairn and N. Pevsner, *The Buildings of England – Sussex*, London 1965, 624-5.

In each of these cases, as at Compton Verney, the house in question had been in the ownership of the same family for a century or more. It may have been that family piety and a respect for the antiquity of the family seat were important factors influencing the design, prompting the retention of old-fashioned courtyard entrances and Great Halls.

In 1752, the fourteenth Lord Willoughby de Broke succeeded to the title at the age of fourteen. He became a Lord of the Bedchamber, and in 1761, married a sister of Lord North, whose family lived at the nearby estate of Wroxton Abbey, Oxfordshire. Lord Willoughby had already commissioned Robert Adam to produce designs for the remodelling of Compton Verney, for one of Adam's eight extant drawings for the house is dated 2 September 1760[16]. It is not clear how the young Lord Willoughby came to choose Adam, then just becoming securely established in London. His future brother-in-law, Lord North, was a junior Lord of the Treasury in the government of the earl of Bute, and Bute was later to emerge as one of Adam's most important patrons. Adam was then engaged at Hatchlands in Surrey, Shardeloes in Buckinghamshire, Kedleston in Derbyshire, and Croome Court in Worcestershire. In all these cases, Adam effectively

16. Soane's Museum, Adam Drawings, vol. 41, 17.

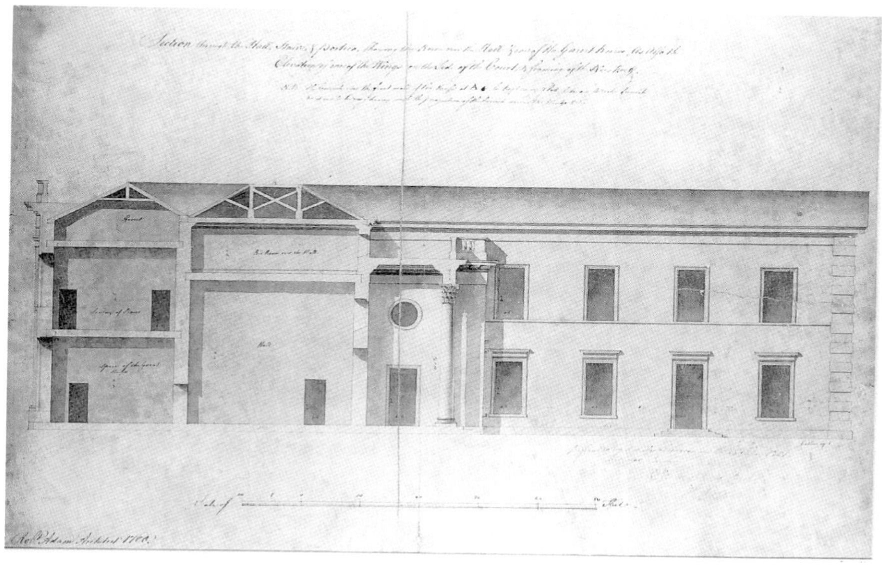

PLATE 25
Cross-section through Compton Verney, looking north, by Robert Adam, 1760 (Victoria and Albert Museum, Print Room, E1 1937 (LD1)).

supplanted an established architect, and Compton Verney would seem to be one of the first jobs where he received the original commission.[17]

Of Adam's nine surviving drawings, only one is dated. The Soane Museum has two elevations showing the east front, with its giant Corinthian portico: one shows square-headed windows as built, the other arched windows, presumably to match the existing Baroque elevations[18] (Plate 23). Then there are three plans of the ground, first and attic floors, which clearly go together (Plates 21 & 22, referred to above). These have the walls which were being retained from the old house clearly marked in a dark colour, and the wings, shown largely as built, in a lighter one.[19] There are important differences between these plans and the house as it was actually rebuilt; several of the principal Baroque interiors seem to have been left as they were, notably the Hall, the Great Stairs and the other West Front rooms. The Soane Museum also has a drawing of wall-elevations for the Great Parlour (the room immediately south of the Hall)(Plate 24), an unexecuted design for a one-storey bakehouse and brewhouse, and a plan of part of the basement just north of the house (largely as built, but since demolished).[20]

There are two more fine Adam drawings for Compton Verney in the Victoria and Albert Museum. One is a cross-section through the middle of the house looking north, signed and dated 1760 (Plate 25). This shows the house largely as rebuilt, the major difference being that the space west of the Hall is marked 'Space of the Great Stair', thus relating to the early plans, which also show the early eighteenth-century staircase left intact.[21] The other drawing is a scheme for the Hall, showing it at its full five-bay length with giant picture-frames, similar to the ones eventually installed[22] (Plate 26). However, this drawing shows arched rather than square-headed windows, and the row of columns at the south end is shown as Doric, not Ionic.

Adam seems only to have produced the designs, with the construction work executed by William Hiorn, an eminent Warwick mason and architect. He and his brother David carried on a considerable practice, working at numerous Midlands country houses, including Arbury (c. 1748 on), Packington (1756-65) and Charlecote (1755-7)[23]. Two estate account books for this period survive, providing patchy references to the work; William Hiorn was paid £200 in 1762, with the main work being carried out, c. 1762-8.[24] The principal masons were Robert and William Wrighton and Samuel Eglinton (1742-88).[25] Stone came from the estate, but also from several other places, including Warwick, Hornton, Gloucester and Painswick. The principal carpenters were William Wilkins and John Maunton.[26]

'Mr Rose Plaisterer' was paid £100 in 1764. This seems to be fairly early in the building campaign and it is not clear that the carcass of the house would by then have been ready; it is possible that Rose was being paid for designs, rather than for executing

17. Colvin, *Biographical Dictionary*, 61-62. Lord North became a junior Lord of the Treasury in 1759; the third earl of Bute became First Lord (Prime Minister) in 1760. However, Bute is not recorded as an active patron of Adam until 1761 when Adam began work on designs for Bute house (later Lansdowne House), Berkeley Square.

18. Soane's Museum, Adam Drawings, vol. 41, 16-17. An Adam elevation, for the south front as built and dated 1760, is reproduced in *Country Life*, 18 October 1913, 534, where it was described as being 'preserved at Compton Verney'; its present whereabouts is unknown.

19. Soane's Museum, Adam Drawings, vol. 41, 19-21.

20. Soane's Museum, Adam Drawings, vol. 41, 18 (The Great Parlour), 22 (Bake- and Brewhouse), and 23 (Cellars).

21. Victoria and Albert Museum, Print Room, E1 1937 (LD1).

22. Victoria and Albert Museum, Print Room, E2 1937 (A77).

23. Colvin, *Biographical Dictionary*, 496-8; A. Gomme, 'William and David Hiorn', in R. Brown, ed., *The Architectural Outsiders*, London 1985.

24. SBTRO, DR 98/1800. This is a book of miscellaneous estate accounts. There are payments for materials and repairs in 1761-5. From 1765 there are summarised 'Bills for Building'; £1,246 for 1765-6, £351 16s 11d for 1766-7, and £908 16s 1d for 1767-8. In 1768-9, £238 17s 3d was spent on 'Sundry Repairs at Compton' and £216 10s 4d on repairing the stables. The detailed accounts for the building work seem to be lost.

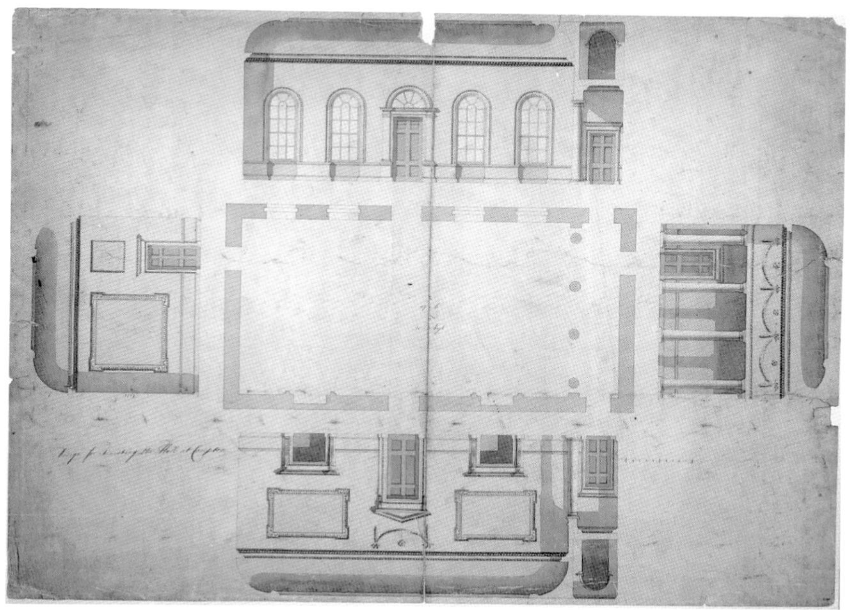

PLATE 26
Design for the Hall at Compton Verney, by Robert Adam
(Victoria and Albert Museum, Print Room, E2 1937 (A77)).

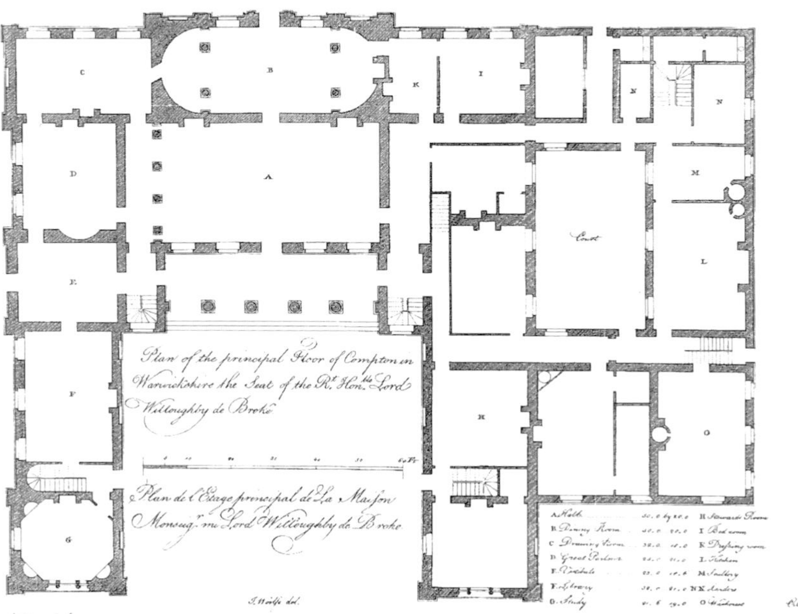

PLATE 27
Ground floor plan of Compton Verney, from *Vitruvius Britannicus*, 1771 (vol. 5, plate 43).

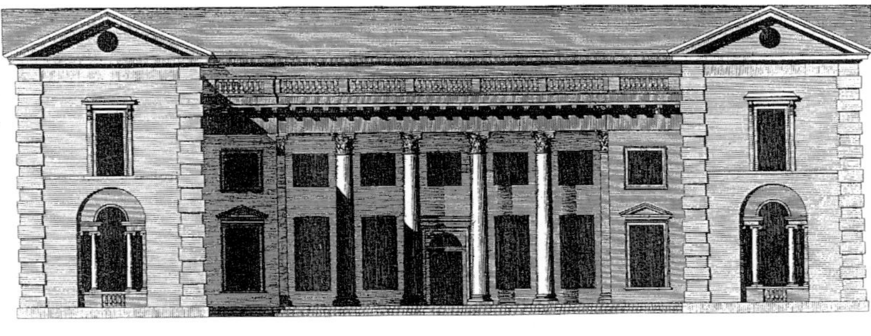

Principal Front of Compton.
Elevation principal de Compton.

J. Gandon del.

PLATE 28
East elevation of Compton Verney, from *Vitruvius Britannicus*, 1771 (vol. 5, plate 44).

PLATE 29
Compton Verney, east front and portico
(photo: Lisa Bowerman).

PLATE 30
Compton Verney, south front
(photo: Lisa Bowerman).

work. It is, in any case, not clear which member of that large and important family is referred to.[27] In 1765-6 payments were made to 'Mr Moore Plaisterer', probably Robert Moore, the leading Warwickshire plasterer of the period, who also worked at Charlecote, Arbury and Warwick Castle.[28]

Work on the ancillary buildings and grounds went on for another thirteen years or more, and is discussed in Geoffrey Tyack's chapter which follows. A ground-floor plan and the east elevation of the remodelled house were published in volume five of *Vitruvius Britannicus* in 1771[29] (Plates 27, 28). This shows that the work as executed varied significantly from Adam's designs. Most importantly, the old great staircase had been torn out, and a five-bay saloon with absidal ends, similar in plan to the Library at Kenwood, had been made in the centre of the west front. As a result the house was left without, and remains without, an impressive main stair. The completed house, though, seems to have been widely admired. Richard Jago, in his long poem *Edge Hill*, written when the exterior of the house must have been barely complete (1767), said:

> .....at his command
> New Pillars grace the House with Grecian pomp
> Of Corinth's gay design. At his command
> On hill, or poain new culture clothes the scene
> With verdant or variegated grove;
> And bubbling rills in sweeter notes discharge
> Their liquid stores.[30]

In 1785 Lord Torrington, usually a sharp critic, said that it was 'as an habitation worth twenty Warwick Castles.'[31] In 1799 the traveller, George Lipscomb, visited it, later writing:

> The exterior of the house is rather neat than splendid, and rooms should rather be called commodious than magnificent; but the pleasure grounds are varied with great elegance, and the water and plantations are delightful.[32]

The remodelled house seems to have remained largely unaltered until 1824. A plan showing alterations to the ground floor, dated in that year and signed 'H.H.', survives in the Victoria and Albert Museum.[33] 'H.H.' is probably Henry Hakewill (1771-1830), a prolific country-house architect who worked all over England, generally in a mild Tudor style or a severe Greek Revival manner.[34] Hakewill switched around the functions of the main rooms; the Saloon on the west front became the dining room, being rather closer to the kitchens, while the door linking this room to the Hall was blocked. The old Dining Room on the south front became the Drawing Room. Hakewill remodelled

25. SBTRO DR 98/1800. There was a large family of masons called Eglinton working in the Midlands in the mid eighteenth century. Samuel Eglinton lived nearby in Kineton; in 1773-4 he and the carpenter, John Mantun, or Maunton, contracted to rebuild Lighthorne Church, also nearby, in a plain Gothic style, at the expense of the fourteenth Lord Willoughby de Broke: Colvin, *Biographical Dictionary*, 337-8.

26. SBTRO DR 98/1800.

27. SBTRO DR 98/1800, 'Mr Rose' could have been either Joseph Senior (c. 1723-80), or his nephew, Joseph Junior (1745-99); there is frequently difficulty in distinguishing between them. Several other members of the family also worked as plasterers in the period. See G. Beard, *Craftsmen and Interior Decoration in England* 1660-1820, London 1981, 279-80.

28. SBTRO DR 98/1800. In 1774 Mr Moore was paid £10 11s 5d for working on the Greenhouse, and for mending a festoon in the Hall. On Moore's career, see Beard, *Craftsmen*, 272.

29. Colen Campbell, J. Woolfe & J. Gandon, *Vitruvius Britannicus of the British Architect*, 5 vols, London 1715-71, v, plates 43-4.

30. G. Tyack, 'Compton Verney'.

31. *The Torrington Diaries*, ed. C.B. Andrews, 4 vols, London 1934, i, 230.

32. George Lipscomb, *A Journey into South Wales*, London 1802, 350

33. Victoria and Albert Museum, Print Room, E4, 1937 (A231).

34. Colvin, *Biograpahical Dictionary*, 444-6.

PLATE 31
Compton Verney, west front
(photo: Chistopher Dalter).

PLATE 32
The Hall at Compton Verney, 1913 (*Country Life*, 18 October 1913).

PLATE 33
Compton Verney, south end of the Hall (photo: Steven Brindle).

Adam's Saloon, taking out the apses, presumably in order to make more space for side-tables and for serving meals; he was probably responsible for the severe doorcases and Ionic columns which remain at either end of the room.

A further bout of alterations was carried out by the eighteenth lord, who inherited in 1862, leaving rather more of a mark on the house to designs by John Gibson, a pupil of Sir Charles Barry.[35] He added various decorative embellishments in a rather heavy Italianate style. The upper windows behind the portico were blocked and the elaborate carved frieze of garlands installed in its place. The roundel in the middle with the family crest of a Saracen's head was added here, and also to the stable pediment. The rather heavy front doorcase is probably by Gibson, and also the heavy doors with arched lights from the forecourt into the wings . Inside, the southern staircase was given a decorative cast-iron handrail. The decoration to the cove of the Hall ceiling seems to date from this period, as does the decorative plaster frieze of a hunting scene above the columns at its south end. Various other surviving pieces of joinery seems to bear the hallmarks of this period.

35. 'John Gibson, Architect, a Memoir', *Journal of the Royal Institute of British Architects*, xvi, 1909, 16.

The house also acquired some of the modern conveniences of the age; in 1869, a gas supply from the Kineton gasworks was laid on.[36] A fire in 1887 must have caused some considerable damage, for the *Stratford Herald* ran an article remarking on the incompetence of the Kineton Fire Brigade: they had taken over an hour and a half to arrive on the scene.[37]

36. Information from Mr Brian Hayton, Compton Verney House Trust, July 1998.

37. *Stratford-upon-Avon Herald*, 30 September 1887; information from Mr Brian Hayton.

Gibson's alterations came in the last period of the family's prosperity, before the agricultural depression reduced its income. In the late 1880s the Verneys were forced to let Compton Verney and moved into a house in Kineton. In 1912 they moved back into Compton Verney; the house was redecorated and equipped for the first time with electric light, powered by a 45 horse-power dynamo, in turn driven by a diesel engine.[38] However, this was an Indian Summer; in 1921 the nineteenth lord was forced to sell Compton Verney, after almost 500 years of Verney occupation. Neglect and erosion followed, a story taken up in the final chapter. It was a pattern being repeated all over England, and for many years it seemed likely that Compton Verney, like so many other houses, was nearing the end of its long history.

38. *Warwick Advertiser*, 22 June 1912; information from Mr Brian Hayton.

The visitor to Compton Verney approaches around the south side of the lake and over Brown's bridge; the last stretch of the drive is straight, on the main axis of the house. Adam, by leaving the east side of the courtyard open, made the dramatic U-shaped entrance court, an effect not often found in mid-Georgian architecture, and perhaps inspired by the work of Vanbrugh, whom Adam greatly admired (Plate 29). Adam's other great and original gesture was the portico, spanning the width of the Hall and framed between the two stair-turrets. The use of the giant Corinthian order is kept simple, without an architrave, and with the wall behind kept very plain – the decorative features there today are of the 1860s. Adam's inspiration for this seems to have come directly from ancient Rome, possibly from Diocletian's palace at Split on the Dalmatian coast, which he had visited in 1757.

On the south front Adam was more bound by the surviving early eighteenth-century work; the left-hand half with its two pediments is entirely of 1714 (Plate 30). Adam responded sympathetically, reproducing the general proportions and most of the details of the earlier work, and, rather surprisingly, producing an asymmetrical design which is nevertheless very effective in oblique views.

The west or garden front is the one part of the Baroque house to remain largely unaltered (Plate 31). The problem of its authorship has already been considered; the use of massive keystones, semi-circular arched windows, heavy plain architraves, and the massive Doric pilasters are reminiscent of various works by Vanbrugh, or Hawksmoor, or for that matter by Hawksmoor and Wakefield. As built, the façade looked down a grand formal garden with a long ornamental pool, to a semi-circular screen of railings and gates giving onto the Kineton road. The north front is the plainest of the four, with only the quoins at the corners for relief; the eighteenth-century stonework remains clearly visible inside Stanton Williams's new gallery wing. Originally, it was flanked by extensive lower service buildings housing the kitchen, still-rook pantry and so on, which are marked on Adam's plan as already existing in 1760.

The Hall is the principal set-piece of the interior (Plate 32). It almost certainly embodies the plan, and some of the shell, of Sir Richard Verney's original fifteenth-century house. As we have seen, the early eighteenth-century hall was a short room, just four bays long, with a gallery across its south end carried by the four columns which still remain (Plate 33). In the 1760s the gallery was enclosed, becoming a first-floor passageway, leaving the south end of the hall somewhat uncomfortably proportioned. John Gibson, around 1863, tried to ameliorate this by filling in the strip of wall between columns and cove with the plaster frieze of a hunting scene.

Robert Adam opened the room up to its present impressive dimensions. The coved ceiling and its main panel are presumably to his design, but the lozenge pattern in the coving seems later, probably from John Gibson's work in the 1860s. The plaster picture-frames on the walls are presumably to Adam's design, and were made to house a series of splendid imaginary landscape paintings by Antonio Zucchi. Zucchi (1726-95) accompanied Robert Adam on his trip to Split in 1757 and came to England at Adam's urging in 1766, becoming his chief decorative painter.[39] He produced decorative canvases for several Adam-designed interiors; those most comparable to the Compton Verney pictures, in size and in subject, are in the Saloon at Nostell Priory (1766-68),

39. E. Croft-Murray, *Decorative Painting in England*, 2 vols, London 1970, ii, 296-7.

PLATE 34
Compton Verney, the Saloon (photo: Malcolm Davies).

the Dining Room at Osterley Park (1767) and in the Music Room at Harewood House (1771).

Zucchi's paintings were large-scale fantasy-scenes with peasants living amongst romantically overgrown ruins, a genre that can be traced back to the landscapes of Nicholas Poussin and Claude Lorraine and beyond. The ones at Compton Verney are recorded in a 1913 *Country Life* photograph of the Hall (Plate 32). It is difficult to make out much of the compositions, but the big canvas on the north wall seems to include Trajan's Column and what may be the Colosseum, while the one on the west wall has an equestrian figure, possibly based on the ancient statue of Marcus Aurelius on the Capitoline Hill. Sadly, Zucchi's paintings seem to have left Compton Verney early this century and their present whereabouts is unknown.

Beyond the Hall, the other principal state-room is the Saloon, adapted by Hakewill as the Dining Room; its present decoration seems more likely to be Hakewill's than Adam's (Plate 34). In its original form, with apses at either end, its plan was very similar to that of Adam's Dining Room (later converted to a Library) at Newby Hall, Yorkshire.

At either end of the Hall are the two main staircases, though they hardly seem commensurate with the size and grandeur of the house. That to the north is surely in its original form of the 1760s, with stone treads and absolutely plain wrought-iron balusters set into them, carrying a simple ramped handrail. That to the south was remodelled by John Gibson and given more elaborate cast-iron balusters, presumably to mark it out as the main stair. The other main reception rooms run along the south side of the house. They are plainly fitted out with simple dado rails, skirting boards and cornices. The doors are mostly small in scale and six-panelled. There are also a number of larger double doors, with scrolls supporting the cornices. The joinery looks to be of various periods: some of it may be eighteenth century, but much was undoubtedly replaced by Hakewill or Gibson, or more recently still. The rooms have some good chimney-pieces, though none of them seem to betray Adam's hand, and they seem to be more in a provincial Rococo style.

The staircase towards the end of the south wing is marked on the plan in *Vitruvius Britannicus* with a somewhat different form; the joinery details suggest that it is fairly recent, indeed probably twentieth century. Beyond is the octagonal Study, again shown on the 1771 plan, though most of its joinery, in particular the corner cupboards, seems to be from Gibson's remodelling . Very little seems to survive of the house's historic fittings in the north wing. The one major survival is a large, plain fireplace with an elliptical arch, and a broad plain architrave. Adam's plan in the Soane Museum marks this room as the Servants Hall, and shows the fireplace marked in black, that is, as part of the new work.

On the upper floors of the house, the depredations of the last seventy years have taken a very heavy toll. Little remains in the way of historic fittings and a good part of what does survive looks to be relatively recent, the machine-cut timber and modern fixings suggesting a date in the 1920s. The eighteenth-century roof-frames seem to survive in large part, though it is not clear whether any of this is from the early eighteenth-century period. One more very interesting historic feature is the lime-ash floor remaining in the south wing attic, presumably installed there because it was cheap and, possibly, also as a fire precaution to prevent spread of fire from the servants' quarters.

On the first and second floors much of the plasterwork and joinery has been stripped out because of dry rot damage revealing certain clues about the early history of the house; at the time of writing (1998) this was still visible. In Adam's south wing, the walls are shown to be entirely constructed of red brick, the external stonework being just a facing, whereas the baroque west front is shown to be of rubble masonry with an ashlar facing. In the first floor rooms on the west front, a number of rather enigmatic clues have been revealed, notably vertical joints between the cross walls and the façade, further vertical joints in the west front itself, and what looks like an earlier, steeper roofline in the two cross-walls. The west wall of the Hall is faced in what looks like mid eighteenth-century brick, but nevertheless has a number of anomalies, such as patches of rubble masonry, chimney-breasts and a blocked window, suggesting that it may once have been an external surface. Finally, at high level in the roof void, areas of the walls and chimney-stacks are rendered and lined with false joints to resemble ashlar masonry. This clearly indicates that these were external surfaces, but it is not clear which period the render dates from, or when these areas of wall were enclosed by the roof. A measured survey of these features would help in interpreting them. In any event, Compton Verney is certainly much older than it at first seems and it has probably not given up all its secrets yet.

CHAPTER FOUR

THE POST-MEDIEVAL LANDSCAPE *at* COMPTON VERNEY

GEOFFREY TYACK

Most students of the English countryside are aware that the landscape is, to an overwhelming extent, not 'natural' but man-made. Nowhere is this more evident than in the landscaped parks which surround so many of our eighteenth-century country houses. What is less widely known is that many eighteenth-century country house landscapes changed quite drastically, often on more than one occasion, before reaching their present state, and that it is sometimes possible, with the help of visual and documentary evidence, to make a detailed reconstruction of their appearance before the almost inevitable arrival of Capability Brown or one of his many imitators. This is happily the case at Compton Verney, where three distinct stages in the creation of the post-medieval landscape can be clearly discerned.

The first stage is represented by an engraving of the house and landscape by the emigré Bohemian artist, Wenceslas (or Vaclav) Hollar, included in the first edition of Dugdale's *Antiquities of Warwickshire* (1656)[1] (Plate 35). The house is shown from a vantage point near the lane leading to the village of Combrook from the Kineton-Stratford road (the present B4086), which follows its course through the valley across a landscape which is noticeably less wooded than that of today. In front of the house is a lake, irregularly-shaped but smaller than today's lake, and behind it, to the north, an open piece of ground surrounded by trees, identified in the legend as 'The Orchard', though it looks more like a stretch of parkland. The area to the left of the road, on the site of the present Park Farm below the Fosse Way, is called 'The Parke' but is planted with what look like young trees in uniform rows: perhaps this was, in fact, the orchard, the mistaken attribution arising from a printer's error.[2] To the right of the house is a small building

1. William Dugdale, *The Antiquities of Warwickshire*, 2nd edn, 2 vols, London 1730, i, 568. The nominal head of the family, Greville Verney, was under age at this time. His uncle, Richard, who succeeded to the estates on Greville's death without issue in 1668, helped Dugdale with the Compton Verney section of the *Antiquities* (above, p.36).

2. I owe this observation to Dr Nat Alcock.

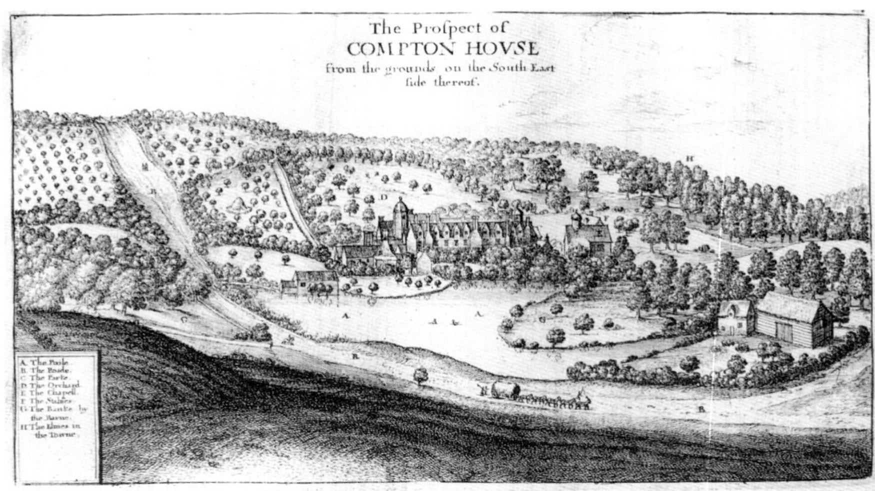

PLATE 35
Compton Verney, from a drawing by Wenceslas Hollar,
published in William Dugdale's *Antiquities of Warwickshire*, 1656.

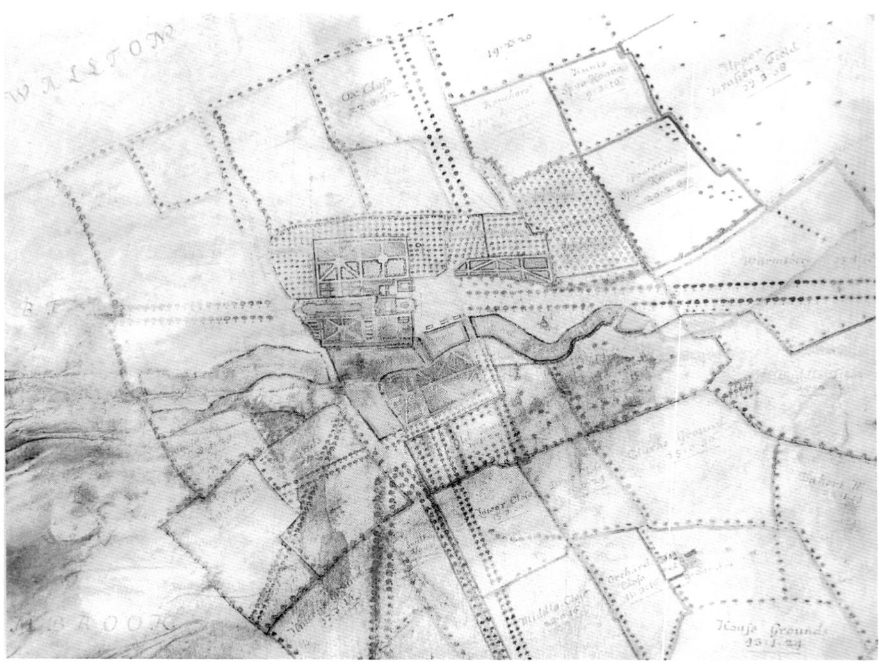

PLATE 36
Compton Verney: the house and its setting, from an estate map by James Fish, 1736
(SBTRO, DR 98/1820).

with a turret called 'The Chapel' – originally the church of the lost medieval village of Compton Murdak – with a stable building behind it. Further to the right there is a large grouping of trees, distinguished by the letter H as 'The Elmes in the Towne'. What can we make of this meticulously detailed and, so far as one can tell, accurate picture?

For all its seeming naturalness, Hollar's view does not represent 'nature in the raw' or anything remotely approaching it. What it shows is, in fact, as much a work of man as the Capability Brown landscape which we see today. Before the fourteenth or fifteenth centuries Compton Verney had been an open-field landscape of the standard south Warwickshire type with a church and village whose site is perhaps alluded to in the enigmatic 'Elmes in the Towne' and in the field known as 'The Old Townes' to the east of the present upper lake.[3] By 1486, however, the population had vanished and the arable land converted to pasture and other uses: a change which the Verney family may have encouraged, and from which they presumably benefited. The landscape shown by Hollar is thus one of seigneurial control.

3. SBTRO, DR 98/1820. See also M.Beresford, 'The Deserted Villages of Warwickshire', *Trans. Birmingham Arch. Soc.*, lxvi 1945-6, 89-90.

The most striking change to the medieval landscape was the creation of the lake on land which had once been part of the deserted village. Its original purpose is recalled by the designation 'The Old Mill Poole' in an estate plan of 1736[4] (Plate 36), and the mill building is clearly shown to the left of the house in Hollar's view. The lake was formed by building a dam on the line of the Kineton-Stratford road, south-west of the house, thus trapping the waters of a brook, a small tributary of the River Dene, which meanders down to the Avon at Charlecote. The initiative for this enterprise presumably came from one of the Verneys, perhaps in the late sixteenth or early seventeenth centuries when small-scale industrial activity flourished throughout the west midlands.

4. SBTRO, DR 98/1820.

The rest of Hollar's landscape has the unmistakeable attributes of a park, with trees dotted around what is otherwise open ground, and a round haystack-like object to the right of the road which might have been a viewing-mound. The park must also have been created by one of the Verneys, possibly Sir Richard, who was in possession from 1574 to 1630 and whose marriage to Margaret Greville led in time to the family's advance into the peerage; it does not seem to have existed when Sir Richard's father died, but it was mentioned in a marriage settlement of 1618 and again in the 1630s.[5] Its precise boundaries are uncertain, but the 1736 estate plan - the first surviving map of the Compton landscape – shows 'The Old Park Grounds' to the east of the field called 'The Old Townes' (Plate 36), suggesting that it originally extended not only to the north of the house, as indicated in Hollar's picture, but also to the south and east, no doubt encompassing what is now Lodge Farm (called the Old Lodge in another plan of 1818).[6] This supposition is supported by eighteenth-century county maps, which show the bulk of the park to the north and east of the Kineton-Stratford road, the land on

5. SBTRO, DR 98/1417, 1657. The park is not shown in either Saxton's or Speed's maps of Warwickshire, and there is no indication when it ceased to contain deer, if indeed it ever had them.

6. SBTRO, DR 98/1832 (Plate 46).

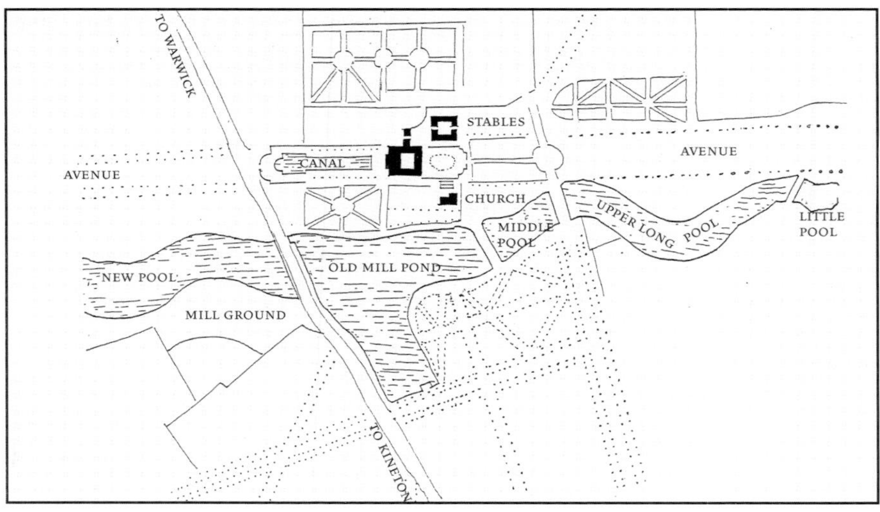

FIGURE 15
Compton Verney, 1736. Redrawn from the estate map of 1736 (SBTRO, DR98/1820).

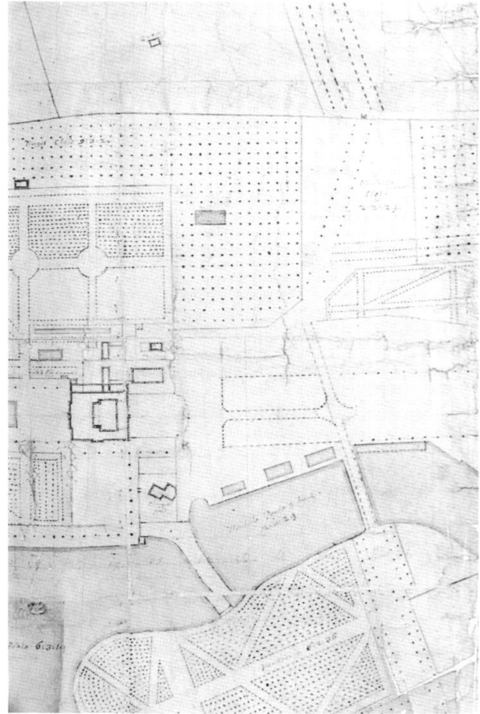

PLATE 37
Compton Verney: the house and its setting, from an estate map by James Fish, 1738 (SBTRO, DR 98/1819).

PLATE 38
Compton Verney, the stable block built to the designs of James Gibbs (photo: Malcolm Davies).

the other (Combrook) side of the road being still mostly under open-field cultivation.

The landscape depicted by Hollar was transformed by George Verney, twelfth Lord Willoughby de Broke, who inherited in 1711 and carried out a major programme of alterations to both the house and its surroundings. In the words of the Reverend William Thomas, who brought out a new edition of Dugdale in 1730, Lord Willoughby 'rebuilt the house at Compton, repaired the Chapel and made gardens and plantations, entirely as they now are'.[7] Hollar's view of Compton Verney does not show anything which we would now construe as a garden, but the 1736 estate plan, by the surveyor James Fish, shows extensive formal gardens to the north and south of the house, together with a rectangular sheet of water or 'canal' between the remodelled west front and the road; this must have existed by 1725, when there are references in an account book to pumping water out of it.[8] The 1736 map also shows the fields on the far side of the road – Warren Ground, Mill Ground and parts of Combrook Field – which were, according to the inscription on the plan, 'proposed to be made into a New Park': something which was not finally achieved until later in the century.[9] A second map by Fish, of 1738,[10] shows an extensive pattern of straight rides or avenues through the surrounding woodland, typical of early eighteenth-century landscaping and clearly part of the recent plantations mentioned by Dr Thomas (Plate 37).

It seems likely that the twelfth Lord Willoughby was also responsible for enlarging the lake to its present dimensions; the 1736 map shows a Middle Pool, an Upper Long Pool and a Little Pool which, taken together with the 'Old Mill Pool' depicted by Hollar, have the same dimensions as the present lake, but with dams demarcating the different sections. The nucleus of the present Lower Lake is also shown on the far side of the road from the house, called, significantly, the New Pool.

There are, unfortunately, no early eighteenth-century views of the gardens at Compton Verney, but the 1736 estate plan is detailed enough to enable us to reconstruct them in our imagination, aided by Henry Beighton's views of other contemporary Warwickshire country-house landscapes, like that of nearby Charlecote, published in William Thomas's edition of Dugdale.[11] Lord Willoughby and his unknown garden designer clearly wanted to beautify the immediate surroundings of the house as well as to impose a sense of formal order onto the landscape as a whole. The rising ground to the north of the house was laid out as a rectangular garden divided by geometrically-aligned paths between beds of flowers or shrubs, with a still-traceable terrace on the southern side overlooking the French-style 'canal'. From the newly pilastered west front – now the most important façade – the canal extended almost up to the road, from which it was divided by gates, and to the south there was another rectangular garden. There were plantations of trees and shrubs crossed by straight paths beyond the lake and and also to the north of the avenue

7. Dugdale, *Antiquities*, i, 566.

8. SBTRO, DR 98/1798.

9. See below. The area is shown as part of a much enlarged park in the next detailed estate plan, of 1818: SBTRO, DR 98/1832.

10. SBTRO, DR 98/1819.

11. A late seventeenth-century bird's-eye view of Charlecote still hangs in the hall there.

PLATE 39
Compton Verney, from the bridge; from a nineteenth-century print.

PLATE 40
The Compton Verney landscape, looking east, earlier this century
(*Country Life*, 18 October 1913).

or 'Great Walk' which led up to the eastern side of the house – then as now the main entrance. The line of the Great Walk was continued west of the road on the axis of the canal, and other avenues stretched to the north and south. This axial planning, so characteristic of the Baroque, complemented the equally formal remodelling of the house.

That assiduous country-house visitor John Loveday observed in 1735 that the gardens were 'well contrived for Use and Convenience', and singled out the view from the house to the pools for special praise.[12] By this time the estate was in the hands of the Honourable John Verney, who became Master of the Rolls three years later in 1738. He commissioned James Fish to produce the estate plans which are so important a source for our knowledge of this phase in the history of the landscape, and he also brought in no less an architect than James Gibbs, who had worked for his nephew the second earl of Oxford, to design a handsome new stable block close to the entrance to the house, on the opposite side of the Great Walk to the medieval chapel.[13] The stables, built by Francis and William Smith of Warwick in 1736-43, were arranged around a courtyard and, according to Loveday, who paid a second visit to Compton in 1740, there were 'Lodging-Rooms, and Rooms for other uses' upstairs.[14] The building is restrained in its architectural character, but the architect showed his hand in the architraves or 'Gibbs surrounds' to the doors and windows, enriched with square blocks of masonry after the fashion of Palladio's Palazzo Thiene in Vicenza. With its completion the Baroque transformation of the landscape came to an end (Plate 38).

The men responsible for creating the present landscape at Compton Verney were John Verney, fourteenth Lord Willoughby de Broke, and Lancelot, 'Capability', Brown, the most famous of all English landscape gardeners. Even in the 1720s, when Lord Willoughby's grandfather laid out his new gardens and avenues, Baroque formality and intricacy were beginning to go out of fashion in England, and in the following decade a new taste for idealised nature with strong classical overtones asserted itself in places like Stowe (Buckinghamshire) and Rousham (Oxfordshire), neither of them far from Compton Verney. Brown was Kent's understudy at Stowe, and in the 1740s and '50s he built up a substantial connection among the Warwickshire gentry and nobility, with work at Newnham Paddox, Warwick Castle, Packington Hall, Charlecote and elsewhere.[15] Other Warwickshire landscapes were meanwhile being transformed in similar vein by Sanderson Miller and members of his circle, among them Radway Grange (Miller's own house), Honington Hall and Farnborough Hall; and Lord Willoughby's brother-in-law, Lord North, employed Miller in the 1740s to improve the landscape of Wroxton Abbey, just over the Oxfordshire border.[16] Lord Willoughby's decision to obliterate a landscape which was only fifty years old might seem absurdly extravagent to us, but in view of his neighbours' activities, and bearing in

12. S. Markham *John Loveday of Caversham*, 1984, 190. An early nineteenth-century picture currently on display in the house shows the same view.

13. Two of Gibbs's drawings are in the Ashmolean Museum, Oxford, Gibbs collection ii, 76.

14. Markham, *John Loveday*, 332.

15. H. Fryer (ed), *Lancelot (Capability) Brown: Warwickshire Commissions*, Warwickshire Gardens Trust 1994. See also A. Wood, 'Lancelot Brown and Newnham Paddox', *Warwickshire History* i, 1969, 3-17; D. Jacques, 'Capability Brown at Warwick Castle', *Country Life*, 22 Feb 1979, 474-6; and G. Tyack, 'Capability Brown and the Packington Landscape', *Warwickshire History*, x, 1997-8, 130-144.

16. A. Wood and W. Hawkes, 'Radway, Warwickshire: the Making of the Landscape', *Journal of Garden History*, vii, 1987, 103-123; L. Dickins & M. Stanton, *An Eighteenth Century Correspondence*, 1910, 266-7 (Honington); G.S. Thomas, *Gardens of the National Trust*, 1979, 134-6 (Farnborough); M. Batey and D. Lambert, *The English Garden Tour*, 1990, 204-8 (Wroxton).

PLATE 41
The greenhouse, since demolished, in 1913
(*Country Life*, 18 October 1913).

mind his court connections and the increase in his income from the Chesterton inheritance, it would have been far more surprising if he had left it alone.

Capability Brown's work at Compton Verney cannot be understood without reference to Robert Adam's transformation of the house (see Chapter 3). By demolishing the east range of the old courtyard, Adam opened the building up to the landscape, and his majestic Corinthian portico supplied a powerfully dominating central motif; Brown's task was to supply a setting worthy of such a bold statement of Roman splendour. His new landscape was intended to be seen as a series of three-dimensional tableaux which gradually unfolded themselves as the visitor approached the house. To achieve the desired effect of expansiveness, the lakes were turned into a single stretch of water by the removal of the existing dams, and a bridge was constructed to take the drive across the site of the dam between the former Middle Pool and Upper Long Pool. It is from here that the house is first seen at its full extent (Plate 39). All vestiges of the existing gardens, including the canal facing the west front and the formal avenues to east and west, were swept away,[17] to be replaced by lawns framed by 'belts' of trees and interspersed with clumps, both deciduous and evergreen. They now include the cedars, possibly planted by Brown, which form an unforgettable part of the Claudian 'framed view' of the house from the bridge.[18] The ancient parish church, which would have blocked both this view and that from the house to the lake, was also demolished, and a new structure built in a less prominent position on the hillside to the north, adjoining a walled kitchen-garden: a striking assertion of purely aesthetic over associational values. Denser planting to the north-west of the upper part of the lake – the area of the 'Elmes in the Towne' in Hollar's view – closed the eastward vista from the house until the onset of Dutch elm disease of the 1970s (Plate 40), and the dam carrying the newly-turnpiked road between the upper and lower lakes was carefully screened by another plantation. As the nineteenth Lord Willoughby, the last member of the Verney family to live at Compton, remarked:

> To look out of the windows on to a ploughed field is by common consent intolerable. A hill of naked pasture-land is less indelicate ... but more often the outline, especially in the Midlands, is awkward and meaningless. So "Capability" decreed that the upper slopes of such hills as would meet the eye when walking in the pleasure-grounds should be clothed with woods or groves of such deciduous forest trees as beech, oak or elm.[19]

Thus the landscape regained its former park-like character.

Brown began work at Compton Verney in 1768, soon after the main work on the house was finished.[20] The progress of the work can be traced both through his own account-book, which records payments of £3,830 between 1768 and 1774, and from the estate accounts.[21] Many of the first payments are for buildings, starting with a new greenhouse on the terrace

17. The less important avenue to the north still existed in 1886 (Ordnance Survey, six-inch map), and traces of the avenue to the south could also be seen on the far side of Warwick-Kineton road at that time.

18. It is not clear when the cedars were planted. They are not shown in Hollar's view and there is no indication of trees on the site in the 1736 estate plan, but they are not mentioned in the late eighteenth-century estate accounts either. A young cedar at the north end of the bridge is shown in the view of the house in J.P. Neale, *Views of the Seats of Noblemen and Gentlemen*, 1st series iv, 1821.

19. R.G. Verney, Lord Willoughby de Broke, *The Passing Years*, London 1924, 3-4.

20. D. Stroud, *Capability Brown*, London 1975, 141-2. He received a first payment of £120 from Lord Willoughby on 19 November 1768.

21. Ibid. Two payments totalling £500 are recorded in Brown's account with Drummond's Bank in 1770-1: P. Willis, 'Capability Brown's Account with Drummond's Bank', *Architectural History*, 1984, 390. The estate account books are in SBTRO, DR 98/1800-2.

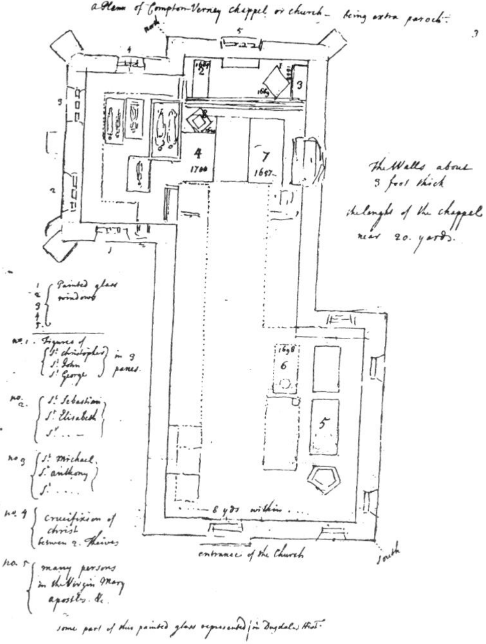

PLATE 42

Plan of the old church at Compton Verney, by George Vertue (British Library, Add. ms. 70438, fol.3.; by permission of the British Library).

PLATE 43

Two panels of stained class, removed from the old chapel on its demolition (For others, see Plate 2).

to the west of the house overlooking the empty stretch of lawn with which Brown had replaced the Baroque water-garden (Plate 41). This elegant structure (since demolished), with its large round-headed windows, engaged Doric portico and Doric frieze enriched with *paterae*, was begun in 1769, when payments were recorded for digging the foundations and supplying Warwick sandstone.[22] The mason was Samuel Eglington, a member of a family of local builders who had worked on the house,[23] and the carpenter John Maunton; Robert Moore of Warwick was paid for plastering the interior in 1775 and for 'colouring the Green House' in the following year.[24] It is not clear whether the design was supplied by Adam or by Brown, who was an accomplished architect in the classical manner,[25] but in the case of the bridge, built between 1770 and 1772,[26] Brown seems the more likely candidate. It is a noble design of three arches, with a balustrade and, originally, sphinxes on the piers, and it forms an integral component of the landscape as viewed both from the house and, with the house in the background, from the upper part of the lake. An ice-house, on the eastern side of the bridge, was built in 1772 and still survives.

Arguably the greatest loss resulting from Brown's activities was that of the ancient church by the lake: the last tangible relic of the medieval village. Fortunately a ground plan of 1737 survives in the notebooks of George Vertue, showing that it comprised a nave with a south aisle and a chancel with a small mortuary chapel to the north[27] (Plate 42). Inside there were several monuments, including one by Nicholas Stone to Sir Richard Verney (d.1630) and his wife Margaret in the form of a tomb-chest surmounted by two recumbent effigies,[28] and a series of stained glass windows dating from the late fifteenth to the seventeenth centuries (Plate 43). Much of the glass was heraldic, but there were also panels showing members of the family, including Sir Richard Verney (d.1527) and his wife, in prayer, and there were six panels of early sixteenth-century German or Flemish glass of religious subjects, including the Crucifixion.[29] The glass and the monument were transferred, together with a marble wall slab with a bust of Sir Greville Verney (d.1668), to the new chapel of 1776-9, which was almost certainly designed by Brown.[30] The building still survives intact on the hillside to the north-west of the house, near the site of the greenhouse, though it has lost most of its original woodwork, together with the stained glass, which was sold by Lord Manton in 1931.[31] Externally plain in the extreme, it lacks the picturesque charm of its predecessor and could easily be mistaken for a domestic outbuilding; but the interior is light and well-proportioned, with large round-arched windows, a flat ceiling on coves, with plaster *paterae* by William Hiatt in the square panels, and a Venetian (or Serlian) window at the east end. The seating faces inwards, collegiate-style, and there is a west gallery resting on Tuscan columns; the space in front of the chancel is occupied by the tomb of Sir Richard Verney and his wife (Plate 44).

22. SBTRO, DR 98/1800, under 'Green House'.

23. His uncle, also Samuel, designed the County Hall at Coventry in 1783-4: H.M. Colvin, *Biographical Dictionary of British Architects 1600-1840*, 3rd edn, New Haven & London 1995, 337-8.

24. SBTRO, DR 98/1802.

25. It is attributed to Adam on stylistic grounds in D. King, *The Complete Works of Robert and James Adam*, 1991, 401.

26. Eglington was paid the balance of his fee for 'finishing the upper bridge' on 8 August 1772: SBTRO, DR 98/1801.

27. *The Notebooks of George Vertue*, Transactions of the Walpole Society, xxx, 1955, 75-80.

28. Stone also supplied the monument to Sir William Peyto (d.1639) in Chesterton church, not far away, and his son John was probably responsible for the design of Chesterton House.

29. Dugdale, *Antiquities*, i, 571; S. Brindle, 'Compton Verney, Warwickshire', English Heritage, n.d.,22-3.

30. SBTRO, DR 98/1802. The mason was Samuel Eglington and the carpenter John Maunton.

31. H.T. Kirby, 'The Compton Verney Glass', *Country Life*, 15 April 1954, 1132-3, where some of the panels are illustrated. Some of the glass is now in the restaurant of the Burrell Museum in Glasgow, but the whereabouts of the rest is unknown.

PLATE 44
Interior of the new chapel, 1980
(National Monuments Record, English Heritage).

PLATE 45
Compton Verney, c. 1820, from an engraving by J.P. Neale, published in 1821.

PLATE 46
Plan of Compton Verney landscape by Paul Pedley, 1818 (SBTRO, DR98/1832).

The first payments for trees and shrubs were made to a Mr Patterson in 1769, and in the following year there were payments for leather and copper for the sluice, for 'digging stone for the fence' – presumably a ha-ha – and for posts and railings at 'the plantation'.[32] Payments for trees and shrubs continued throughout the 1770s, with 200 elms being bought on 23 December 1776; the 1776 accounts also record 'mounding the clump', ditching round the 'large clump' and the 'other clump' and trenching in the 'new plantation'. References in the later 1770s to plantations at Combrook and the 'Windmill Ground', near the road to Kineton, make it clear that trees were being planted not only in the immediate vicinity of the house but also elsewhere on the estate,[33] a policy which went hand in hand with the progress of inclosure, one result of which was to give the formerly open landscape of south Warwickshire a more wooded appearance which it retains to the present day.

32. SBTRO, DR 98/1800.

33. SBTRO, DR 98/1802.

The improvement of the landscape continued sporadically throughout the rest of the century. Samuel Eglington was paid £21 in 1788 for building a 'pavilion or seate on the broad walk at Compton',[34] complete with columns, a frieze and a pediment. This structure has disappeared without trace. In 1797 the nurserymen John and Robert Howey of Putney supplied a variety of new and, at the time, exotic trees and shrubs, including pines, firs, laurels, rhododendrons and Swedish junipers,[35] and in 1799 George Lipscomb remarked that 'the pleasure grounds are varied with great elegance, and the water and plantations are delightful. In the greenhouse we were shewn a choice collection of exotics'.[36] Some of this planting may have taken place on the south side of the lake, close to the present visitors' car park; an estate plan by Paul Pedley of 1818 – the first detailed map of the post-Brown landscape[37] (Plate 46) – shows a fairly dense block of trees here, traversed by paths which are clearly shown in the first Ordnance Survey map of 1886. By the 1820s, judging from the view from the far end of the upper lake published by J.P. Neale[38] (Plate 45), the landscape close to the house looked much as it does today, save for some lack of maintenance in the more distant portions and the thinning of trees as a result of Dutch elm disease.

34. SBTRO, DR 98/1654/172.

35. SBTRO, DR 98/1654/191.

36. G. Lipscomb, *Journey into South Wales... in the year 1799*, London 1802, 350.

37. SBTRO, DR 98/1832.

38. *Seats of Noblemen*, 1st series iv, 1821. The west front is shown in a slightly earlier view in the Aylesford Collection, Birmingham City Reference Library, views of Warwickshire houses, i, fol. 136.

The most important changes in the nineteenth century were to the more distant parts of the landscape, especially on the far side of the Kineton-Stratford road, where there was a major extension of the park. Here the presiding spirit was the Honourable Henry Verney, younger son of the fourteenth or 'good' Lord Willoughby. He took over control of the estate in lieu of his elder brother, who was insane, before his father's death in 1816, and in 1815 he came to an agreement with William Whitmore, the Birmingham-based engineer of the Birmingham-Stratford Canal, to enlarge the lower lake to its present size, an undertaking which involved the building of the dam which can be seen today from a footpath just outside Combrook village. Relations between the two men

PLATE 47
The obelisk, erected c.1848, marking the family vault in the medieval parish church (photo: Malcolm Davies).

were strained in the extreme, and Whitmore was dismissed in 1818 before the dam was completed.[39] But the lake is shown with its present dimensions in the 1818 estate plan (Plate 46), and in 1821 Henry Verney, who had succeeded as sixteenth Lord Willoughby in the previous year, was credited by Neale[40] with having added 'considerable plantations', together with 'an expanse of water called Combrook Water' [i.e. the lower lake]. Pedley's map shows the Park extending on both sides of the Lower Lake as far as Combrook, over the lands of the present Park Farm, with a 'belt' of trees alongside the Fosse Way – called the 'Foss Rides' in the first edition of the six-inch Ordnance Survey map (1886) – and a substantial plantation called 'The Rides' stretching south from the lake to the lane from the Kineton road to Combrook. Though some of the original open park-like character has been lost, these features can still be clearly seen today.

39. R. Chaplin, 'The Landscape Lakes at Compton Verney', *Warwickshire History*, i, 1970, quoting letters in WCRO, CR 556/312.

40. *Seats of Noblemen*, 1st series iv, 1821.

Victorian changes to the landscape were relatively minor. The only significant change in the immediate vicinity of the house was the construction of a small obelisk of Cornish granite, formerly at Place House, Fowey, above the old family vault on the site of the medieval church by the sixteenth Lord Willoughby in about 1848[41] (Plate 47). A small boathouse nearby, which still survives, is shown in the first edition of the six-inch Ordnance Survey map of 1886. An avenue of wellingtonias to the east of the bridge dates from 1856,[42] but the main focus of attention of the seventeenth Lord Willoughby, who succeeded his father in 1852, and of his successors, appears to have been the estate rather than the landscape near the house, which was now entering its most mature phase. The sixteenth lord's widow employed John Gibson, who also carried out work in the house, to rebuild the church at Combrook in the Gothic style in 1866, and this survives largely intact as an excellent example of an estate church of that period. It is probably also to Gibson – who worked extensively at Charlecote for Lady Willoughby's sister – that we owe the picturesque estate cottages and school which can be seen in the village today. These formed an important part of the patriarchal landscape described with such nostalgic affection by the nineteenth lord in his autobiography, *The Passing Years*.

41. A drawing survives in SBTRO, DR 98/1745-7.

42. Information from Brian Hayton.

Both the nineteenth Lord Willoughby and his father seem to have devoted more attention to the Compton Verney kennels than to the landscape, but they respected Brown's achievement, as can be seen both in *The Passing Years* and in the illustrations to the first (and only) account of the house in *Country Life* for 1913.[43] The Verneys' inter-war successors at Compton, Lord Manton and Samuel Lamb, maintained the pleasure grounds to a high standard, and Lamb also planted quantities of trees on the far (Combrook) side of the road, with visually questionable results. After the Second World War, when the house suffered grievously, the immediate landscape setting still survived largely unchanged under the stewardship of Harry Ellard, though much of the

43. *Country Life*, 18 Oct 1913, 528-35.

surrounding land was sold. And it is Brown's landscape, with the house framed by trees rising up above the placid waters of the lake, which remains most abidingly in the memory of the modern visitor to Compton Verney.

CHAPTER FIVE

A Seventeenth-century Landscape:

THE CHESTERTON ESTATE *and the* WILLOUGHBY DE BROKE PAPERS

PHILIP J. WISE

At first sight it might appear to be strange to include a paper on the Chesterton Estate in a volume devoted to the subject of 'Compton Verney – a history of the house and its owners'. However, in 1746 Margaret Peyto died and in her will she left her estate at Chesterton to a distant cousin, John Verney. Thus the future fourteenth Lord Willoughby de Broke inherited not only the Chesterton estate, but also a large collection of family papers amassed by the Peytos over several generations. Amongst these are a group, mainly accounts, which relate to the construction and maintenance of various buildings at Chesterton including a windmill, a water mill and a great house. These papers provide a vivid insight into the development of the estate during the seventeenth century and are a rich source of information for the local historian.

The first building to consider is the windmill itself (Plate 48). It stands in splendid isolation on a hilltop, visible from both the Fosse Way and the Avon Valley to the west, the M40 to the south and the Feldon to the east. It is a classical building, six square pillars with round-headed arches supporting a circular tower covered by a low dome. Today the ground floor is open although early photographs show a wooden structure which must have contained a stairway giving access to the first floor. This is lit by three windows while the cap has a small dormer window balancing the sails. This prominent position has attracted the interest of writers since the early nineteenth century, resulting in a widely held view that this building was designed by Inigo Jones in 1632. The earliest occurrence of this attribution appears to be in the writings of the Reverend Thomas Ward (1770-1850)[1], and this claim is repeated by Ribton-Turner in 1893, W. H. Hutton in 1926 and the writer of the *Victoria County History* in 1949[2]. More recently Howard Colvin

1. Ward states that 'On the summit of a small hill stands the large stone windmill erected in 1632 by Sir Edward Peyto after a design by Inigo Jones' (BL Add. ms. 29264, fos 189-90).

2. C.J. Ribton-Turner, *Shakespeare's Land,* London and Leamington 1893, 303; W.H. Hutton, *Highways and Byways in Shakespeare's County,* London 1926, 65; *VCH, Warws.*, v, 42.

PLATE 48
The windmill at Chesterton (photo: Philip Wise).

has suggested that the windmill might have been the work of either Nicholas Stone (1586-1647), who was Inigo Jones's master-mason and designer of garden sculptures and church monuments, or Sir Edward Peyto (1590-1643), the owner of the Chesterton estate in the early seventeenth century.[3]

Nicholas Stone is widely acclaimed as one of the most accomplished sculptors of the early seventeenth century. His 'Notebook' records the designs of three monuments in Warwickshire – for Sir Richard Verney (d. 1630) at Compton Verney in 1631, for Sir Thomas Puckering (d. 1636) in St Mary's, Warwick, in 1639 and, most significantly, for William Peyto (d. 1619) in St Giles's Church, Chesterton, in 1639[4]. Stone also worked as a master-mason under Inigo Jones during the building of the Banqueting House at Whitehall Palace in 1619. It is certainly possible, therefore, that Stone was the designer of Chesterton windmill, although there is no surviving documentary evidence.[5]

Alternatively, it has been convincingly argued that Sir Edward Peyto was his own architect.[6] The estate papers include two relevant documents in support of this argument. Firstly, there is a licence granted on 30 April 1613 by the Privy Council to Sir Edward Peyto, 'to travayle into the lands beyond the seas' for 'the space of three yeares for his better experience and knowledge in the languages'.[7] By an interesting coincidence Inigo Jones was accompanying Thomas Howard, second earl of Arundel, on a tour of Italian cities in this year and it is almost certain that Sir Edward would have followed a similar itinerary. Secondly, the catalogue of the library at Chesterton, compiled in 1733, has survived and includes a number of architectural text-books which may have belonged to Sir Edward Peyto.[8] This view of an educated gentleman is confirmed by the inscription on Sir Edward's memorial in Chesterton Church which describes him as '...very skilled in sound learning, especially in mathematics' (*Vir bonarum literarum maxime mathematicarum peritissimus*). Lastly, the enterprising nature of Sir Edward is shown by a series of accounts which relate to the cultivation of the woad plant at Chesterton.[9] The ending of French supplies of woad in 1638 apparently encouraged him to meet the demand from London's dyers by growing the plant himself. All in all Sir Edward Peyto probably had the education, experience and enthusiasm to design his own windmill.

Almost as much attention has been given to an apparent contradiction between the date the structure was erected and its earliest recorded use as a windmill. The date 1632 appears on a lead panel above the window in the cap, but the building was thought not to have functioned as a windmill until 1637.[10] The estate accounts record in October 1637: 'Paid for pack thridd to mend the sailcloth 4d', and later in the same year, 'Paid to Thomas Bond for 20 foot of stone used at the windmill 3s 4d'.[11] This gap of several years has prompted suggestions, by, amongst

3. H.M. Colvin, 'Chesterton, Warwickshire', *Architectural Review* cxviii, 1955, 115-7.

4. P.B. Chatwin, 'The Later Monumental Effigies of the County of Warwick', *Transactions of the Birmingham and Warwickshire Archaeological Society* lxii,1933, 140-1, 145-6.

5. A payment to a 'Mr Stone' does appear in the estate accounts. On 22 February 1638 is recorded: 'Pay'd to your wor[ship]; for to give to Mr Stone £4'. This may have been a deposit for the design of William Peyto's tomb, for which Nicholas Stone was paid £150 in 1639: SBTRO, DR 98/1710, fol. 21r.

6. Colvin, 'Chesterton', 116; E.G. Baxter, 'Chesterton Windmill', *Warwickshire History* i, no.6, 1971, 21.

7. SBTRO, DR 98/1663.

8. SBTRO, DR 98/1741. Among the folio and quarto volumes listed in William Peyto's library are the following: Leon Battista Alberti (Paris 1553 and Venice 1565), Vitruvius (editions of 1567 and 1662), Palladio (Venice 1601), Scamozzi (Venice 1615) and Philipert de L'Orme (Paris 1626). There are also a number of folios of 'cutts', or engravings, of the fountains, triumphal arches, palaces and other monuments of Rome.

9. B.M. Baggs, ed., 'Woad Accounts for the Manor of Chesterton 1638-1641', in R. Bearman, ed., *Miscellany* 1, Dugdale Society Publications xxxi, 1977, 1-14.

10. Wilfred Seaby noted this lead panel in 1935, establishing that it pre-dates the re-roofing of 1965-71. The 1632 date does not appear on the stone-work of the windmill as has been stated by Baxter ('Chesterton Windmill', 22).

11. SBTRO, DR 98/1710, fos 3r, 11r.

others, Nikolaus Pevsner, that the structure may have been an observatory or a gazebo.[12]

12. N. Pevsner & A. Wedgwood, *The Buildings of England – Warwickshire*, Harmondsworth 1966, 230.

This was the state of knowledge before 1993 when a previously unrecognised set of accounts for the windmill was found in the Willoughby de Broke papers.[13] This quarto account book for 1633-1634 was originally catalogued as a record of wood-sales to people in Chesterton and the surrounding villages. Further examination revealed other accounts relating to the 'wyndemill' presented in two different forms – payments to named individuals and as a running list of expenses. These accounts are not always easy to follow today and similar difficulties appear to have been experienced at the time of their preparation. A note in the accounts by Sir Edward Peyto himself, bemoans their disorganised state and ends: 'to conclude they are soe confused that they might not bee understood'.[14]

13. SBTRO, DR 98/1708.

14. SBTRO, DR 98/1708, fol. 88r.

References to the 'wyndemill' occur in the accounts for the four months from 28 May to 29 September 1633. Nine men are listed as being involved in some way with its construction: John Richardson and his son, who were stone masons; Mr Westly and his son, builders; William Gelder and his man, carpenters; Thomas Priest, a roofer; Mr Saunders who supplied the sailcloth and Richard Robinson who cleared the site after the windmill was finished. Considerable detail is presented in these accounts. For example, the Richardsons were paid for digging stone at the quarry for half a day to supply the windmill as well as at least one and a half day's work at the site itself, while sailcloth for the windmill was bought at 9d. per yard (Plate 49). An attempt has been made by the writer to calculate the amount of time spent in building the windmill and the cost of its construction.[15] The results obtained were 50½ days' and £9 15s 9d, but neither figure is likely actually to represent the total amounts involved in building the windmill. It is inconceivable that only half a day was needed to quarry stone for the windmill or that it could be built in only eight weeks. It is certain therefore that we have only part of the building accounts covering the later phase of the mill's construction in the summer of 1633. However, these accounts have confirmed that the structure was erected originally as a windmill in 1632-3 and not as a folly or other estate building which was later converted.

15. P.J. Wise, 'New Evidence for the Building of Chesterton Windmill', *Warwickshire History* ix, no. 4, 1995, 159-162.

It is clear from a study of the 1637-8 Chesterton accounts in the Willoughby de Broke papers that the windmill required regular maintenance during the mid-seventeenth century. As might be expected, repairs to and replacement of the sailcloths and sails appear. In the period 25 March 1637 to 30 March 1638 we find: 'Pay'd in parte for the sayle clothes £6 0s 0d', while an entry for 10 June 1638 reads: 'Goodwife Smyth for mending the sayle cloathes for the myll 4d'.[16] Later, on 12 August 1638, John Birknell was paid 1s 6d for one and a half days' mending the wooden sails themselves.[17] Other maintenance is implied by payments in December 1637 for the sharpening of

16. SBTRO, DR 98/1710, fol. 26r; DR 98/1711, fol. 91v.

17. SBTRO, DR 98/1711, fol. 96v.

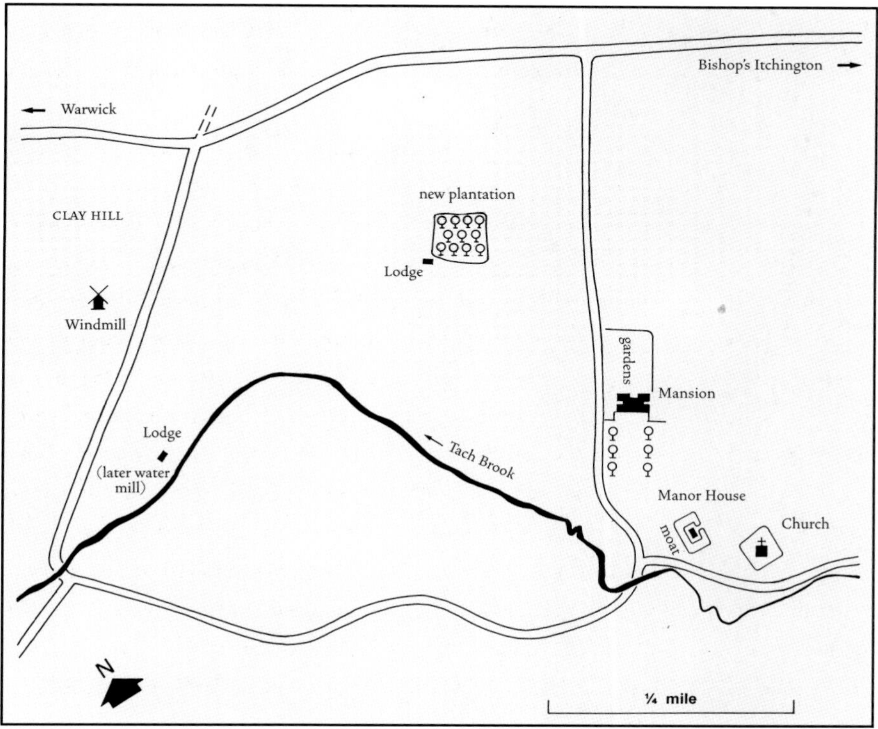

FIGURE 16
A reconstruction of the Chesterton estate
as it might have appeared in the seventeenth century
(drawing: Howard Brooks).

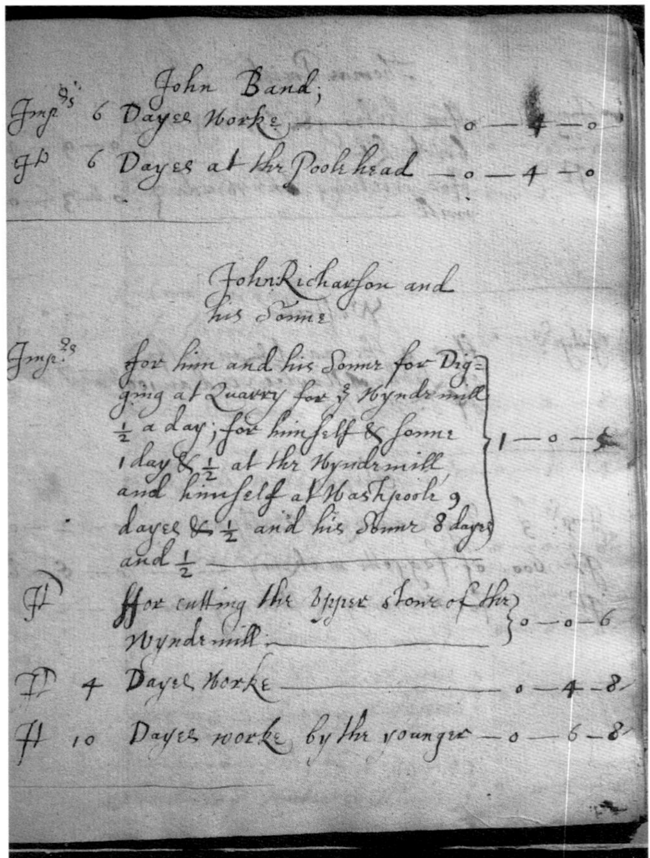

John Band;

Imp. 6 Dayes Worke ——— 0 — 4 — 0

It 6 Dayes at the Poolehead — 0 — 4 — 0

John Richarson and his Sonne

Imp. for him and his Sonne for Digging at Quarry for ye Wyndemill ½ a day; for himselfe & Sonne 1 day & ½ at the Wyndemill and himselfe at Washpoole 9 dayes & ½ and his Sonne 8 dayes and ½ ——— 1 — 0 — [illegible]

It ffor cutting the Upper stone of the Wyndemill ——— 0 — 0 — 6

It 4 Dayes Worke ——— 0 — 4 — 8

It 10 Dayes worke by the younger — 0 — 6 — 8

PLATE 49
Page from the 1633/34 accounts showing payments for the building of the windmill (SBTRO, DR 98/1708).

PLATE 50
The water mill at Chesterton (photo: Philip Wise).

millpicks (iron tools used to dress millstones) and in April 1638 for 'wyitt leather' and 'a pound of soope' (soap) which were probably used to lubricate the moving parts of the mill machinery.[18] Major repairs must have been necessary in May 1638 for on the 27th there is a list of six craftsmen, including the builders John and Thomas Westly, who were paid a total of 16s 8d for thirty days work 'about the windmyll'.[19]

The water mill has received less attention than the windmill, but has a similarly detailed history[20]. The building known today as the water mill lies just below Windmill Hill. At an unknown date the ground floor of this building was converted to house the water mill machinery by the adaptation of a rear staircase passage to house the waterwheel and the insertion of a mezzanine to take two pairs of stones. This must have occurred by about 1770 for the estate map clearly shows the building described as the 'mill' and its accompanying pool.[21] However, even a cursory inspection reveals that the 'water mill' has had a more distinguished past. The front elevation 'has the appearance of a small, elegant country house' with a symmetrical design of a central pedimented doorway on Tuscan columns and, above, a statue niche between single pairs of four-light windows with prominent hoods (Plate 50).[22] To the side there is a door set within a rusticated frame with an oval light above, but no pediment, and two more windows of similar design to those on the front elevation at first floor and attic level separated by a string course. The rear elevation was altered when the waterwheel was inserted and is also partly covered in foliage, but may have originally had six small windows arranged in two rows of three to light the ground and first floors. Inside, the ground floor consists of one large room with a passage behind it which once contained a staircase. The ceiling beams have prominent chamfer stops and are finely moulded. The first floor was partitioned into two rooms, each with a doorway leading to the rear passage and in one room there is a large fireplace. Again, the ceiling beams are decorated with chamfer stops. The rear passage has a doorway at its eastern end which now gives access to a later brick cottage, but which may have originally opened onto an external staircase. Overall, the exterior architectural details suggest an early seventeenth-century date and this is confirmed by the design of the chamfer stops on the ceiling beams. There is also an intriguing collection of graffiti inside the mill including one example which consists of the initials WP and EP and a crudely carved date which might be 1622.[23] In conclusion it seems inconceivable that such an elaborate building as this was designed for the purpose of housing a water mill.

Yet there was certainly a water mill at Chesterton in the seventeenth century as one appears in the estate records.[24] At the same time as the construction of the windmill was taking place in the summer of 1633, a Richard Cockbole was paid 4s 4d for six and a half day's work at the water mill. This was repair work to the mill dam and included the

18. SBTRO, DR 98/1710, fol. 13r; DR 98/1711, fol. 87v.

19. SBTRO, DR 98/1711, fol. 90v.

20. B. Job, N. M. Clarke and T. Booth, 'Chesterton Watermill', *Wind and Watermills*, xv, 1996, 28-59. This paper contains excellent photographs and drawings of the water mill.

21. SBTRO, DR 98/1823.

22. D.T.N. Booth, *Warwickshire Windmills*, Midland Wind and Watermills Group, 1979, 45-6.

23. Illustrations of these graffiti are reproduced in Job, Clarke and Booth, 'Chesterton Watermill', 33, figs 3,4. Could WP be William Peyto and EP Edward Peyto?

24. The earliest reference is in 1554 according to the *VCH* (v, 42).

PLATE 51
The lodge at Chesterton, from a drawing by Thomas Ward, c.1830
(British Library, Add. ms. 29264, fol. 190; by permission of the British Library).

PLATE 52.
The gateway at Chesterton giving access to the churchyard from the mansion house (photo: Philip Wise).

supply of sand and lime.[25] Later, on 14 January 1636, Nicolas and Thomas Bond were paid £3 0s 2d for the 'pavier in the water mill 289:foote at 2 ½d the foote'.[26] On 17 December 1637 the estate paid out one shilling for '4 wedges for the water mill', while in 1638 a Mr Batchelour was paid 6d for carrying 'the spindle of the water mill to Southam'.[27] Lastly, a conveyance by Edward Peyto of various lands to members of the Verney family on 20 November 1647 refers to a 'water corn mill'.[28]

25. SBTRO, DR 98/1708, fol. 17r-17v.

26. SBTRO, DR 98/1709, fol. 24r.

27. SBTRO, DR 98/1710, fos 13r, 23r.

28. SBTRO, DR 98/1093.

If this seventeenth-century water mill which appears in various documents is not the existing water mill where was it located? And what was the original purpose of the building later converted into a water mill? Neither question is easy to answer due to limited evidence from both documentary and other sources. The 1647 conveyance does not record the location of the water mill, unlike the windmill which is described as being on 'Clay Hill'. There is an item in the December 1637 accounts relating to the payment of 4d to a Mr Mills for '½ day making a damme in Clay Hill', but in the absence of an explicit reference to the water mill at this location it is unwise to put too much weight on this reference. An alternative location might be proposed in the area close to the church and medieval manor house. Here, amongst a number of water features, is a mill leet which runs into the Tach Brook close to Ewe Fields Farm.[29] However, the evidence is by no means conclusive and further archaeological work is required to confirm the existence of a water mill at this location. At present, therefore, the site of the seventeenth-century water mill must remain unknown.

29. C.J. Bond 'Chesterton Magna', unpublished fieldwork notes, Warwickshire Museum Sites and Monuments Record.

Turning to the original purpose of the 'other' water mill it is reasonable to suggest that this might have been built as a lodge by Sir Edward Peyto who succeeded his father William in 1619. A man who was capable of adding one unusual building to his estate could have contributed a second, but in the absence of documentary proof it is difficult to be certain. Against this theory is the existence of another lodge on the estate although, as shall be seen, this is possibly of an earlier date.

That there was at least one lodge on the Chesterton estate is known from the estate map of about 1770 and a rather romantic account by the Reverend Thomas Ward written during the first half of the nineteenth century. The estate map shows a lodge on an elevated site backed by the 'New Plantation' and this accords with Ward's description of the building as 'standing on an eminence and backed by a small plantation'.[30] Ward continues that the building 'had a whimsical effect the stone being all white'. His illustration of the lodge shows a Jacobean building, square in plan with 'windows corbelled out over the angles like the barbizans of a Scottish castle'(Plate 51).[31] This has been compared by Colvin to the Triangular Lodge at Rushton, in Northamptonshire, built by Sir Thomas Tresham in 1593-7. If this lodge at Chesterton was built very early in the seventeenth century then it is likely that it was

30. SBTRO, DR 98/1823; BL Add. ms. 29264, fol. 190.

31. Colvin, 'Chesterton', 116.

PLATE 53.
Chesterton House, from an estate map of c. 1770 (SBTRO, DR 98/1823).

built to the order of William Peyto (died 1609) rather than his son Sir Edward.

Still surviving is the Peyto gateway, an impressive rusticated and pedimented brick archway set into the north wall of the churchyard (Plate 52). This provided a private access for the Peyto family from their house to the church. The date of the gateway is by no means certain as there is no documentary evidence for its construction. It is traditionally said to have been designed by Inigo Jones and is at least of a similar style to the three decorative archways built by Jones in the period 1615-1625.[32] However, most authorities place the date of the Peyto gateway rather later in the seventeenth century.

Lastly, there is Chesterton House, described by Nikolaus Pevsner as 'the grand and curious mansion of the Peytos'.[33] Sadly this building was demolished in 1802, but its site and appearance are known from the estate map of c.1770 and from a series of air photographs taken in 1975.[34] Chesterton House was located near the top of the south-facing slope to the north of St Giles's Church. A drawing on the map shows the entrance facade of nine bays with the centre emphasised by a flight of four steps up to the doorway, closely spaced half-columns and scroll ornaments above (Plate 53). The building was of two floors of equal height over a basement, the lower columns of Ionic order and the upper Corinthian. The upper-floor windows were surmounted by triangular pediments and the roof eaves hidden behind a balustrade with pinnacles.[35] Tyack has written: 'In no other Warwickshire house of its date were the classical orders used with such coherence and understanding'.[36] The plan of the house shows up clearly from the air as a cropmark. It is a large rectangular building with a continuous entrance front, but projecting wings and recessed centres on the other three sides. Internal subdivisions are visible and the central part of the house appears to be two rooms deep which could have been an entrance hall containing a grand staircase, as suggested by Colvin, with a saloon behind.[37]

At least some of the building accounts for Chesterton House survive in the Willoughby de Broke papers and they indicate that work began in the early spring of 1657. The first group of relevant accounts were kept in two forms, firstly as a list of payments to named individuals and secondly as moneys spent on building materials. For example, Thomas Band, the younger, was paid £1 0s 0d for fifteen days work in April 1657 while on 8 June 1657 the sum of 6s was paid to Edward Cottill for 900 nails at 8d per 100.[38] Also surviving is 'a bill of all the carpenter's works concerning the bilding' covering the period 8 March 1659 to 29 May 1662. The carpenters employed were four members of the Gelder family – John, Robert, Richard and Edward. In a month selected at random, July 1661, the total wages paid by the estate was £31 9s 10d.[39]

The design of Chesterton House, like that of the windmill, has been attributed to Inigo Jones as it was assumed by some that both buildings dated to the 1630s.[40] The surviving accounts for the House, however, record its construction between 1657 and

32. J. Summerson, *Inigo Jones*, Harmondsworth 1966, 66. Only the decorative archway for the Great House of Lionel Cranfield at Chelsea survives.

33. Pevsner & Wedgwood, *Warwickshire*, 230.

34. SBTRO, DR 98/1823; J. Pickering, Air Photographs SP3558 F, J-R, Warwickshire Museum Sites and Monuments Record.

35. A drawing in the Ward Collection of Chesterton House differs from this representation. Here there are eleven bays rather than nine with the wings being shown with three bays rather than two. The other main difference is that the balustrade is ornamented with urns. Overall the appearance is of a lighter, more vertical design rather clumsy in comparison with that shown on the estate map. However, as Ward's drawing was produced after 1815, some years after the house had been demolished, it is likely to be less accurate (BL Add. ms. 29264, fol.190).

36. G. Tyack, *Warwickshire Country Houses*, Chichester 1994, 49.

37. Colvin, 'Chesterton', 116.

38. SBTRO, DR 98/1540/1, fos 1r, 11r.

39. SBTRO, DR 98/1540/3.

40. See for example Hutton, *Highways and*

1662 and, given that Jones died in 1652, he cannot have been the architect. Instead, the surviving documentary evidence suggests that Chesterton House is the work of John Stone (1620-1667), the son of Nicholas Stone, already proposed as a possible designer of the windmill. John Stone was certainly employed by the Peyto family at this period: on 7 November 1660 he received from Mrs Elizabeth Peyto £5 'in full payment as well for all worke done for her as for particularly a grave stone sent downe of her husband deceased'.[41] This was Edward Peyto, the son of Sir Edward, who had died in 1658 at the early age of thirty-two. At his death the designs for the new house were clearly not complete for in October 1659 Elizabeth Peyto gave £1 to 'Mr Stone for drawing the draught of the head of the pillars for Chesterton'. In the following year she paid John Stone £2 'for the 2 capitalls of the arch at the staires' and a further £6 as part 'of the bargaine he made for the 10 capitalls of the lower row of pillars'. Further entries show payments in 1660 to Caius Gabriel Cibber (1630-1700), a Danish sculptor who was employed in Stone's workshop.[42] As well as these documentary clues to the identity of the architect of Chesterton House, the style of the building itself also points to John Stone as its author. Howard Colvin notes its similarity to the Banqueting House in Whitehall built by his father Nicholas to the design of Inigo Jones. Other architects, of course, copied Jones's buildings, for example Sir Roger Pratt at Coleshill in Berkshire, but the continuous patronage of the Stones, father and son, by the Peyto family over some twenty years strongly supports the identification of John Stone as the architect in this case.[43]

41. SBTRO, DR 98/1540/6. This is the black marble slab in the nave floor of Chesterton Church.

42. BL ms. Egerton 2983, fos 26-133, quoted by Colvin, 'Chesterton', 115.

43. Colvin, 'Chesterton', 116.

In 1600 the Chesterton estate had belonged to the Peyto family for over two hundred years and was about to see its greatest period of development as successive generations of Peytos undertook the construction of new buildings. These included perhaps two lodges, a windmill, a monumental gateway and ultimately a mansion. The names of many of the estate craftsmen employed on these projects have come down to us in the surviving family papers. By contrast, and perhaps rather surprisingly, we cannot be certain of the identity of the master-masons or architects who designed the buildings which so enriched the Chesterton Estate in the seventeenth century.

I should like to thank Dr Robert Bearman and his staff at the Shakespeare Birthplace Trust Record Office for their assistance and patience, Steven Wallsgrove for his comments on Chesterton water mill, Brian Merriman for allowing access to the water mill, and my wife Annemieke for her help with the fieldwork and general encouragement.

CHAPTER SIX

Portrait of a 'Diehard': GREVILLE VERNEY, NINETEENTH LORD WILLOUGHBY DE BROKE

ROLAND QUINAULT

Greville Verney, nineteenth Lord Willoughby de Broke, was the last member of his family (and the last Warwickshire peer) to play a prominent role in local and national politics. He was born in 1869 and was a Member of Parliament for the Rugby division of Warwickshire from 1895 to 1900. He succeeded to his father's barony in 1902 and thereafter was generally known as 'Willoughby' – which he preferred to his full title. He became a national figure in 1911 when he was one of the leaders of the Tory 'Diehard' peers who opposed the Parliament Bill in the House of Lords. Thereafter he remained active in national and local politics until his early death, at the age of fifty-four, in 1923.

Willoughby's political career has been variously assessed by historians. In 1935 George Dangerfield, in an influential book, described Willoughby as an aristocrat whose face 'bore a pleasing resemblance to a horse' and who 'was not more than two hundred years behind his time'.[1] Modern assessments of Willoughby have been rather more flattering, but more complex. Gregory Phillips has described Willoughby as a traditional landed aristocrat who used the new tactics of political democracy to preserve the *status quo*.[2] Alan Sykes has argued that Willoughby sought to bring the Conservative party back to basic Tory principles: the defence of the Church and the Crown, and the practice of *noblesse oblige* – the duty of the privileged to protect those less fortunate than themselves.[3] David Spring has recently observed that although we have much more information about Willoughby's role as a national politician than as a great landowner, he was 'far more in love with the hunting field and English country life than he was with the daily grind of the professional politician'.[4]

1. George Dangerfield, *The Strange Death of Liberal England*, London 1935, 43-4.

2. Gregory D. Phillips, 'Lord Willoughby de Broke and the Politics of Radical Toryism 1909-1914', *Journal of British Studies*, xx, 1980, 205.

3. Alan Sykes, 'The Radical Right and the Crisis of Conservatism Before the First World War', *The Historical Journal*, 26, 1983, 665-8.

4. David Spring, 'Willoughby de Broke and Walter Long: English landed society and political extremism, 1912-14', in Negley Harte and Roland Quinault (ed.), *Land and Society in Britain, 1700-1914*, Manchester 1996, 173, 176. For Willoughby's career and the Warwickshire agricultural context, see also Roland Quinault, 'Warwickshire Landowners and Parliamentary Politics c. 1841-1923', unpublished D.Phil. thesis, University of Oxford 1975.

Most of what we do know about Willoughby's personal life in Warwickshire comes from his memoirs, *The Passing Years*, which were published, after his death, in 1924. The book gives an amusing, evocative and wistful account of life on the Compton Verney estate in the later Victorian period, which Willoughby described as 'English country life at its best'. In a typical passage, he described the life of his grandfather, the seventeenth baron:

> His pre-occupations were fox-hunting, shooting and coaching, and the catching of pike, perch and eels in the lake at Compton on off days. He had no taste for county or Parliamentary business, nor indeed for any other business except the business of being a country gentleman.[5]

5. Richard Greville Verney, Lord Willoughby de Broke, *The Passing Years*, London 1924, 9.

Willoughby's father, who succeeded to the barony in 1862, also loved rural life at Compton Verney. He owned 12,621 acres in Warwickshire and about 5,500 acres in other counties, which gave him a total gross annual rental of nearly £24,000 in 1872.[6] This provided the eighteenth baron with a comfortable income which enabled him to indulge his passion for hunting. He was an outstanding Master of Foxhounds of the Warwickshire Hunt which, under his direction, was one of the foremost hunts in England.

6. John Bateman, *The Great Landowners of Great Britain and Ireland*, London 1883, 480.

Willoughby, as his father's heir, had a privileged upbringing. He recalled that 'As soon as I could hear anything I was told that I was born with a silver spoon in my mouth'.[7] Nevertheless his childhood at Compton Verney was traditional and comfortable, rather than spoilt and luxurious:

7. Willoughby, *Passing Years*, 1.

> Roast beef and beer formed the background to an ample, but not lavish, domestic economy that was in harmony with the character and tradition of the place, which is neither Castle, nor Hall, nor Towers, nor Court, nor Manor, nor Abbey, nor yet one of the stately homes of England, such as Raby Castle or Chatsworth. It is just Compton Verney.[8]

8. Willoughby, *Passing Years*, 6.

In his memoirs, Willoughby presented an idealised picture of landed life in south Warwickshire from the 1850s to the 1880s. That period was certainly a prosperous one for local landowners and farmers, but it was not quite as tranquil as Willoughby recalled. He was was too young to remember, for example, the agricultural labourers strike in south Warwickshire in 1872. This was organized by Joseph Arch of Barford, near Stratford, and it developed into a national movement dubbed 'the revolt of the field'. Arch was a nonconformist Liberal, who was supported by urban radicals like Joseph

PLATE 54
Lord Willougby de Broke, Master of Foxhounds, 1910;
from a photograph in *The Passing Years*.

Chamberlain and he organized strikes on the estates of leading south Warwickshire Tories like Sir Charles Mordaunt of Wellesbourne. The Verney estates were not singled out in the same way, although Willoughby's father was an ardent, if unvocal, Tory. Nevertheless, Willoughby later noted that Compton Verney was too close to Birmingham to be pleasant for a peer.[9]

9. Willoughby, *Passing Years*, 167.

The comfortable economic existence of the Verneys and other landowning families was undermined in the later 1870s and 1880s by a prolonged agricultural depression. A sharp fall in wheat prices, due to the import of cheap corn from America, coupled with a succession of bad harvests, made arable farming on the heavy clay soil of south Warwickshire no longer profitable. In 1879 Willoughby's father wrote to his county neighbour, Lord Hertford:

> I have had to make a great reduction in rent and shall be poorer for the present by from £1,500 to £2,000 a year. I only hope it will be for the present only, but I fear that our outlook is most gloomy.... Nothing on earth but a measure of protection can save us, and I fear we shall not see that at present. That it will come, I feel certain. Every word and prophecy of Bright's and Cobden's at the time of the repeal of the Corn Laws has proved utterly false, and people are beginning to see it more and more every day.[10]

10. Warwickshire County Record Office, Seymour of Ragley papers, CR 114A/725/2: Lord Willoughby de Broke to Lord Hertford, 21 September 1879.

In 1882 Lord Willoughby publicly suggested that the only way to relieve agriculture was to impose a 5 shilling duty on imported corn.[11] In 1887 he renewed his plea for a corn duty at a Warwick county meeting convened to consider the current agricultural distress. He claimed that the land of the county was fit for growing corn and nothing else.[12] But by 1890, he had reluctantly come to the conclusion that protection was 'quite outside the pale of practical politics'.[13] The decline of his agricultural income left him financially embarrassed and in 1887 he let Compton Verney and sporting rights to 5,000 acres to the financier, Sir Ernest Cassel, for £400 a year.[14]

11. *Warwick Advertiser*, 4 February 1882.

12. *Wark. Advert.*, 29 October 1887.

13. *Wark. Advert.*, 7 June 1890.

14. Information from the 20th Lord Willoughby de Broke; and see above, p. 47.

Willoughby's father realized that the world was changing and he advised Greville 'not to look askance at those who did not happen to see the world through Warwickshire spectacles'.[15] He sent his son, not to local schools – like Rugby – but to a prep school at Winchester and then to Eton. From there Greville went up to New College, Oxford, where he soon gravitated to the Bullingdon Club, the home of the smart sporting set. He described his life at Oxford as 'an easy degree, cricket, hunting and driving four horses'.[16]

15. Willoughby, *Passing Years*, 42.

16. Willoughby, *Passing Years*, 165.

While Willoughby was receiving an education away from home, the political predominance of the Tory landowners in south Warwickshire was undermined by the 1884 Reform Act which gave the vote to male householders in county constituencies. Hitherto the rural electorate had been mainly composed of farmers who regarded the

Tories as natural champions of the agricultural interest. But the majority of householders in rural constituencies were agricultural labourers, most of whom supported the Liberal party and the policy of Free Trade which ensured cheap food prices. The 1885 Redistribution Act divided south Warwickshire into two parliamentary divisions: Stratford and Rugby. Lord Willoughby de Broke was the largest landowner in the Rugby division, but his influence over the new constituency was limited. Many of the local agricultural labourers disliked the close association of the Tory party with their employers, the farmers, while the development of Rugby as a railway centre and the strength of rural nonconformity also strengthened local support for the Liberal party. When, in 1885, a Tory lecturer spoke at Kineton – the centre of Verney influence in the district – the audience rejected his views and Lord Willoughby de Broke hastily left the chair on the excuse of another engagement.[17] At the general election, later that year, a Radical Liberal, Henry Cobb, was returned with the help of Joseph Arch, the leader of the agricultural labourers' union. After the election, Lord Willoughby's brother, the Honourable and Reverend W.R. Verney, advised the Tories to woo the labourers by establishing in every village branches of the Primrose League, reading rooms and allotments for the labourers.[18] Lord Willoughby acted on this advice and became the chairman of three new institutions in Kineton: the Primrose League, the Working Men's Club and the Allotment-holders' Association.[19]

17. *Wark. Advert.*, 18 April 1885.

18. *Wark. Advert.*, 19 December 1885.

19. *Wark. Advert.*, 23 October 1886.

When Greville Verney came down from Oxford, in 1893, he was immediately adopted as the Tory candidate for the Rugby division of Warwickshire. This foray into local parliamentary politics had no recent precedent, for no Verney had stood for the county since the seventeenth century. Greville later described the division as 'a straggling rural constituency, about thirty miles long and fifteen miles broad, consisting of about ninety villages and the town of Rugby'.[20] He wooed the electors by touring the villages in a carriage and 'comfortable evenings at home had to give way, with distressing frequency to the village meeting'.[21] This was no exaggeration, for in 1894 the Rugby Conservatives held no less than sixty-four meetings and distributed 64,000 pamphlets.[22] Greville got married just before the writs were issued for the 1895 election and his honeymoon outing was a campaign drive around the constituency.[23] He was elected by a majority of 284 – an improvement of 523 over the Tory vote in 1892. The President of the Rugby Conservative Association observed: 'It has been a hard nut to crack and it has taken ten years to do it'.[24] Nowhere had the turn of the electoral tide been more marked than at Kineton, where the Radical Club had closed before the election and been turned into a public house.[25]

20. Willoughby, *Passing Years*, 178.

21. Lord Willoughby de Broke, *The Sport of Our Ancestors*, London 1921, 6.

22. West Midlands Conservative Association, Leamington, *Annual Report of the Midland Union of Conservative Associations*, 1894, 16.

23. Willoughby, *Passing Years*, 179.

24. Hatfield House, Papers of Robert Cecil, 3rd Marquis of Salisbury: Lord Denbigh to Lord Salisbury, 26 July 1895.

25. *Wark. Advert.*, 30 November 1895.

Greville was only twenty-six when he was elected to Parliament and he appeared to have a promising political career before him. His enthusiasm for the House of Commons, however, soon waned. In 1898 his father became seriously ill and, since it was likely that Greville would soon inherit the peerage, he decided, in 1899, not to stand for election again. When Greville succeeded his father, in 1902, he inherited a much depleted patrimony. Between 1875 and 1900 agricultural rents in south Warwickshire had been reduced, on average, by nearly forty per cent and in 1902 Rider Haggard described the landowners of Warwickshire as 'considerably crippled'.[26] Thus Willoughby was confronted with severe financial problems which were to dog him for the rest of his life.

26. H. Rider Haggard, *Rural England*, London 1902, i. 412, 421.

Willoughby took his seat in the House of Lords in 1902, but he played little part in its affairs before the landslide victory of the Liberals at the 1906 general election. Soon afterwards, when he was out hunting, he met a friend who said to him: 'it is the most terrible revolution of modern times. They are going to take all the nice land away from you Compton Verney way and put a stop to fox-hunting'.[27] Willoughby dismissed the idea as ridiculous, but it was not long before he became worried by the policy of the new Liberal government towards the House of Lords. The large Liberal majority in the Commons soon came into conflict with the large Tory majority in the Lords and Willoughby was drawn into the conflict. In 1907, the Liberal government declared its desire to reform the House of Lords. This prompted a Tory peer, Lord Newton, to produce his own reform scheme in which life peers would outnumber hereditary peers. Willoughby was opposed to any reform of the Lords and was 'astonished to find that masters of foxhounds were not included in Lord Newton's list' of peers eligible to sit in the re-constituted House of Lords. Newton also proposed to exclude peers who had only been elected once to the House of Commons – so Willoughby would have been excluded for that reason.[28] Willoughby amplified his views on Lords reform in an article in the *National Review*. He accepted the principle of life peerages, but stressed that the hereditary system ensured independence of thought and action.[29]

27. *Wark. Advert.*, 31 July 1909.

28. *Parliamentary Debates*, 4th series, clxxiii, 1907, 1250-1.

29. Lord Willoughby de Broke, 'A Plea for an Unreformed House of Lords', *The National Review*, xlix, 1907, 770.

Willoughby opposed the 1908 Liberal Licensing Bill, which placed restrictions on the drink trade, partly because he disliked the temperance movement and partly because his wife was the daughter of a wealthy brewer. He attended a meeting of Unionist peers at Lansdowne House, which he described as the first occasion when the Tory leader in the Lords took the backbench peers into his confidence:

> Some of us who had never spoken in the House of Lords and who had never been consulted about anything outside our own counties, met each other fresh from the hunting field and were able to compare notes about the past season and to discuss the

PLATE 55
Lord Willoughby de Broke, pulling the strings of the 'Die-Hard' followers of Lord Halsbury; cartoon in the *Morning Leader*, October 1911.

possible winners of the spring handicap .... the backwoodsmen were in no mood to listen to any tampering with the liquor traffic.[30]

30. Willoughby, *Passing Years*, 246.

Willoughby was even more strongly opposed to Lloyd George's 1909 Budget, which proposed not only higher duties on alcohol but also a controversial new tax on the unearned increment of land. He later wrote:

> I am determined to do all I can for the leadership and responsibility of the owners of agricultural land. ... I should never have had a try at public speaking unless the Lloyd-Georgian school had found a prophet in the Chancellor of the Exchequer. When he came out at Limehouse I felt bound to take a hand; he has given a lift to the powers of darkness, but he will not prevail.[31]

31. House of Lords Record Office (HLRO), Willoughby de Broke papers, WB/11: Willoughby to Mrs Bontwood, 1 November 1914.

Willoughby's hostility to the 1909 Budget was shared by most Warwickshire landowners and Sir Grey Skipwith even declared that Lloyd George ought to be shot.[32] In May 1909, there was a by-election in the Stratford division, when the Tory candidate had an easy victory.[33] This result encouraged Willoughby to believe that the Tories would win the next general election, so he had not 'the slightest anxiety' when the Tory peers rejected the Budget and thus forced the Liberal government to call a general election.

32. *Wark. Advert.*, 4 December 1909.

33. *The Times*, 3 May 1909.

Willoughby believed that the tariff reformers were largely responsible for persuading the Unionist peers to reject the Budget. He was a strong supporter of tariff reform – the protectionist and imperialist fiscal policy which Joseph Chamberlain persuaded the Tories to adopt in the mid-Edwardian period. The tariff reformers advocated a tax on foreign corn similar to that which Willoughby's father had advocated in the 1880s. Nevertheless Willoughby knew that protection was very unpopular with the agricultural labourers in Warwickshire. He had made no mention of protection when he was the Tory candidate for the Rugby division, and in 1902 he had witnessed the hostile reaction of the villagers of Tysoe to a temporary corn duty.[34] But by 1909 he believed that opinion in the rural villages was everywhere turning in favour of tariff reform.[35]

34. Willoughby, *Passing Years*, 242.

35. *Wark. Advert.*, 16 January 1909.

Before the January 1910 election, Willoughby joined other Tory peers in a national platform campaign against the Budget, in which he also denounced the whole tendency of radical legislation:

> The Radical policy meant Ireland for cattle drivers, Atheism for school children, £500 a year for paid officials, water for the working man and the British empire for the foreigner.[36]

36. *Wark. Advert.*, 18 December 1909.

He introduced himself as a 'real live peer fresh from the backwoods', thus proudly adopting the term 'backwoodsmen' which Lloyd George had applied to the rural Tory peers who had made a rare visit to Westminster to vote down the Budget. Yet Willoughby's own life-style was not particularly bucolic. He was passionate about fox-hunting, but he had little knowledge of agriculture or estate management. In the Edwardian period, he lived at Woodley House, in Kineton, which was close to the railway station and he made frequent visits to London both on business and for pleasure. He loved the West End theatre and he persuaded the trustees of his estate to build the St Martin's Theatre, which opened in 1916. He was also a director of several speculative companies, but he appears to have made little or no profit from them. During the Budget debate in the Lords, Willoughby claimed that he had already been impoverished by the 'Manchester school' economic policies of recent Liberal governments.[37] Yet in 1910 he was sufficiently prosperous to be able to take up residence again at Compton Verney, where he held regular house parties until the First World War.

37. *Parl. Debates*, 5th series, Lords, iv, 1909, 775.

At the January 1910 general election, the Tories did well in Warwickshire. They retained Stratford, where Willoughby had become President of the Conservative Association, and they also regained the Rugby division. But the Liberals remained in power, thanks to their alliance with the Irish Nationalists and Labour. Consequently Willoughby felt more should be done to stir up Unionist feeling in the country. In the autumn of 1910 he started the 'Reveille' movement with Henry Page Croft, a Ware maltster and a keen tariff reformer. The 'Reveille' movement failed to have a significant electoral impact, but it helped to raise Willoughby's national profile. He outlined the aims of the movement at a dinner in London attended by 100 Members of Parliament and peers. He advocated a 'scientific' tariff, imperial preference, industrial insurance, the purchase of small holdings on easy terms, and poor law reform. The 'Reveille' movement reflected the fears of grass-roots Tories that their leaders would make a compromise deal with the Liberal government on reform of the Lords. Willoughby later observed that 'a real quintessential Diehard never entirely trusts his leaders not to sell the pass behind his back'. The break-down of the 1910 inter-party constitutional conference reflected the strength of Diehard opposition to any compromise settlement.

Willoughby strongly opposed the Liberal government's Parliament Bill when it came before the Lords in 1911. He followed family precedent in this respect, for his great grand-uncle, the sixteenth baron, had been one of only twenty-two peers who voted against the third reading of the 1832 Reform Bill. Willoughby formed a luncheon club for those Tory peers who were prepared to fight to the end to prevent any reform of the House of Lords. It was at one of these lunches that Curzon coined the famous comment: 'we will die in the last ditch before we give in'. Willoughby became the unofficial whip of the 'ditchers',

PLATE 56
Lord and Lady Willoughby de Broke, as they appeared in a performance of *The Duke of Killicrankie* at the Theatre Royal, Leamington, in 1907.

but they were undermined when Asquith persuaded the king to create peers, if necessary, to force the Parliament Bill through the Lords. A split then developed between the 'ditchers' who were determined to fight on and the 'hedgers' who thought that discretion was the better part of valour. Willoughby wasted no time in running after the hedgers – which he described as 'hunting badgers with foxhounds' – but he scoured the backwoods for peers who would vote against the Bill. Nevertheless many peers – including four of the seven Warwickshire peers who had opposed the 1909 Budget – abstained at the third reading of the Parliament Bill which was duly passed.

Willoughby expressed his feelings about the peers' surrender in a pantomime staged in the hall at Compton Verney in 1913. Dressed in his peer's robe and coronet, he played the part of the Censor who vetoes bad plays – a reference both to his interest in the theatre and to his support for the Lords' veto. He declared:

> When I was but a youth, a headstrong youth,
> I left the hunting field of Warwickshire
> To play the game of party politics
> And got the punishment of party hacks.[38]

38. *Wark. Advert.*, 18 January 1913.

Underlying Willoughby's resistance to the reform of the House of Lords was a firm belief in the hereditary principle. As a Master of Foxhounds, he found 'few studies so interesting as the study of heredity, especially of horses and hounds'. He believed that 'like should be mated with like, with just enough outcross to guard against the danger of inbreeding'.[39] He told the House of Lords that he had been brought up 'in the midst of stock-breeding' and that he 'was prepared to defend the hereditary principle ... whether ... applied to peers or ... foxhounds'.[40] In 1922 Willoughby declared that 'the hereditary principle is ... the only really sound principle on which you can found any institution ... whether it is the monarchy, or the House of Lords, or a pack of foxhounds, the three most important institutions in the country that I can think of'.[41]

39. Willoughby, *Passing Years*, 76-8.

40. *Parl. Debates*, 5th series, Lords, v, 1910, 323.

41. *Parl. Debates*, 5th series, Lords, li, 1922, 566

Willoughby's belief in breeding led him to take a strong interest in the eugenic movement which sought to improve the human racial stock. The study of eugenics was pioneered by Francis Galton, who was influenced by the work of his cousin, Charles Darwin, on evolution. Galton became a Fellow of the Royal Society and a knight and his influence was at its height when he died in 1911. Soon afterwards, Willoughby claimed that evidence of 'the value of the transmission by heredity of statesmanship was to be found in Galton's work'.[42] Willoughby knew the Galton family, for Francis Galton had been brought up on his father's estate at Claverdon, near Warwick, and his brother, Darwin, was a typical local squire who was fond of hunting and stock-breeding.

42. Lord Willoughby de Broke, 'The Restoration of the Constitution', *The National Review*, lviii, 1912, 865.

Willoughby also studied the works of other eugenists, including the Whethams, who predicted that the aristocracy would soon become extinct because of the sharp decline in their birth-rate. They claimed that the House of Lords contained a very high percentage of men of great ability and argued that the great hereditary families were a valuable national asset.[43] Willoughby also much admired the physician, Dr C. W. Saleeby, whom he described as 'one of the greatest prophets of eugenics in this country'.[44] Saleeby was not interested in party politics, but he encouraged Willoughby to take an interest in public health. Saleeby wanted new legislation to mitigate the deleterious effects of alcohol and venereal disease – which he termed 'racial poisoning'. Willoughby supported Saleeby's campaigns for the passage of an Inebriates Bill (which was passed in 1913) and for state action against venereal disease during and after the First World War. Willoughby was President of the Stratford-upon-Avon Hospital in 1914, when he declared that 'the health of the nation should be the first consideration of the statesman and everyone else'.[45] In 1918 he repeated Saleeby's call for a Ministry of Health which he thought would be 'national salvage all round'. Shortly before Willoughby died, he told his son: 'if my life is spared I want to devote the rest of my life to eugenics'.[46]

43. W. C. D. & D. C. Whetham, *The Family and the Nation*, London 1909, 139, 100.

44. *Parl. Debates*, 5th series, Lords, XXX, 1918, 928.

45. *Wark. Advert.*, 17 October 1914.

46. Information from the 20th Lord Willoughby de Broke.

Willoughby's interest in eugenics was also linked to his concern with national defence. He feared that the declining national birth-rate would undermine Britain's military position since he believed that the most powerful nation would be the one which could place most men in the field. Willoughby, together with his wife and Saleeby, was a member of the National Birth-Rate Commission, which was established in 1913 to investigate the causes of the decline in the birth-rate.[47] The enormous mortality during the First World War made Willoughby even keener to encourage population growth by improving medical services.

47. C. W. Saleeby, *The Progress of Eugenics*, London 1914, 130.

The passage of the Parliament Act prompted Willoughby to reconsider the role and character of the aristocracy. He wrote to Saleeby in 1912:

> It must be Willoughby tout court, if you please. The re-arrangement of ideas carries with it a re-estimation of values. Rank was conferred on a man and his heirs for service to the state. We must regenerate this distinction. In the new Toryism, each man and woman will be known, not by who they are, but by what they are. ... What has he done for his country? ... The new aristocracy that shall be, are those who can answer this question in a satisfactory manner. I hope I may get into its ranks. You are there already.[48]

48. Shakespeare Birthplace Trust Record Office (SBTRO), DR 145/1: Willoughby to Saleeby, 6 November 1912.

In 1913 Willoughby claimed that 'National Toryism aims at the establishment of an aristocracy not of birth, or of brain, but of instinct and character'.[49] He called for an alliance between the people and the peers against the plutocrats with whom the workers

49. *National Revival: A Re-statement of Tory Principles*.

PLATE 57
Lord Willoughby de Broke, campaigning on the Ulster question, 1913.

were 'justly engaged in a righteous warfare'.[50] He believed that the upper classes should be the first to come forward 'to sacrifice something for the public good'.[51] This prompted him, in 1914, to introduce a Bill into the House of Lords which he described to Saleeby:

> It is called 'The Responsibility of the Rich' or the 'Conscription of the Comfortable Classes'; short title 'noblesse oblige.' It imposes military training on the richer willy nilly, and leaves it voluntary for the poor. This is the first step to the creation of a Carlylean aristocracy.[52]

Willoughby told the Lords that the Bill was designed to increase the military strength of the country. He defined the rich as those with an income of £400, together with members of the public schools, universities and higher professions. The Bill was fully debated, but it was opposed by most Unionist peers because, as Lord Roberts pointed out, the poor would regard it as an attempt by the rich to monopolise military power.[53] The Duke of Bedford told Willoughby that he favoured arming the classes against the masses, but he didn't think that it would be prudent to say so in public.[54] In 1915 Willoughby advocated giving the vote to all servicemen – a proposal which accorded to his idea of an aristocracy of service.[55]

Like other Tory Diehards, Willoughby cared passionately about national defence. He inherited an interest in military matters from his father, who had commanded the fourth troop of Warwickshire Yeomanry, which was made up of fifty-four troopers who were all his own tenants.[56] Willoughby became a lieutenant in the Warwickshire Yeomanry in 1891 and a major in 1908. He resigned his commission in 1910, but he commanded the second line yeomanry from 1916 to 1918.

In 1906 Willoughby joined the National Service League, which had been founded by Lord Roberts and others, to advocate compulsory military service and to ensure 'the moral and physical condition of the people'. The military and eugenic aims of the league strongly appealed to Willoughby. His concern with national defence was apparent during the debate over the Liberal Budget in 1909. He regarded tariff reform as one aspect of national defence and thought that the best speech against the Budget was by Curzon who stressed the supreme importance of national defence.[57] Willoughby himself declared that 'the great question we had to consider in the near future was what part we were going to play in any matter of European conflict'.[58] His interest in the army was matched by his interest in the navy. In 1909 he presided over a Warwickshire county meeting which supported the two-power standard of the Royal Navy.[59] In 1911, at the request of the Imperial Maritime League, he presided over a conference of parliamentarians concerned with the maintenance of food supplies in wartime.[60] In 1912, at a Leamington meeting to celebrate the eightieth birthday of Lord Roberts,

50. *Parl. Debates*, 5th series, Lords, xv, 1914, 606.

51. *Wark. Advert.*, 25 October 1913.

52. SBTRO, DR 145/4: Willoughby to Saleeby, 8 February 1914.

53. *Parl. Debates*, 5th series, Lords, xv, 1914, 461-7, 585.

54. Private papers of 20th Lord Willoughby de Broke: Bedford to Willoughby, 5 March 1914.

55. *Parl. Debates*, 5th series, Lords, xx, 1915, 167.

56. Willoughby, *Passing Years*, 43.

57. Willoughby, *Passing Years*, 262-4.

58. *Wark. Advert.*, 31 July 1909.

59. *Wark. Advert.*, 10 April 1909.

60. *Wark. Advert.*, 11 November 1911.

Willoughby declared that 'If history is going to be written in red ink in the next ten years we are going to look to it that we and our friends are going to come out top and not Germany and her friends'.[61] In a speech on patriotism, in 1913, Willoughby quoted Kipling on the duty of each man to his country.[62] Like Kipling, Willoughby combined a love of the British Empire with personal knowledge of India which he visited in 1898 and 1922.

61. *Wark. Advert.*, 5 October 1912.

62. *Wark. Advert.*, 25 October 1913.

Willoughby's interest in national defence encouraged him to take up the cause of female suffrage. His wife was an active local leader of the Conservative and Unionist Women's Suffrage Association, which had been founded, in 1908, by the Countess of Selborne. Willoughby declared his support for female suffrage at Warwick in 1913. He noted that the first part of the empire to give votes to women – New Zealand – was also 'the principal pioneer in imperial defence of a practical kind'. He also sympathized with the militant tactics of the suffragettes, observing that 'all great causes, including Christianity, have been won by militancy ... by the possibility of the appeal to physical force ... I myself am a militant by nature'.[63]

63. *Wark. Advert.*, 13 February 1913.

In 1914 Willoughby supported Lord Selborne's female suffrage Bill on the grounds that if the Lords helped the women, they might help the Lords against the Liberal dominance of the Commons. He advised the Tories to make sure that they had the 'first cut off the joint' of the future female electorate. He also supported the Bill on eugenic grounds, arguing that the 'mothers of the future race' should be heard when there was the threat of a European war.[64]

64. *Parl. Debates*, 5th series, Lords, xvi, 1914, 84-9.

When the 1917 franchise bill came before the Lords, Willoughby supported female suffrage on eugenic and military grounds:

> If this war has proved anything at all it has proved that the nation which in the long run can bring to maturity the greatest number of healthy men and women and place them in the field will eventually win in the great racial struggle of which this war is only the beginning. It is for this reason highly desirable that we should seek the assistance of women in framing our imperial policy and legislation forthwith.[65]

65. *Parl. Debates*, 5th series, Lords, xxvii, 1917, 506-7.

He also noted that Mrs Pankhurst's Women's Party supported both the empire and the union with Ireland.

Willoughby was a very strong supporter of the union of Great Britain and Ireland for both personal and political reasons. His mother was the daughter of a large landowner in County Cork, and her brother, Arthur Smith-Barry, was one of the leaders of the Irish Unionists in the 1890s. Willoughby believed that the passage of the Parliament Act had 'resolved constitutional government in this country into a pure question of powder and shot' and had provoked the militant resistance of the Ulster Unionists to home rule for

Ireland.[66] In 1913 he became chairman of a new organization, 'The British League for the Support of Ulster', which was intended to provide trained fighting men to assist the Ulster Volunteer Force. The league gained the support of some prominent British Unionists, including Milner and Amery, but provided little effective support for the Ulster Unionists. They had no lack of trained volunteers, but they did need weapons, so Willoughby tried to buy carbines from a West End gun shop.[67]

66. *Parl. Debates*, 5th series, Lords, xv, 1914, 38.

67. Information from the 20th Lord Willoughby de Broke.

Willoughby, as the son of a southern Unionist, wanted not just Ulster, but all of Ireland to remain part of the United Kingdom.[68] In the spring of 1914, he hit on a new constitutional device to prevent home rule. He told the Lords that if they rejected the annual army act which regulated military discipline, they would prevent the government from ordering the army to coerce Ulster and, hopefully, force a general election on the home rule issue. He advised Tory candidates to appear before the electors with tomahawks in their hands and say 'we stand firm for the Union'.[69] His comment prompted a cartoon by Max Beerbohm which showed Willoughby in Red Indian dress with a tomahawk in his hand. Willoughby's strategy was soon overtaken by events, because 'the Curragh mutiny' dissuaded the Liberal government from using troops to coerce Ulster into accepting home rule.

68. *Parl. Debates*, 5th series, Lords, xiv, 1913, 926.

69. *Parl. Debates*, 5th series, Lords, xv, 1914, 43-4.

The implementation of the Home Rule Bill was delayed by the outbreak of the First World War in August 1914 and then by the formation of a Coalition government in 1915. Nevertheless the Diehards remained fearful that the Tory leaders in the coalition would abandon the Union. In May 1918, Willoughby and Diehard peers warned that the public would abandon the Conservative party if it supported Irish autonomy.[70] Willoughby believed that events since 1912 had made the case for the union much stronger.[71] By 1920, however, most Unionist peers were ready to accept autonomy for southern Ireland and Willoughby was now in a minority on this issue. Lord Curzon noted that 'the backwoods in which my noble friend ranged at the head of a formidable band some years ago are now relatively deserted'.[72] One of Willoughby's last public acts before his death was to convene a meeting at Leamington to draw attention to the plight of the southern Unionists in the Irish Free State.[73]

70. Maurice Cowling, *The Impact of Labour, 1920-24*, London 1971, 463.

71. *Parl. Debates*, 5th series, Lords, xlii, 1920, 461.

72. *Parl. Debates*, 5th series, Lords, xlii, 1920, 667.

73. *Wark. Advert.*, 22 December 1923.

Like other Diehards, Willoughby opposed Tory participation in the post-war Lloyd George coalition government. Until October 1920, he was the Whip of the Independent Unionist Peers who took their lead from Salisbury, rather than Curzon.[74] Willoughby did not think that either the Russian Revolution, or the threat of socialism, made it advisable to support Lloyd George's government. He did not fear Bolshevism in England, since he believed that native patriotism and common-sense would always triumph.[75] He welcomed the fall of the Lloyd George coalition in 1922 as the end of a temporary and unnatural alliance between Tories and Liberals. He declared that 'the protection of the constitution,

74. HLRO, WB/12: Salisbury to Willoughby, 29 October 1920.

75. *Wark. Advert.*, 14 February 1920.

of Church and State ... was the rock bottom of the Conservative party and nothing else'.[76] Willoughby, like other members of his family, was devoted to the Church of England.

76. *Wark. Advert.*, 4 November 1922.

In 1923 a new Tory candidate was required for the constituency of Warwick and Leamington. Willoughby, as the chairman of the Warwickshire Conservative Association, asked his son and heir, John, to stand, but he replied in a one-word telegram: 'no'. His father remarked that he had never known such a marvellous offer to be turned down so succinctly.[77] Willoughby presided over the meeting to select the new Tory candidate and was largely instrumental in securing the nomination of Captain Anthony Eden. He was an agreeable candidate to Willoughby for many reasons. Eden's father was a baronet and Master of Foxhounds in County Durham who – like Willoughby – hated bureaucrats and plutocrats, but got on well with the workmen on his estate.[78] Willoughby was also attracted by Eden's war record and social outlook. Eden had been the youngest brigade-major in the army and had won a Military Cross at Ypres. He was also a devout Anglican who opposed disestablishment and easier divorce, while he regarded fox-hunting as God's gift to free-born Englishmen.[79] Eden easily won Warwick and Leamington in 1923 and retained the seat until he retired from the premiership in 1957.

77. Information from the 20th Lord Willoughby de Broke.

78. Timothy Eden, *The Tribulations of a Baronet*, London 1933, 21.

79. Margaret Blunden, *The Countess of Warwick*, London 1967, 275.

Willoughby agreed to make many platform speeches for the Conservative and Unionist party before the 1923 general election, but his exertions brought on laryngitis which led to his sudden death. His wife linked his death not just to his physical exhaustion, but also to his feeling that 'there was little now left for which to fight'.[80] He had been disheartened by the end of the union with Ireland and the disestablishment of the Church in Wales, but the saddest blow of all for him was a personal one. The First World War had put further strain on his depleted finances and forced his family to live in one wing of Compton Verney. The high taxation occasioned by the war further undermined his financial situation and in July 1921 Willoughby sold Compton Verney and 5,000 acres to a northern industrialist, Joseph Watson. Willoughby retained the Chesterton estate and continued his local activities, but the emotional shock of parting with his family's ancestral home was considerable. His wife wrote after his death:

80. Willoughby, *Passing Years*, xvii.

> During the last few months of his life, he had been much struck by the lamentable results arising in many cases from the passing of family places – the lovely old homes of England – away from those who had been born and brought up in them, and who possessed by tradition the natural instinct to act as friend and neighbour to all those living on the estate. The new owners who have acquired so many of these beautiful places seemed to him to be missing much real happiness, both for themselves and for those around them. He had meant to make a very earnest effort to put before them what an ideal relationship

it could be, and to appeal to them at least to try the old traditional ways of friendly intercourse and interest in one and all living on their land.[81]

81. Willoughby, *Passing Years*, xv.

Willoughby intended to deal with this theme in the final chapter of *The Passing Years*, but died before he could do so. The contrast in outlook and values between an aristocrat and a *nouveau riche* industrialist was, however, addressed in two plays by John Galsworthy – *The Skin Game* and *Loyalties* – which were premiered at Willoughby's St Martin's Theatre in the early 1920s. Galsworthy, like Willoughby, had been at New College, Oxford, and shared his enthusiasm for fox-hunting, but not his Toryism. Willoughby's interest in the theatre remained to the end of his life and in one of his last speeches in the Lords, he called, 'as a Warwickshire man', for government support for the Shakespeare Memorial Theatre at Stratford.[82]

82. *Parl. Debates*, 5th series, Lords, liv, 1923, 794-5.

Willoughby has been regarded, in retrospect, either as an archaic reactionary, or as a classic example of the new Edwardian 'Radical Right'. In reality, neither the 'reactionary', nor the 'radical', label fully describes him, because he employed modern political methods and policies to uphold traditional Tory values. Although he was an aristocrat, his outlook had more in common with grass-roots Toryism, than with élite Conservatism. He was generally mistrustful of the party leadership and represented a tradition of independent rural Toryism which had deep roots in Warwickshire. Like Charles Newdegate, a Tory Member of Parliament for North Warwickshire for most of the Victorian period, Willoughby asserted his political independence whenever the leaders of his party appeared to abandon Tory principles. Willoughby's outlook kept him from seeking any public office which would hamper his freedom of speech and action.[83]

83. Willoughby, *Passing Years*, xvii.

Much of Willoughby's world did not survive his death, yet some of the problems and challenges which he faced are still with us nearly a century later. Indeed, if Willoughby was alive today, he would have been struck by the parallels between the current political situation and that which existed after the Liberal landslide of 1906. He would have been horrified by the ban on most hereditary peers sitting in the House of Lords and even more by the Bill to outlaw fox-hunting. He would doubtless have played a leading role in organizing the Countryside Demonstration and in protesting against urban intervention in rural affairs. On the other hand, Willoughby would have been heartened by the restoration and adaptation of Compton Verney – a blend of the best of the old and the best of the new which, in his own way, he tried to promote.

CHAPTER SEVEN

After The Fall:

COMPTON VERNEY
1921 – 1998

MARTYN JAMES

In September 1921, Richard Greville Verney, the nineteenth Lord Willoughby de Broke, was forced by adverse financial circumstances to leave his ancestral home for the last time, and the house together with an estate of some 5,000 acres of rich Warwickshire farmland, including several farms and dozens of cottages, was sold. The new owner was a newly rich industrialist and alleged war profiteer, the soap and wartime shell manufacturer, Joseph Watson, who was created Baron Manton of Compton Verney (a new peerage) in Lloyd George's 1922 New Year's Honours List.

Watson's wealth derived from the family's businesses in Leeds, created by his grandfather, initially in tanning, and expanded by his father and uncle into candles, soap and grease: these he had taken over from them on incorporation into a limited company in 1897. His main business rival had been Lever Brothers of Port Sunlight. The two companies had for a while entered into a cartel arrangement called the Soap Trust but this eventually broke down and led to a fierce battle for market domination from which Lever Brothers emerged triumphant in 1913.

At the outbreak of the war in 1914 Watson set aside his interests in soap manufacture and became chairman of the National Shell Filling Factory at Barnbow, near Leeds. It was through his war work that he initially came to the notice of Lloyd George, then Minister of Munitions in the Asquith government. Barnbow was the most important factory of its type in the country and, following the Shell Scandal of 1915, would have had a large role to play in increasing shell production from 25 million a year in 1915 to 223 million a year in 1916.

Watson, however, was unable to subdue completely his commercial instincts and ploughed £800,000 into an ultimately unsuccessful speculation in linseed oil in 1916. This forced him to sell his shares in his soap business to Lever Brothers for a similar sum in order to recoup some of his losses, and he withdrew from business to lead the life of a country gentleman. He sold more of his business interests in 1919 for a further £680,000 to a Dutch margarine manufacturer, and eventually assembled estates totalling 20,000 acres. In addition to establishing an agricultural laboratory for experimental work in animal nutrition, plant breeding and soil problems, he became a well-known figure on the turf, owning race-horses, playing polo, hunting, shooting and entertaining county society. The purchase of Compton Verney was a defining moment in his ambition to be accepted as a member of the landed gentry, rather than as a nouveau riche arriviste, and the conferment of a peerage a mere four months later confirmed his place in the upper échelon of English society.

Immediately he acquired the estate, Baron Manton began a major modernisation programme. Beginning in the spring of 1922, bathrooms were put into all the first-floor bedrooms, extensive re-plastering was undertaken and much of the Victorian richness of the rooms was destroyed. Much of what we see today, including the rather plain interiors of the first-floor rooms (where the plasterwork remains) dates from this period. Unfortunately, Baron Manton was not to live to see the changes he had instigated. He was killed in a fall from his horse whilst out hunting on the estate on the 14 March 1922, and was buried at Offchurch near Leamington four days later. He left four sons and estate valued at £1 million gross, and was succeeded by his eldest son, George Miles Watson (1899-1968). The will was proved in June, but the first baron's complex affairs were not finally settled until seven years later, in June 1929, when the second Baron Manton sold the estate and the Watson family relinquished all interest in Compton Verney. Interestingly, the Compton Verney estate of 5,064 acres, including the mansion and 621 acres of parkland, was sold 'by direction of the trustees of the late Rt. Hon. Lord Manton' suggesting that the total estate, of which Compton Verney was a part, was being broken up and distributed among the members of his family.

A final coda to the Watsons' short tenure of the estate following almost 500 years of ownership by the Verneys, concerns the medieval stained glass,which had originally graced the family chapel near the lake. When this was demolished in the 1770s as part of the landscaping of the new park, the armorial glass depicting members of the Verney family and their coats of arms had been re-instated in the new chapel built by Capability Brown to the north of the house. This was removed by George Watson, in what some might regard as an act of architectural plunder, prior to vacating the house in 1929, and in 1931 it was sold in four lots by Christies. One lot can today be found in the County

PLATE 58
Compton Verney in the 1920s: postcard by 'Antona'
(Oxfordshire County Council Photographic Archive).

Museum at Warwick, and another is displayed in the café at the Burrell Collection in Glasgow. The whereabouts of the rest is unknown.

The new owner of the estate was Samuel Lamb, a cotton magnate with mills in Lancashire and Argentina. Lamb was frequently out of the country on business or otherwise engaged in running his mills in Manchester and consequently had little time to spend at Compton Verney. His wife, Gita, however, lived at the house when she was not in London for the Season, and was apparently a difficult and exacting employer who demanded high standards from her staff. A former housemaid recalls one incident when Mrs Lamb, apparently dissatisfied with a flower arrangement in the Saloon, threw the vase and its contents through a closed window. Coming from an Austrian aristocratic family, she was accustomed to running a large household, with servants above and below stairs, gardeners, nurserymen and chauffeurs, and to entertaining on a large scale. Mrs Lamb was also an accomplished horsewoman who rode to hounds in the Willoughby de Broke tradition, and, although her husband did not share her enthusiasm for fox-hunting, he did spend money and effort on new tree-planting on the estate, establishing about 2,000 new trees by the end of the 1930s.

In the thirties, Compton Verney hosted lavish weekend parties which were attended by Hitler's ambassador to Britain and subsequent Foreign Minister, Joachim von Ribbentrop, and other influential, pro-German members of British society. Many, such as Sir Thomas Beecham, were in support of the Ribbentrop Bureau's unsuccessful 'charm offensive', an attempt to forge an English Alliance for Germany amongst the English upper classes whom von Ribbentrop mistakenly believed to be the real rulers of the country.

THE SECOND WORLD WAR

The outbreak of the Second World War ushered in a new and unwelcome phase in the history of Compton Verney, and a period of decline in its fortunes that continued until very recently. In October 1940 the house was requisitioned by the Ministry of Home Security, and the Lambs moved to Whitchurch near Stratford-upon-Avon. Mr Lamb, doubtless concerned about damage to the fabric of the house, stipulated that only officers should be billeted in the main building with other ranks being housed in the stable block or elsewhere, and this stipulation was adhered to for at least the first year of army occupation.

Research and development for camouflage against air attack had restarted in 1936, and the Munich crisis in the autumn of 1938, coupled with the threat of imminent war, led the Air Ministry to set up an experimental camouflage section at Farnborough under the direction of Dr R. E. Strahling. At the start of the war, responsibility for camouflage was transferred to the Home Office and shortly thereafter to the new Ministry of Home Security, which was responsible for all aspects of Civil Defence.

The camouflage unit was moved to Leamington Spa in October 1939, and in May 1940 became part of the Research and Experiments Department. The department was concerned with studying explosions, fire behaviour, smoke screens and fire decoys, and more generally with developing methods of preventing aerial reconnaissance and of screening sensitive industrial sites from the Luftwaffe. Compton Verney was turned into a fully-equipped research establishment where the department's scientific work could be grouped and co-ordinated. The house provided living accommodation for the staff, and rooms for workshops and laboratories; the grounds space for field trials in the fundamentals of smoke production. The facilities opened in January 1941, with seven officers forming the scientific and technical staff, together with laboratory assistants, clerks, mechanics and labourers, all of whom lived on site.

Only a few months later, however, in September, the scientific work was moved to new premises near Leamington Spa. The house was taken over by L4 Division and became solely a training school for the skilled operators of the generators used to produce smoke screens. As a result about a hundred more Pioneers were billeted in the attic rooms in addition to those already in the stable block. By March 1943, the threat of aerial attack had significantly diminished, and the Government ordered a reduction of fifty per cent in the camouflage deception programme. The house was transferred to the War Office and came under the command of the Army School of Chemical Warfare, which led to extensive hutting being erected at the front of the house. By 1944, about 200 men were accommodated in the attics and the stable block, and twelve officers on the first floor of the main building. In order to service the requirements of this large body of men, a large sewage plant had been built in the grounds, which remains to this day.

It was not just Mr Lamb who was concerned about the effect of army occupation on Compton Verney. The house had been listed by the National Trust as being of sufficient architectural and historical importance not to be occupied by the military if at all possible, and the Ministry of Works, which was at that time responsible for listed buildings, warned in September 1941 that, once occupied by military units, no adequate protection could be given to it. An inspection a few weeks later noted that there was wear and tear to the main building, damage to the portico columns, to the stairs – apparently from bumping beer barrels up and down – and to the tesselated floor of the Hall which had been used as a mess room. The Ministry of Works had had the foresight to remove the paintings for safekeeping, and to box in the carved wooden fireplaces.

At the end of June 1945 James Lees-Milne, then acting Secretary to the National Trust, visited Compton Verney whilst on holiday in the area. He wrote to the Inspector of Ancient Monuments informing him that most of the balustrade to the 'Adam' bridge had been knocked off. The army initially disclaimed any responsibility for this, but, following a claim by the Lambs' gardener that he had seen the damage being caused by lorries, and by Pioneers celebrating VE day, the Ministry of Works agreed to pay for new replacements at a cost of around £600, it being thought too difficult to try to recover the original stonework from the lake. In the summer of 1948 an inspector from the Ministry of Town and Country Planning reported that part of the ceiling in the Hall had fallen down. This was due to a blocked gutter over the portico, but since the War Department had de-requisitioned the house in January, on this occasion it was left to Mr Lamb to deal with the repairs.

THE POST-WAR PERIOD

By the time the army vacated the house three years after the end of the war, Compton Verney had ceased to be a desirable country house and family seat. There was damage to the interior, including a large hole in the Hall ceiling, and the neglected parkland bore witness to the effects of military occupation. In addition to the sewage plant there was a large pump house adjacent to the lake, a small arms weapons pit and a guard room. Most of the huts were still standing on the front lawn, and the whole site was surrounded by approximately 300 tons of barbed wire. An additional hazard was posed by the numerous smoke bombs left lying around the property, one of which was discovered by the groundsman when he was pruning a tree in 1995.

The Lambs never returned to Compton Verney, preferring to live more comfortably at Whitchurch. Mrs Lamb died in 1954 and Mr Lamb decided to sell what had become a neglected and semi-derelict property three years later. The house was stripped of its remaining contents and left as an empty shell. It was in this condition that it was bought in March 1958 for £9,000 by a rather eccentric self-made millionaire, Harry Ellard (1898-1983), who paid a further £28,000 for an unspecified amount of land in its vicinity. Mr Ellard's wealth stemmed from his engineering firm, Ellard's Pressings Ltd, based in Wednesfield, a suburb of Wolverhampton, which he had built up from a workshop in his back garden. The business prospered during the war, and Ellard invested heavily in property in the immediate post-war years. In addition to Compton Verney he also owned the 1,700-acre Broadstone Estate near Chipping Norton, and two farms in the Cotswolds. He never married and lived in a bachelor flat in another of his properties, the Regency Club in Solihull.

Under his ownership the house entered upon a period of what might be called benign neglect. No attempts were made to repair or restore the house or its grounds following the

PLATE 59
Filming Peter Hall's *A Midsummer Night's Dream*, 1969:
Barbara Jefford and Derek Godfrey as Hippolyta and Theseus (right),
with the musicans as huntsmen (Shakespeare Centre Libary).

depredations of the war years nor were any further outrages perpetrated upon it. Apart from allowing the house to be used occasionally as a film set – a television adaptation of Iris Murdoch's *The Bell* was filmed here, as was a production of *A Midsummer Night's Dream*, for which it was necessary to construct a grand staircase in the Hall – Mr Ellard was content to let Compton Verney slumber gently in its park.

He visited the house every Thursday, driving an eleven-year-old Austin 1300, bringing with him scraps from the restaurant at the Regency Club which were fed to a litter of pigs which he kept here. These were looked after by the groundsman, who also grew fruit and vegetables in the kitchen garden. The pigs were reared for pork which, together with the garden produce, were served on the dining tables of the Regency Club. Mr Ellard kept a caravan at the back of the butler's cottage, where he would make tea for friends who occasionally came to visit him. His groundsman recalls asking him why he wanted the house, to which his reply was that he just enjoyed possessing it. He possessed the house, in fact, for twenty-five years until his death on Christmas Day 1983. His funeral was attended by 170 mourners, many of them his employees, and his ashes are buried beneath a commemorative tablet, near the lake, on the site of the old chapel.

In 1984 the house with 122 acres was sold by his executors to Period and Country Houses Ltd, a company with a reputation for restoring and developing large country houses. Having acquired Compton Verney, its directors lost no time in putting into effect their development plans, and from March 1985 submitted an avalanche of planning applications to the local authority. Firstly, the West Lodge was sold, followed by the kitchen garden and some fields adjacent to it, for housing. In 1987 a planning application was made to convert the mansion house, the brewhouse and part of the stable range into a hotel, with the butler's cottage as a manager's house, and in 1992 a further application was made to turn the eighteenth-century stable block into houses. At the same time, a complementary project was mooted to build an opera house in the field adjacent to the 'Adam' bridge. Planning consent was obtained for the houses, which now stand in the old kitchen garden, and for the conversion of the stable block, but by 1993 the attitude of the planning authority had hardened; the possibility of converting the mansion into a hotel had receded, and Period and Country Houses Ltd decided to put the house on the market. This coincided with efforts being made by Peter Moores, of the Littlewoods Pools family, to find somewhere to display his art collection and to develop an art museum. Due to its size and location, close to large centres of population, with good access to the motorway network, and yet in an enviable rural setting, Compton Verney was an appealing prospect.

The house and forty acres was purchased in 1993 and a charitable trust, the Compton Verney House Trust, created to oversee the restoration and conversion of the building to its new use, whilst respecting as far as possible the architectural integrity of the house and its setting. An initial budget of £7 million was made available to complete the first phase of the project, and on 9 April 1998 Compton Verney opened its doors to the public for the first time. Since then almost 60,000 visitors have been able to admire the works of art on display, and to see for themselves the transformation of the ground floor rooms of the house.

As this book passes through its proof stage, much work still remains to be done to restore the rest of the house, the grounds and the other buildings on the estate. The-ice house is to be turned into a hibernaculum for Compton Verney's bat population, and the complex of buildings to the north of the house, including the butler's cottage, the brewhouse and the old carriage house will become an education centre to enable an expansion and development of the already strong links with the educational community. The chapel and the 'Adam' bridge require urgent structual repairs, and the conversion of the upper floors of the house and the installation of an environmental control system throughout the building have still to be tackled. While this work is in progress the house is closed to the public, but after decades of neglect and uncertainty, Compton Verney is now in safe hands and can look forward with confident anticipation to re-opening as a fully operational major arts venue in the spring of 2003.

SOURCES:

Compton Verney House Trust archive material, including an unpublished lecture by Brian Hayton and unpublished research by Richard Thorpe and Barbara Clegg

FURTHER READING:

A.R. Astbury, *History of the Research and Experiments Department.*

A. Bullock, *The Ribbentrop Memoirs*, 1954.

G. Hartcup, *Camouflage: a history of concealment and deception in war*, 1979.

Ministry of Works (n.d.), *Ministry of Home Security*, 1939-1945.

R. G. Verney, *The Passing Years*, 1924.

INDEX

Index of persons and places (in Warwickshire, unless otherwise stated)